Diaspora &

Theory, Culture & Society

Theory, Culture & Society caters for the resurgence of interest in culture within contemporary social science and the humanities. Building on the heritage of classical social theory, the book series examines ways in which this tradition has been reshaped by a new generation of theorists. It also publishes theoretically informed analyses of everyday life, popular culture, and new intellectual movements.

EDITOR: Mike Featherstone, *Nottingham Trent University*

THE TCS CENTRE
The Theory, Culture & Society book series, the journals *Theory, Culture & Society* and *Body & Society*, and related conference, seminar and postgraduate programmes operate from the TCS Centre at Nottingham Trent University. For further details of the TCS Centre's activities please contact:

Centre Administrator
The TCS Centre, Room 175
Faculty of Humanities
Nottingham Trent University
Clifton Lane, Nottingham, NG11 8NS, UK
e-mail: tcs@ntu.ac.uk
web: http://tcs.ntu.ac.uk

Recent volumes include:

The Body and Social Theory
Chris Shilling

Religion, Realism and Social Theory
Phillip A. Mellor

The Body in Culture, Technology and Society
Chris Shilling

Globalization and Belonging
Savage, Bagnall and Longhurst

Diaspora & Hybridity

Virinder S. Kalra,
Raminder Kaur
and
John Hutnyk

SAGE Publications

London ● Thousand Oaks ● New Delhi

SAGE Publications Ltd
1 Oliver's Yard
55 City Road
London EC1Y 1SP

SAGE Publications Inc.
2455 Teller Road
Thousand Oaks, California 91320

SAGE Publications India Pvt Ltd
B-42 Panchsheel Enclave
Post Box 4109
New Delhi 110 017

British Library Cataloguing in Publication data

A catalogue record for this book is available from the British Library

ISBN 0 7619 7396 6
    0 7619 7397 4

Library of Congress control number available

Typeset by C&M Digital (P) Ltd., Chennai, India
Printed on paper from sustainable resources
Printed and bound in Great Britain by Athenaeum Press, Gateshead

Contents

Introduction   1

1   Home and Away: Social Configurations of Diaspora   8

2   Cultural Configurations of Diaspora   28

3   Sexual Limits of Diaspora   51

4   Hybrid Connections   70

5   Hybridity and Openness (or, Whose Side Are You On?)   87

6   Journeys of Whiteness   105

7   Transnational Terror   127

References and Bibliography   139

Index   152

Introduction

It is not that we have been forced to change our minds, or the ways we work, but the gap between the time of this book's conception and its context of publication is large. The reassertion of borders and the closing down of multiple perspectives in the current political climate has undone the progressive potential of the terms with which we were to engage. We began this work in 2000, when, given the cultural promises of diaspora and hybridity, it was still possible to discern the beginnings of a transformation in the cultural certainties of the homogeneous, autochthonous nation. A hesitant but real expectation heralded the advent of hybrid forms of culture, working at the point of cultural translation, which many believed were going to disturb the settled formations of white supremacist capitalist patriarchy (to borrow from bell hooks). We have agreed to show the traces of this optimism, which may still be found in parts of this book, but on the whole, our gauche enthusiasm has been dashed in the face of the global war on terror, the inauguration of new fear-driven security clampdowns, extra-legal detentions and incarcerations, bombing raids and imperial occupations – a case of 'perpetual war for perpetual peace' (Vidal 2002). It seems that when the Unites States of America finally joined the rest of the world in having to face the insecurity of a uni-polar globe, the adequacy of theory was put to the test. The grim sequence of events following the attacks on the World Trade Center and the Pentagon have remade a world in which boundaries and borders are even more vigorously policed, the activities of diasporic peoples have been seriously curtailed, and a once applauded hybrid creativity seems meek and mild in the face of an aggressive neo-liberal conservatism.

Is this, then, the obituary of the terms of diaspora and hybridity? Should this book be read as an ode to the time when the terms carried some resonance? Certainly this is not our intention. Rather, we wish to pursue an agenda that provides some insight into how these tools could, and may still, provide assistance to those struggling for social justice and equality. While we are critical of the (in)adequacy of current theorisations of diaspora and hybridity, this does not mean that, given the correct organizational context and praxis, they cannot yet emerge as useful modes of engagement for progressive struggle. What is absolutely clear is that we are living in an era that requires a defence of diasporic Muslims/Asians (and their varied substitutes among the demonized 'others' of our times – asylum-seekers for one) and a promotion of hybrid forms of collective action. It is a sad fact that creative responses are not often forthcoming from the schools of cultural studies and the humanities. The institutions that sponsor and promote the circulation of key academic terms seem less likely than ever to be places that encourage critical questions (or answers) about (to) the urgent politics of today. Rather, there is an ever starker contrast between the symbolic capital used by those building coalitions to 'Stop the War' and those using the language of diaspora and hybridity.[1] This is regrettable, but, as this book will illustrate, it is not unexpected, given the intellectual histories of these terminologies.

This is not a textbook in the sense that it offers a comprehensive overview of the literature on the uses and abuses of hybridity and diaspora. This would be an impossible task, given the appearance of an ever-increasing number of publications that are either exploring or making passing references to these concepts. It would also be disingenuous as our perspective would necessarily favour certain approaches over others. Rather, our concern is to consider those texts that most persuasively illustrate how academic works can be used to relate diaspora and hybridity to some form of social change and to the pursuit of equality. To contextualize our stance, we offer provisional definitions of these terms and a review of the main theoretical viewpoints, with the caveat that the use of the terms 'diaspora' and 'hybridity' is often discipline-specific. If we sometimes seem overtly critical of the work that diaspora and hybridity can do, it is because our intentions are specific. No doubt the inclusion of hybridity and diaspora in certain academic fields has opened up a range of possibilities for intellectual activity, but the main effort of this book is to seek possibilities that go beyond the comforts of arm-chair rumination/thinking. Our emphasis on criticism for change provides the reader with frameworks with which to assess the various arguments, theories and narratives under review, and to explore implications for action. It follows that we are not attempting to offer some sort of balanced view. Nor do we conceal where our politics lie. By making this transparent, the reader has adequate information to judge the nature of our intervention.

Within this directive, familiar terrain on hybridity and diaspora is covered and issues of identity, social relations and historical change are made present. Our concern is to delineate the way in which diaspora and hybridity have certain commonalities in their relationship to notions of migration and disjuncture and to show how these have come to be articulated in terms of the subversion of naturalized forms of identity centred on the nation. This is not to dismiss the power of nationalism, nor to valorize the identity-building activities that are signified by hybrid or diasporic processes. It is rather to indicate the nature of the dialogue between the two; perhaps also to highlight the often violent nature of this dialogue, and the costs associated with the production of hybridity and the formation of diaspora.

We also note the unspoken racialized assumptions involved in diaspora and hybridity. Too often these terms have been used to avoid confronting issues of racial inequality and so they become substitutes for talking about the racial or minority ethnic group without having to enter into the sullied world of institutional politics. We attempt to expose this kind of posturing and also turn the lens of diaspora on to the study of whiteness, posing questions as to why it is the movements and settlements of peoples of colour that have attracted so much attention in the literature on diaspora and hybridity. This focus on whiteness, like all the categories that are used in this book, does not preclude the changing nature of social identification. As we will show, the term diaspora was first used to describe Jewish people, a group that in certain contexts appear as 'white' and in another appear as racialized 'others'. Our point of critical departure is to note how inadequate this shifting knowledge is when confronted with the ongoing plight of, for example, the Palestinian people.

The book begins by considering the idea of diaspora in a relatively conventional mode, tracing what is often called the classical diasporas of Jewish and Armenian peoples. Our intention is to introduce key facets of the concept without limiting the various uses to which diaspora has been put. In particular, the criticisms that diaspora offers towards settled notions of immigration and ethnicity are scrutinized. By comparing concepts related to diaspora, we are also able to home in on those features that consistently arise when the term is deployed. We note how diaspora more often than not evokes two social spheres of interaction – the place of residence and the place from which migration has occurred. Agency, in these multiple locations, is in the diasporic group which exhibits some form of collective mobilization around the tensions between home(s) and abroad(s). It is the ongoing political, economic, social and cultural ties between multiple institutionalized spaces that characterize diaspora. Citing examples from social movements, articulating national liberation and organized through diasporic networks, such as those of the Kashmiris and Kurds, our first chapter explores these political connections in detail. We also consider economic ties, recognizing that the limit of diaspora's usefulness as a tool for progressive politics is reached when those same networks are used for consolidating new forms of capitalist accumulation attendant with neo-liberal policy. In the end, there is nothing inherently progressive in the contours that make up diaspora's social life, but the historic role that diasporas have played in progressive mobilizations stands as testimony to its potential.

Broadly, we find a theoretical divide between those who use diaspora as a descriptive tool (such as Safran 1991 and Cohen 1997) and those who apply it as a process (such as Gilroy 1993a and Clifford 1994). This distinction divides the first chapter from the second. There are consequences in this division for both main theoretical approaches to diaspora, where one approach is more interested in categorization and the *post hoc* implications of this, while the other finds diaspora as a way to critique the categories and essentialisms involved. This theoretical divide is also played out in terms of those areas which come under empirical scrutiny. In Chapter 1 we note political and economic implications of diasporic formations, whereas in Chapter 2 our attention shifts to the more cultural aspects of diaspora. These wide, sweeping distinctions are necessarily heuristic and the importance of politics and economics to cultural production is not forgotten. Rather, the distinction is maintained as a means of critique of an approach to diaspora that is overly focused with textual concerns which emerge from some cultural studies work and is common to Clifford as much as it is to Safran, to descriptive just as much as to processual approaches to diaspora.

The notion of belonging and the imposition of a single idea of belonging to the nation are potentially brought under question by diaspora. The nation is the foil against which we attempt to delineate various conceptualizations such as 'diasporic consciousness', 'multivocality' and 'deterritorialization'. Each of these notions attempts to unsettle and unpack the problems associated with having multiple belongings or no sense of belonging at all. These somewhat abstract concepts are considered through the cultural arenas of music, film and literature. Cultural creativity is also a site for the ferment of hybridity, in a way that many claim offers great potential for resistance to the politics of homogeneity. We note that in an era where cultural industries increasingly form the most dynamic and profitable parts of capitalist production, diasporic cultural works fall into familiar patterns of marketing, management and consumption. The moments where these works provide inspiration or form part of a wider mobilizing campaign become more and more squeezed. This does not render diasporic cultural products forever to Theodor Adorno's graveyard of popular culture, but forces a recognition that all culture is available for exploitation even where its intentions are not that way inclined.

In Chapter 3, we ask whether being a man or woman, boy or girl, makes a difference to the experiences of living in new lands, and whether there is any scope here for equality, not only between diasporas and host societies, but also within diasporic contexts. We consider the legalistic and economic reasons for the migration of men and women to new terrains. We look to see how this has impacted differentially on the lives of men and women with the example of case studies such as marriages between Punjabi men and Mexican women in the early twentieth-century USA, and the 'maid-trade' – that is, the migration of domestic labourers or sex workers – in the twilight of the twentieth century. The latter enquiry also permits us to ask why labour migration is conventionally not seen as part of diaspora studies. The movements of 'maids' and sex workers raises the issue of citizenship in establishing new diasporas. This is a potentially contested site in the making of what may be called silent/silenced diasporas that, by way of negotiating the institutional limitations placed upon actual people's lives, opens up diaspora to critical practice and politics.

The case of genital mutilation of sub-Saharan African Muslim women in Britain permits us to consider how far diasporic women have been struggling not only with the rights for women, but also with the education of their men: in addition, there is the burning question of how much of this issue to expose to mainstream society. We also ask why, classically, men have been excluded from studies of gender? Why is it that masculinity is implicitly taken for granted whereas femininity has been rigorously studied? We look to some work that addresses this absence. Finally, in our challenge to monolithic identities, we briefly turn to the developments in queer theory, whose main thesis suggests that homosexuality is not the opposite of heterosexuality. We observe how 'Otherness' inflects the lives of non-heterosexuals in diasporic communities, while at the same time calling into question issues of boundary with regard to the variety of possible identities. Ultimately, we are a complex residue of several, often overlapping, identities today – described best by Gloria Anzaldúa as 'heterogeneous identities' (Anzaldúa 1987). The fact that we prioritize one over the other at any one time is to do with the socio-political circumstances of the enunciation.

In Chapter 4, we begin by providing a link between hybridity and the previous discussions on diaspora. Insofar as hybridity is often located next to diaspora, and because the cultural mix that hybridity invokes is a 'problem' for conceptions of both the host culture and the diasporic arrivee, hybridity marks diaspora in varied ways. This chapter explores these co-ordinates through a close reading of a number of key texts on hybridity and a comparison with organized politics around issues of race and ethnicity. This task initially offers a description of the term 'hybridity' and its uses in anthropology, cultural studies and related fields, followed by a critique of assumptions (those of purity, of marginality and identity) that underpin much of hybridity theory. A discussion of cultural creativity, syncretism, diffusion, race and biology (the history of migration, language, culture and 'blood') leads on to a consideration of how syncretism and hybridity seem to do duty as terms for the management of the more esoteric cultural aspects of colonialism and the global market. The argument focuses on cultural creativity – innovation and authenticity, ownership of cultural forms and of technological modes of cultural mix – with examples drawn from film and television. In this way, we are able to underscore how lack of attention to political and economic difference makes possible celebrations of hybridity as the fruit of late capitalist globalization.

In Chapter 5, we further evaluate the relation of host and guest, home and away, here and there, and do so with reference to the nation and the cross-border theory of 'post-nationalism'. We begin with a consideration of what is and what is not considered hybrid, and why there is good reason to consider the selective ascription of hybridity to the marginal and not the centre. In this way, we note that border theory, for example, highlights hybridity but is notably absent from discussions of campaigns against the detention camps which maintain borders. This links hybridity to more explicit political terminologies and construes hybrid artefacts as commodities of difference in the context of transition – urbanization, privatization, trinketization. Urbanization in particular is picked up as the terrain upon which more problematic dimensions of hybridity-talk are cast. Our theoretical attention is drawn to one of the founding figures of hybridity theory: Homi Bhabha, whose stance is subjected to scrutiny. Given an agenda anticipated in a redistributed future, the subsequent discussion then advocates more militant approaches and wonders what must be done with the hybrid today if we are to take seriously Marx's old point of not just interpreting the world but wanting to change it.

In pursuit of radical questioning, in Chapter 6 we again review the main propositions on diaspora and hybridity, but this time in relation to a subject that rarely gets a mention when it comes to race and diaspora studies – the position and movement of white people. We do this not just to say that this is a group (or set of groups) that has been overlooked and therefore needs to be taken into consideration. Rather, we highlight the invisibility of such groups in regimes of supremacy to do with whiteness. We also question whether diaspora can adequately account for the variety of movements associated with white people, as with (settler) colonialism, tourism and travel, retirement migration and expatriate cultures. Our foray on this terrain first considers studies on whiteness as such and then focuses on the ways certain diasporas have been permitted to 'disappear', often ambivalently, due to a variety of features, such as skin colour, religion, economic status and the particularity of history. We go on to address the ambiguous cases of the Jewish and Irish diasporas. In a consolidation of the discussion of hybridity in the previous chapters, Chapter 6 pursues the question of hybrid racial mixtures, their institutionalization within racial hierarchies, and considers why only raced people are seen to be altered in processes of hybridity: we look to the cases of the Anglo-Indians in colonial and post-colonial India in comparison with the liaisons between Europeans and Native Americans in the so-called New World from the seventeenth century. The obsession with racial purity has led to the suppressions of the fact that millions of white people in the USA have multiracial roots. As with the dynamics of whiteness in general, invisibility and the suppression of hidden histories leads to regimes of supremacy which need to be dismantled.

Our final chapter does not act as a conclusion, but is rather a way of asking whether hybridity and diaspora can help us in the struggle against the forces of imperialism that are, with apparent impunity, re-enacting nineteenth-century colonial policy. As a new emperor surveys a domain on which, yet again, the sun never sets, we choose 'Transnational Terror' as the title of the closing chapter. This is intended to evoke both the question of just who the terrorists are in this context and to address how the transnational dimension of the activities of the US administration, of New Labour's UK Inc., and of the 'coalition of the coerced' have changed or transformed our understanding of diaspora and hybridity. At the nexus of these processes is a conflation between terrorists, Muslims and asylum-seekers/refugees. These new pariahs are intimately caught up in a web of conceit that reworks the connections that exist between all people, and thus remakes those who dare to step outside the reformed, concrete-blocked and sacrosanct borders of Western nation-states. Terrorists and asylum-seekers are those without a home, without status (as those in Camp X-Ray in Guantanemo Bay, the immigration 'centres' at Woomera and Baxter in Australia, the detainees at Belmarsh, UK, or at Kumingting in Malaysia, and too many more) and therefore those who are out of the pale of rights that are granted to people with qualifications and papers. The enactment of the Patriot Act in America and the equivalent acts in Britain are examples of legislation which seeks to legitimate de-diasporization – the breaking of transnational links – revocation of citizenship and what, in Britain, was always a dream of the right: repatriation. At a time when the kind of key thinking that has been developed to understand hybridity and diaspora is most needed, scholarly work seems overly concerned with issues of a purely cultural type, too closely related to the particular, and not able to deal with the transnational dimension of the 'threat'. We need to read these terms critically in order to act, and our book is designed as an intellectual tool to clear a space for action. The various forms this action takes are still to be suggested, of course. And we are not explicitly prescriptive here. Our task is one we see as an evaluation of earlier theorizing with a view to engagement in the now. This is, for us, the basis for any engagement at all. We do not claim all the answers, or even all the right questions about hybridity and diaspora, but we do think we have, at least, to ask.

Note

1 Evidence for this can be seen by the various literature produced by these movements. Stop the War websites have a conspicuous lack of engagement with terms such as diaspora and hybridity. In the UK, see www.stopwar.org.uk and in the USA www.notinourname.net.

1

Home and Away: Social Configurations of Diaspora

> I want to begin by asking how resistance is itself to be understood? (Gilroy 1991: 3)

> It is good to swim in the waters of tradition, but to sink in them is suicide. (M.K. Gandhi, Navajivan, 28 June 1925)[1]

If words could change the world, then 'diaspora' is one of those terms that promised much but delivered little. Events have neutralized the purchase of many agreed conceptual staples and today it is transnational networks (often labelled 'terrorist') that have entered into the social science and broadsheet vocabulary. Such a change of terminology – not for the first time – marks a transition in the significance of diaspora for a whole range of cultural, social and political formations. Thus, our aim is to present theory and illustrations that allow us to gauge whether the conceptualization of diaspora has helped to enhance or has diverted attention from issues of social justice, and to ask if this has offered either hope or disappointment for those engaged in struggles for equality.

The contemporary significance of diaspora as an area of study that emerged alongside related intellectual movements in the academy such as post-colonial studies and the ubiquitous and poorly defined processes of globalization. There are many links between these areas and it is only possible to indicate briefly where the main moments of overlap occur. Phil Cohen (1999) itemizes academic interest in diaspora by quantifying articles and books that have a diasporic title or theme. Pre-1990, there was little academic interest in the term 'diaspora', and the few publications with diaspora as a theme were primarily concerned with the historical Jewish or African experience. Post-1990, there is a mass proliferation of written work as well as a huge diversification in terms of those groups who come under the diaspora rubric. The breadth and diversity of diaspora now stretches from queer theory, where sexuality is the site of difference from which settled notions of belonging are challenged, to economic network theory, where diasporas are examples of effective entrepreneurial networks.

Our perspective is opposed to the kind of study which advocates research and commentary that remains solely concerned with trends in the world of academic writing. The point, not made by Phil Cohen in his survey of diaspora use, is that the period of exponential increase in interest in the concept also coincides with events such as the fall of the Berlin Wall in 1989 and the subsequent new political terrain in which the foreign policy interests of the USA are unfettered by competition with the Soviet Union. Since the end of what was commonly called the Cold War, a credible global opposition to the US administration has not emerged in any renewal of communism, but rather with Islamism, which, it can be argued, has its own version of diaspora in the notion of the *umma* (Sayyid 2000b). Teasing out the relationship between these events and trends in the conceptual and socio-political frameworks of diaspora is a theme that will be running through all the chapters of this book, though the particular issue of the Islamic diaspora will be taken up explicitly only in the final chapter.

This chapter outlines the conventional view of diaspora, beginning with the Jewish experience. We then address the question of diaspora as a social form by looking at some of the other terms that hover around it, such as 'immigration' and 'ethnicity'. Notions of ethnicity, immigration, settlement and race are all found to intersect and dissect conceptualizations of the diaspora. Following this tour of terms, we will then return to two key themes. First, that of the relationship between home(s) and abroad(s), which will be examined in terms of economic, political and social ties. Secondly, our critical perspective on diaspora demands an assessment of how the term contributes to strategic thinking concerned with addressing the condition of the dispossessed and marginalized in our uneven world.

Convenient convention

In a conventional mode, diaspora is related to the Greek gardening tradition (as is hybridity), referring simply to the scattering of seeds and implying some description of dispersal. While the etymology of seeds and sperm as carriers of both culture and reproductive capacity is central to this description of diaspora, these themes are taken up in Chapter 3. Rather, we take the accepted site of the Jewish experience of forced exile as a starting point for discussing diaspora. In Jewish historiography, the source of diaspora experience begins in the sixth century BC with the destruction of the First Temple and Jerusalem. The expulsion of Jews from the city and their subsequent exile to Babylon has become one of the central Jewish cultural and political narratives. This is despite the fact that there were already Jewish settlements in many parts of the region, notably in Egypt and Greece, at the time. By the fourth century BC there were more Jews *outside* rather than inside the region of Jerusalem (Ages 1973). Nevertheless, the association of the term 'diaspora' with loss or exile or some sort of suffering has meant that the Jewish experience has come to be seen as the prototype diasporic experience. This description of a group is seductive as it allows people living all over the globe to articulate a connection with each other and to think themselves connected, to a greater or lesser extent, with a piece of land (whether this be mythical or actual). Of course, we are aware that in the

Jewish case this has also precipitated tragic consequences and injustice for the peoples of Palestine. Ironically, given the intimate connections between the exile of Jewish peoples and the concept of diaspora as trauma, this has not prevented the creation of another victim diaspora in the Palestinian people.[2] This may have something to do with the Jewish diaspora occupying an ambivalent place in racial hierarchies, an aspect explored in greater detail in Chapter 6.

The classical form of diaspora, then, relates to forced movement, exile and a consequent sense of loss derived from an inability to return. This is also conventionally applied to the mass movement of Africans via slavery to the Americas. Zygmunt Bauman (2000) notes that it is only through the work of African studies scholars in the 1960s that the term 'diaspora' comes into academic use and this is specifically in relation to the Jewish and African experiences. Indeed, the use of Babylon as a signifier of the oppressor is often found in invocations of the experiences of slavery from diasporic black communities (Gilroy 1987). A vast literature traces the history of slavery, but the cultural outcome of the Atlantic trade is best explored in Paul Gilroy's *The Black Atlantic* (1993a) and Ronald Segal's *The Black Diaspora* (1996). This association of movement and migration with trauma, and containing within it a constant loss and yearning for an obtainable home, is one of the main foci of critiques of the classical model of diaspora. For instance, this model is unable to deal with highly qualified Chinese migrants to the engineering sector in the USA, migrants who have no bars on their return, yet organize themselves in many ways which we would call diasporic. Despite these difficulties, the association of victimhood with diaspora does lead to the inclusion of other groups, such as the Armenians who suffered forced displacement at the beginning of the twentieth century at the hands of Turkish expansionism (Cohen 1997).

In all of these cases, a defining characteristic is a blockage to 'return' – that there is a difficulty, if not an absolute bar, in returning to the place of migration. Forced exile becomes essential to the heightened sense of longing for home and is central to this understanding of diaspora. Even in those cases where the bar to return is dissolved, such as the movement of African-Americans to Liberia at the behest of Marcus Garvey in 1920, this return journey is not usual. The sense of attachment or, in some way, connection to the land from which exile was forced operates, at the very least, as a powerful metaphor. The idea of forced exile also applies to contemporary migrations and movements. The events in the Balkans in the 1990s witnessed forced movement and resettlements of people to almost all parts of Europe and North America. The dissolution of the former Yugoslavia into Bosnia, Kosova, Serbia and Slovenia means that many peoples are living close to their former homes, yet are not able to return. The displacement of people as asylum-seekers and refugees also brings with it the difficulty of returning home. South African political activists often found their way to Britain and were banned from returning to South Africa during the apartheid era. It is only recently that the concept of diaspora has been deployed in the context of refugee studies (see Wahlbeck 2002). Significantly, the status of refugee ties in with the notion of an exiled diasporic, as the only country a UN-recognized refugee passport does not allow the bearer to travel to is the homeland.

It is useful to abstract the idea of force as a motivation for migration and thus the potential creation of a diaspora in the contemporary world. There are numerous examples in the late twentieth century of ethnic and nation-alist politics creating groups of displaced peoples. In 1994, the internal strife in the African state of Rwanda led to the creation of over a million refugees.[3] Indeed, the more general point that the action of nation-states can lead to population upheaval and disengagement from a locality is important to note. However, it can be argued that, other than in some trading communities, migration of all sorts carries with it varying degrees of com-pulsion. These may not be directly traced to the actions of a nation-state, but do relate to the inequalities created by capitalism, such as the demand for labour, the rise of poverty or famine and the basic demand for better social and economic conditions. Unlike exile, migration, as such, does not necessarily mean that returning home is barred, even though not being able to return may act as a powerful source of nostalgia for home. As we will see later, home, or what Avtar Brah (1996) calls 'homing', is fundamentally connected to the deployment of the term 'diaspora'.

Frameworks

In the relationship between 'home and away' that marks out diasporic understandings, 'away' signifies some sort of loss, and can be generalized into a representative typology or definition of what a diaspora might be. Robin Cohen (1997) builds upon the framework developed by William Safran (1991) to provide a list of conditions which, when satisfied, allow for the application of the diaspora label. In viewing diaspora as a mode of categorization, we find a number of problems. As the following criteria illustrate, there is an inherent bias towards certain types of experience:

1 dispersal and scattering (from a homeland);
2 collective trauma (while in the homeland);
3 cultural flowering (while away);
4 a troubled relationship with the majority (while away);
5 a sense of community transcending national frontiers (home and away); and
6 promoting a return movement (away to home).

The application of this method is akin to a game of 'name those people': what such lists allow commentators to do is take a group divided by class, gender, age, etc. and lump them together in a flexible, but vague, self-confirming category. Robin Cohen's *Global Diasporas* (1997), spends a lot of time describing groups of people, their movement, their subsequent set-tlement and social engagements in exactly this way. The volume contains extensive detail about various migratory groups which Cohen then tries to encapsulate in a neat framework. As a challenge to this, in the parenthesis attached to the categories in the above list, we have characterized Cohen's criteria in each case as a relationship between the homeland and the place of dispersal. Our reason for doing this is to illustrate one of the fundamental flaws in the exercise he attempts. Crucially, the dynamic presented by Cohen oscillates around the idea of a homeland. There is little space left to talk about those groups who, for whatever reasons, are compelled to leave one place for another, subsequently settle and then have no formal relationship with their place of 'origin'. Nor does the recourse to origins make room for those 'displaced' people who may not even have a homeland (perhaps they are not a diaspora after all?).

Cohen's hermetic theoretical framework suffers from over-ambition. In addition to the above criteria, he further classifies diasporas in terms of a set of core features. There are, accordingly, five different forms of diasporic community:

1   victim (African and Armenian);
2   labour (Indian);
3   trade (Chinese and Lebanese);
4   imperial (British); and
5   cultural (Caribbean).

Even though Cohen is not simplistic in the application of these divisions, acknowledging as he does that there are overlaps and that things can change with time, the nature of this project is to develop a metanarrative which accounts for a world of movement and settlement in an orderly way. It is our argument that Cohen's typology demands too much from the term 'diaspora' and delivers too little of the analytical usefulness of the category. For example, to reduce an Indian diaspora to labour migration immediately anticipates that this is the key factor in shaping the contours, cultures and settlement of the entirety of that diaspora. This is, of course, not true, as there are a myriad of other factors that go into such processes of creation. To talk of an Indian diaspora in these terms loses sight of those other aspects of Indian migration and settlement which constitute the diasporic form (even when applying Cohen's rules of what a diaspora is). The structural incoherence at the heart of Cohen's conceptual scheme renders diaspora subject to criticism from both those who question the ethnography (such as Anthias 1998) and those who question the theory (such as Clifford 1994; Brah 1996).

If there is a useful aspect to this kind of grand narrative, it is to provide detailed historical material and to point out issues that are worth exploring and that can be taken up in other contexts. For example, the historical longevity of the diasporic construct is one that predates the modern formation of the nation. In this sense, diaspora could be utilized to indicate transnational forms, formations and processes that take into account larger geo-political shifts and historical patterns of struggle (civilizational clashes, changes of mode of production, etc.). Diaspora is not limited to any particular historical period in that we have examples of pre-colonial, colonial and post-colonial diasporas (even while privileging this as a historicizing framework). Cohen's work is a useful starting point because he offers many examples and case studies which provide at least a base from which to think about diaspora. This approach is also strongly people-centred in that links created by capital and commodities and, more recently, through media channels such as television and newspapers are not made a priority, though obviously this has both advantages and disadvantages. Ultimately, however, such a definitive schema is unable to even partially answer the question of whether diaspora as a term helps us in thinking about movement and change with any clarity, let alone providing the intellectual tools needed to transform society along lines that enable the pursuit of social justice.

Another framework is offered by Steven Vertovec (1999), who approaches the subject of diaspora not so much through the categorization of peoples, but with attention to the ways that multiple meanings of diaspora are generated through ethnographic work. From his work in Trinidad and Britain, Vertovec offers three definitions as types:

1 diaspora as social form;
2 diaspora as a type of consciousness; and
3 diaspora as a mode of cultural production.

Our focus in this chapter will be on diaspora as social form; the next chapter will concentrate on cultural issues. A concern with diaspora as consciousness will straddle both chapters. For Vertovec, diaspora as a social form has three aspects. First, it consists of specific social relationships related to common origins and migration routes. Secondly, there is a tension of political orientation between loyalty to homeland and to that of the host country. Thirdly, there are particular economic strategies that mark certain diasporic groups in terms of mobilizing collective resources. The context in which these aspects are played out are also threefold: (i) the global stage upon which transnational ethnic ties are maintained; (ii) the local state in which settlement has taken place; and (iii) the homeland states, or where forebears come from.

It may be that the distinction between social and cultural forms offered by Vertovec provides a useful set of categories for organizing the literature. This matrix is privileged for its classificatory elegance rather than for offering a way of comprehending social groups or conceptualizing diaspora in analytical terms. At the time of writing, there are at least three major sociology/cultural studies journals (*Diaspora, Public Culture, Transnational and Transcultural Studies*) and numerous books on the subject. It is quite apparent that diaspora as a concept has gained productive purchase in a range of fields that traverse the social sciences and humanities. Diaspora as social form plays out across the traditional interests of sociology, political science and economics, while diaspora as consciousness and mode of cultural production foregrounds theoretical and ethnographic texts in anthropology, cultural studies, literature and the arts. However, although the models of diaspora presented by Vertovec may serve well to categorize the literature, they do less to address the limitations that might be placed around the concept and they do not point us in the direction of its possible progressive uses. Indeed, this final point can also be made about the work of Cohen. To move beyond these frameworks requires a sidelong glance at concepts that have been critiqued by the emergent interest in diaspora, such as immigration and ethnicity. In so doing, the usefulness of disapora in terms of both theory-building as well as relating to political struggles comes to the fore.

Diaspora, immigration and ethnicity

Perhaps the most closely related concepts to diaspora and ones that have come under some scrutiny through the lens of diaspora are those of immigration and ethnicity. 'Immigrant', as a term to describe communities, has fallen into disrepute for a number of reasons. First, it marks groups who have never migrated but are the offspring of migrants as not belonging to a particular place. The word 'immigrant', rather than relating to an actual event of movement, becomes a euphemism for 'not from this place', or for 'one who belongs somewhere else'. Where large settler populations have existed for some time, this conceptualization of immigrant carries less analytical weight but remains a political tool for marginalizing or racializing a group. Secondly, it implies a one-off event that people migrate from one place and settle in another, end of story. However, research has now shown that migration can entail a number of shifts and movements and actually may even entail an incomplete process (Papastergiadis 2000). The critical questions we would ask here are clear: Does diaspora help us think of groups as more settled than the term 'immigration' implies? Or does it emphasize difference by highlighting transnational affiliations? In other words, if we draw attention to the diasporic nature of a population, does that serve as an excuse not to think of them as belonging to the settler nation, which then falls into the same trap as calling a group 'immigrant'? Diaspora certainly shifts our discussion away from viewing migration as a one-off, one-way process, but it is not clear whether this is a positive embracing of transnational affiliation or a defensive posture by communities in the face of a hostile host saying 'you do not belong'. For now, let us assume a positive perspective.

Combined with a hyphenated, hybrid identification, it can be argued that diaspora allows us to move beyond the static, fixed notion of immigrant. For instance, French-Algerians or Dutch-Guyanese are better descriptions than Algerian immigrants to France or Guyanese immigrants to Holland. In both these cases, the Algerian and Guyanese diasporic communities continue to be settled in Europe as well as maintaining ties with Algeria and Guyana, so the term 'immigrant' seems inadequate. At this level of descriptive accuracy, 'diaspora' is perhaps a better term. It also allows us to see migration not as a one-off event with one-way consequences, but rather as an ongoing process of building links and relationships at the material and cultural levels. We are talking here about a relationship that, to a greater or lesser extent, changes both the sending and receiving countries. This relationship has many connotations which are absent when thinking in immigration terms alone. America is often described as a land of 'immigrants', which quickly allows for the disavowal of the rights of indigenous peoples, but also glosses over the stark disparities that exist between racialized groups in the 'United' States today. If America were renamed a land of 'diasporas', would this change those relationships? Perhaps not in any fundamental manner, but it might destabilize the dominance of an American nationalism and white supremacy which can easily accommodate new migrants, as long as they accept the American way of life. This is what Vijay Prashad calls 'the new immigrant's compact with America' (Prashad 2000: x), which offers benefits as long as new arrivals do not destabilize the primary racialized hierarchies. In this way, to be called diasporic can only be constituted as a threat when it interrupts the black/white divide, something that has recently occurred with the racialization of Arabs, Muslims and South Asians in the USA.

Perhaps, more fundamentally, the appellation of immigration carries with it sets of larger institutional connotations, such as laws, regulations and reciprocity between nation-states. Legislation governing the movements of people can often be reduced to nation-states maximizing either monetary or human capital resources: so you may migrate to Canada if you have $100 000 to invest in that country or you can move to Sweden if you are a qualified medical doctor. In both cases, the immigration system is oriented towards creating benefit for the receiving end. The same is true for earlier periods of immigration into Europe and the Americas, where labour shortages have always required new sources of workers – either rural to urban migration or in international migration.[4] Diasporic formations sit uneasily in this mechanism because they imply that there is some benefit for the homeland in terms of remittances, social ties and ongoing economic relations. Legal and institutional mechanisms governing diasporas are few and hard to find. This is one of the reasons for the popularity of the term 'transnationalism' in academic discourse, as this is more attuned to the impact of diasporic formations upon legislation and state institutions. The diversion away from institutional structures to cultural matters is a critique that can also be levelled at diaspora and, perhaps even more so, at hybridity (as we argue in Chapter 5).

A turn away from institutional structures does not necessarily mean a lack of concern with politics. Certain diasporic formations can sit easily in the political culture of a nation-state while others do not. The clearest example of this is demonstrated by the aftermath of the attacks on the World Trade Center and the Pentagon on 11 September 2001. Although it was seen to be relatively safe for certain sections of the Jewish diaspora in America to support and work with the Israeli state in pursuing its policies of assassination and genocide against the Palestinian people, those who settled in the USA from Muslim countries (even those supporting the USA, such as Pakistan) were subject to registration with the authorities, general harassment and detention. Operating different policies for different diasporic groups in no way contradicts the foreign or domestic policy interests of the USA, but is an example of the way in which diasporic groups are treated unevenly by the state as a matter of strategy.

Diasporic understandings can add many dimensions to the study of immigration, but these are, on the whole, complementary rather than competing accounts. In contrast, when analysing the related term 'ethnicity' – at least as it has been used in the British context – it can be argued that diaspora provides a more disruptive critique. Even though the study of ethnicity has generated a huge amount of literature, it has come under scrutiny from a number of quarters. Studies of Britain's minority ethnic groups have often focused on the creation and maintenance of group boundaries, drawing on the work of anthropologist Fredrik Barth (1969). This perspective on boundaries has been criticized by those who see ethnicity as overly concentrating upon cultural aspects to the denigration of politics (CCCS 1982) and by those who have more contemporary concerns about essentialism (Brah 1996). Here, the emphasis is on the way ethnicity draws attention to certain processes by which boundaries are maintained and fixed. Much state and public discourse reproduces groups that are differentiated in terms of gender, class, etc., in terms of simple categorizations such as Black and Asian. This then has ramifications for how these people are treated (see Sharma and Housee 1999).

In contrast, diasporic understanding, by focusing on transnational links and emphasizing a multiplicity of belongings and identities, can challenge the fixity of identity invoked by ethnicity. Floya Anthias, however, is cautious about such claims for diaspora:

> The perception of diasporas as breaking 'the ethnic spectacles' with which the world was previously viewed, may vastly underestimate the continuing attachment to the idea of ethnic and therefore particularist bonds, to a new reconstructed form of ethnic absolutism. (Anthias 1998: 567)

In other words, diasporic groups are just as likely to operate within the bounds of ethnic absolutism as any other group. For example, Black Muslims in the Nation of Islam or Sikh separatists may organize and exist as transnational groups, but they are also engaged in the process of building and maintaining quite rigid boundaries. The reason for this, according to Anthias, is because ethnic diaspora necessarily invokes the by now familiar idea of a lost 'homeland':

> Diaspora entails a notion of an essential parent – a father, whose seed is scattered. ... The original father(land) is a point of reference for the diaspora notion: it is this constant reference point that slides into primordiality, however much it is refined and reconstructed as in Clifford's work. (Anthias 1998: 569)

Theoretically, therefore, diaspora and ethnicity may share more in common than is often acknowledged. For Anthias, the target of critique is James

Clifford, Stuart Hall and Paul Gilroy, all of whose work we will examine in more detail in the next chapter. For our present purposes, it is sufficient to note that the problems of essentialism do not disappear with the invocation of diaspora and certainly diasporic and ethnic groups are not mutually exclusive categories.

Diaspora does, however, differ markedly from ethnicity in terms of where it draws our attention. Ethnicity reinstates the nation-state as the legitimate social sphere in which boundaries are made. In some ways, ethnicity is like the smaller version of the nation, in that the processes described to bind an ethnic group are often similar to those used to describe and bind the nation. Also, the space in which ethnicity is allowed to exist is often determined by the policies and institutional procedures of a nation-state. For instance, in the Netherlands all children are allowed to learn their mother tongue in state schools regardless of whether it is Kurdish, Dutch or French. This is in contrast to the French system where non-European languages are not deemed appropriate for teaching in school, or in England where they are called 'community languages'. Policies of nation-states play a dialectical role in the creation and maintenance of ethnic groups. It is here that diaspora can be seen as almost a contradictory force to ethnicity, as it draws attention away from the single nation-state and towards a potential multiplicity of nation-states or regions within states. As we shall see later, the idea of ethnicity, as with that of the nation, is more difficult to sustain when the analysis moves away from a single society. It is in this context that diasporic understanding allows us to survey different kinds of identity formation, as well as of social organization. If there is any single theme that emerges from a study of diaspora, it is that of its multi-locational qualities, or the interaction between homes and abroads which cannot be reduced to one place or another. It is this couplet that allows us to outline the substantive implications of diaspora for politics and economics.

Homes/abroads

If diaspora implies a relationship between more than one society, one culture, one group of people, then this is a useful starting point for considering how it has impacted upon politics and economics. There are crudely three social spheres which can be identified:

1 the dispersed group who have some form of collective identity or process of identification;
2 the contexts and nation-states in which these various groups reside; and
3 the nation-states to which an affiliation is maintained, through a series of social, economic and cultural ties.

This 'triadic relationship' (Saffran 1991) forms a central feature of diasporic formations and debates. From this triadic perspective, diaspora contains within it a central tension which invokes at *least* two places – once again, home and abroad.[5] Perhaps the best illustration of this are the activities of community organizations that have emerged all over Europe, providing services for these diasporic groupings, often funded by the state or by charitable institutions. These organizations embody a certain diasporicity. In the major cities of Europe, associations abound with titles such as the Pakistani Society, the Turkish Association, Ukrainian Centre, Sikh Community and Youth Service, the Chinese Association, and so forth. These organizations may be syncretic in their practices (we would argue that this is inevitable) but they certainly have little difficulty in directly relating to their homelands. The fact that they are equally concerned with immigration advice and welfare information, as well as the latest information from 'home', means that they do not fit easily into the idea of ethnic associations which can exist without any transnational ties and are usually constituted and run within the institutional confines of the countries in which they are located. These organizations literally straddle a 'here and there', offering ways of being in 'the abroad' (making a home) as well as providing connection with 'out there' (another home).

Diasporic organizations also illustrate how home is not a stable category (in the next two chapters we will look at the idea of 'homing' in more detail). As we have indicated in our intervention of Cohen's typology at the start of this chapter, in diaspora studies there is often a use of the homeland connection as a central source for understanding the way a community organizes. However, there is tremendous variety in the nature of connections with a homeland, from a very close engagement (such as with Kashmiris in the UK) to a less materially close relationship (as with the Tamils in South Africa) to minimal interaction in terms of visiting and material ties (as demonstrated by the historical position of Indians in Guyana and the Caribbean (Ramdin 2000)). In each of these cases, the relationship to 'India' of what we could probably only at a stretch collate as the Indian or South Asian diaspora varies tremendously according to the era of migration, the circumstances associated with migration and settlement, and the subsequent technologies available for communication.[6] Perhaps more fundamentally, this relationship can become stronger and weaker depending upon changes to the political relationships between the respective countries and access to both material and other forms of cultural contact. For instance, dual citizenship for the Indian diaspora resident in certain countries was made available in 2003 and is likely to make the relationship closer for those who can take up such status.

When exploring the relationship between 'home' and 'away', there is a need not only to consider relationships between individual actors or members of diasporic groups; there are also legislative state frameworks, alongside the working of markets which enable or disable the creation of ongoing relationships. One example of this is the difference between the Indian and Pakistani governments' approach to the legal status of, and therefore nonresident 'national' involvement allowed for, people in their respective diasporas.

The Indian government up until 2002 resolutely disallowed dual citizenship and in fact it was illegal for those without an Indian passport to own land or be engaged in any formal manner in the politics or economy of the country. This is despite the fact that many migrants from India may have entitlement to ancestral land. In contrast, the Pakistani government has always recognized dual citizenship and, as such, the Pakistani diaspora has a much closer and intimate economic and political connection with Pakistan. Indeed, one of the MLAs (Member of Legislative Assembly) of the former ruling party in Punjab, Pakistan, had residence in both the UK and Pakistan, as well as two passports. This example reflects how state structures and legal frameworks can restrict, enable or create certain diasporic effects and activities.

Another aspect of homeland in diaspora studies that we need to address is the supposed unchanging nature of the homeland. Before 1991, for example, there was only an Ethiopian diaspora, but since then there is now another independent state called Eritrea. In the post-war migration to Britain from South Asia, up to 1972 there was only a Pakistani and Indian diaspora. After the struggle for independence, a third country, Bangladesh, came into formation and thus a new diaspora formed. Strictly speaking, both the Eritrean and Bangladeshi diasporas were not constituted through migration, exile, trade or any of the other reasons previously given, but nominally arose due to the creation of new nations.

The instability of ideas of home and abroad can be partially attributed to the commercially driven increased use of information communication technologies (ICTs) and the decreasing costs of travel, which have enabled the movement of people, information and goods to take place in greater volume. Developing interconnectivity across international borders has meant that those with access are now able, to various extents, to maintain connections, deepen relationships and broaden networks with lesser investment in terms of time, cost and effort. Though the question of infrastructure remains central to the enhanced use of technologies of communication, and there remains many that are excluded from the transnational ecumene, there is no doubt that extended diasporic connections have arisen as ICTs have become more ubiquitous. This is not to say that it is ICTs that have somehow created diasporas in the sense of virtual communities on the internet, but rather the combination of cheaper travel and greater ease of communication has supported what was already present (see Kaur and Hutnyk 1999).

However, the impact of ICTs repeats the old story of the centrality of the nation-state in diaspora studies. It is the use of new technology, with its ability to transcend state borders, which is highlighted. This is indeed a hangover of the exile thesis, in which context there are barricades to return or limits on maintaining transnational links. Movements from village to city and upward mobility from working to middle class also evoke some of the temperaments of diaspora. An elite family sitting in Nairobi watching satellite television and drinking coke in their air-conditioned apartment may, in that setting, have more in common with their cousins sitting in a flat in London than with a grand-uncle living in their ancestral village in Sokoto state. But this does not necessarily mean that the Nariobi-ite has had to question affiliation with the village in quite the same way as his London cousins may do. Questions of racism, loyalty to the nation and belonging all become pertinent in transnational migration, questions which have their counterpart in rural–urban migration but do not always carry quite the same urgency or the same threat (although it can be urgent and threatening in different ways, of course).

Political connections

The problem that nation-states have with diasporas has to do with the ideal of loyalty. In the modern era, the nation-state is supposed to be the principal body of affiliation for all those who live within its borders. This is the manner in which the nation can then represent the interests of those it claims to represent. Diasporas complicate this easy formulation. In 1990, Norman Tebbit summed up this problem by asking who British Asians would support in a cricket match, England or a South Asian team.[7] This question of divided loyalty presented in these terms is of course a gross and stupid simplification, in that people have rarely held unswaying and singular loyalty to their nation-states (especially where cricketing prowess is concerned). The famous maxim from the *Communist Manifesto* (Marx and Engels 1848/1987) asserts that 'the working men [*sic*] have no country' as the nation-state does not serve the interests of the working class but those of the bourgeoisie. Similar critiques of the masculinist nature of the affiliation to the nation have been made by feminists (see Anthias and Yuval-Davis 1989; Chatterjee 1995). But the diasporic context has a special significance here because the loyalties in question are concerned with other nation-states. In this sense, unlike Marxist and feminist critiques, diasporic questioning often remains within the domain of nation-states. Yet, crucially, it is the fact that it is those residing in one place but influencing another that becomes problematic.

It is in the realm of politics that the activities of diasporic groups, in what Benedict Anderson (1994) has termed 'long distance nationalism', have had some major impact. However, the activities of these groups in influencing their homelands do not necessarily follow a progressive or even transgressive set of political aims. According to Yossi Shain (2002), the impact of the American-Jewish diaspora on the politics of Israel has been to promote a peaceful solution. However, this activity is belied by the way in which the American government maintains the largest share of its military grants ($16 billion in 2003) as handouts to the Israeli state. This example reminds us that despite the activities of diasporas, inter-state relations tend to work towards mutual maintenance rather than criticism. This is also exemplified by the coming together of the British and Indian governments in the treatment of Sikhs and Kashmiris who have been vociferous supporters of secessionist movements in India (Goulbourne 1991).

The role of diasporas in homeland politics becomes all the more apparent when there is conflict at play. Often these conflicts become more prominent when large diasporas are involved. The successful struggles of the Eritrean people for nationhood received scant attention in the Western media when compared to those groups who had diasporic connections. The list that Arjun Appadurai often reels off in his various commentaries include the Kurds, Sikhs, Tamils and Kashmiris – groups that all have a significant presence in Euro-America and therefore with relative ease of access to media and those deemed powerful in the New World Order. Yet, this process is not that new: the Irish in America have long been both material and ideological supporters of the Irish Republican Army (see Chapter 6). We have already twice noted the Jewish case. Anthias (1998) illustrates how Cypriots abroad differ according to whether they are Greek or Turkish in terms of their preferred political solution to the question of Cyprus. Yet, in all of these cases it is premature to dismiss the role of the nation-state. The influence and impact that a diaspora can have at the level of *realpolitik* depends largely on the structures of the particular nation-state in question. Ostergaard-Nielson (2000) shows the lack of success that Turkish and Kurdish groups have when lobbying the German and Dutch parliaments. The reason for this is due to the foreign policy of these states towards Turkey and Kurdistan, and the community's inability to apply pressure through lobbying. In contrast, Yossi Shain (1999) demonstrates how Northern Ireland, Cyprus and Israel are all kept high on the political agenda in the USA through well-organized lobbies led by diasporic groups. The American political culture is premised on various vote-banks which are incorporated into the lobbying system as a vehicle for expressing state agendas. What becomes evident from this comparative work is the sustained role of the nation-state in framing and enabling the political activities of diasporic groups, even where this is to have a transnational impact.

Attempting to balance the role of the nation-state, the organization of a diaspora and the roots of an ethno-national conflict calls for analysis of some depth, which many accounts often fail to develop. For example, the Sikh secessionist movement calling for a Khalistan was heavily supported by and influenced by the diaspora in the UK and Canada (see Tatla 1998). Yet, the reasons for this large participation cannot be solely reduced to expressions of sympathy directed against the actions of the Indian state in the Punjab. In the 1980s when the then Prime Minister of India, Indira Ghandi, ordered a military attack on the Golden Temple in Amritsar, to ostensibly remove 'terrorists' who were based in its precincts, there was considerable outrage among US and British Sikhs. To name such sympathies as deterritorialized ethnicity is a reduction that does not account for the fact that separate processes can produce a similar outcome. In the Sikh case, support for the Khalistan movement from the diaspora was at least partly due to debates about the 'loss' of Sikh identity in the British context. The ideological revivalism that was associated with the Sikh secessionist movement resonated with settler-migrant concerns. At the same time, the impact of capitalism on rural livelihoods led to similar questions about Sikh identity in the Punjab. These separate processes came together due to an ongoing dialogue in a diasporic space, the significance of which led the Indian government to accuse the diaspora of causing all the problems in the Punjab – a useful way of avoiding their own culpability.

Perhaps an even more extreme example can be found among those engaged in the struggle for an independent Kashmiri state in the north of India and Pakistan. One of the main organizations engaged in political activism in the region found its origins in Birmingham, UK, in the newly forming diaspora.[8] The Jammu and Kashmir Liberation Front emerged after a meeting of activists from (Azad) Kashmir and Britain. This organization then later worked in Pakistan-administered Kashmir before crossing the border into Indian-administered Kashmir to become one of the main secular organizations fighting for liberation. Yet, the circulation of ideas and people that fostered this struggle has remained a closed case to the plethora of books written about the Kashmir situation. It is perhaps because diasporic analysis is too difficult to carry out in a context where international relations are still determined by inter-state concerns and diasporic involvement is seen as illegitimate or an unwelcome interference.

Diasporic formations engaged in long-distance conflicts over territory do not demonstrate what Appadurai has called 'a beyond to patriotism' (1996: xx). The Sikhs and Kurds are not looking for a new way to live with difference. Rather, they are concerned with gaining their own nation-state. In an era where many argue that the nation-state is no longer all that relevant (see Held et al. 1999), it is worth considering why these struggles are so prevalent and important. This desire for nationhood among certain diasporas poses some problems for those theorists who have argued an anti-national line, and all the more so for those who at least have highlighted the tension that exists between notions of diaspora and the nation-state. Appadurai's weak example of Kashmiri Pandits as a group who are *not* demanding their own state despite being in exile does not mean that all diasporas involved in conflict with their homeland states are inevitably concerned with the perceived respect that comes from the family of nation-states.[9] Indeed, this is the central contradiction of all mobilizations for statehood that gain much of their force from diasporas; they are always open to the criticism that it is the diaspora's concerns about identity which are being played out, often violently, in the homeland.

Once again, there are historical antecedents to the role of diasporas in political formations. The first Pan-African Congress took place in Paris in 1919 and the largest of these events was held in Manchester in 1945. The international struggle against colonialism and imperialism never respected extant nation-state borders. Indeed, the British policy of exiling those who were deemed a danger to the Crown led to the creation of revolutionary diasporas. The Ghadar movement was a revolutionary movement of the 1900s in India with the aim of overthrowing British imperialism. Many of its members were exiled to North America where they continued their work of anti-imperialist struggle, finding a receptive American public, which had rid itself of the British in the late eighteenth century as a result of the Revolutionary War. Considering latter-day developments, such as the deportation of *émigré* communists after 1917 (including Emma Goldman), it is ironic to think that the US Constitution and the USA itself has been seen at times as a haven for revolutionary exiles.[10]

Economic ties

One of the reasons for the increasing attention paid to diasporic ties may be because they are now recognized as significant conduits for the flow of money. As previously discussed, the notion of migration contains with it the idea of transfer of people from one place to another. In many ways this involves a loss to the sending country, especially if the person migrating has been educated to a post-secondary/high-school level. This has been called the 'brain-drain' because it implies a loss of resources, often for those countries that most need them. However, the flows in the other direction come in two forms: these are as remittances and as investment in productive capacity, that is, businesses. These forms of flow can be illustrated by comparing the Indian and Chinese diasporas. According to Devesh Kapur:

> The ratio of foreign investment [in China] by the Chinese diaspora is nearly twenty-fold that of the Indian diaspora [investment in India]. However, remittances by the Indian diaspora are about seven times that of the Chinese diaspora ($49.8 billion and $7.6 billion respectively between 1991 and 1998). (Kapur 2001: 275)

The difference here may be due to the relative size of an established entrepreneurial class among the Chinese diaspora and the large proportion of rural migrants among Indians (although this is now changing due to newer migration to the USA). In either case, we are still talking about substantial amounts of money which have a considerable impact on the receiving economies.

This recent courting of diasporas by governments of the South has arisen because of their need to capture large flows of capital which can have a positive, if not major impact upon economic development. This, however, demands that remittances are used for a 'national' rather than local process of development and this is clearly not the case with most remittances. Rather, the impact of remittances is localized to those areas of mass migration. For instance, certain parts of Mexico (Gutierrez 1999) and parts of Pakistan (Kalra 2000) have benefited greatly from remittances, but this phenomenon has not been widespread or even. In the case of the investment from overseas Chinese, only certain provinces in China, such as Guandong and Fujian, have benefited (Weidenbaum and Hughes 1996).

Diasporas tend to want to invest in the localities from which they come rather than in more general commercial development initiatives. This is another example of the discrepancy between nation-states which have particular plans for their diasporas and the groups themselves, who may pursue very different agendas.

The investment patterns of diasporic populations may not concur with national agendas of development but they do resonate with the current phase of global capitalism, which creates uneven regions within nation-states as well as between them. Indeed, diasporic capital organization seems to fit into another trend of the new logic of advanced capitalist organization, that which favours small-scale networks over large, vertically-integrated forms of production (see Castells 1996). Large organizations are seen as unresponsive to the requirements of contemporary consumers, who want more individually tailored and customized products. The supposed rapidly changing nature of the market place can therefore benefit from networks of small producers who can respond quickly to market change and at the same time can harbour specialist knowledge. In this way, the flexibility and diverse capabilities of smaller companies are maintained while the marketing and sales muscle of the co-ordinating firm makes for a mutually beneficial relationship. While this ideal of the networking firm is closely bound up with the ideology of neo-liberalism, it is not too difficult to see how diasporas, with their links across nations, can be seen as tools for the facilitation of economic growth. Kapur (2001) persuasively argues that diasporas are able to provide both local knowledge and credibility when firms wish to expand from the West into the developing world. This is particularly the case with the penetration of large information technology (IT) companies such as Microsoft and Hewlett Packard into India. Much of this process was facilitated by Indian IT professionals located in Silicon Valley in California.

Diaspora emerges, then, as it becomes useful to the market, or to the new logic of global finance capital. As Gayatri Chakravorty Spivak remarks:

> a new US immigrant was recently promoted to an executive position in a US-based transnational. She will be helpful in the emerging South Asian market precisely because she is a well-placed Southern diasporic. (1999: 310)

Much of this kind of activity is seen among the professional diaspora, now converted from brain-drain into 'brain-gain'. This shift in scholarly attention still tells us little of the economic activities of the majority of diasporic groups, who are the service sector workers of the developing world (and the Third World in the First). Ranging from Latino agricultural labour in California to Nigerian peddlers in Athens, Tamil flower sellers in Frankfurt and Bengali waiters in London, these groups constitute a seemingly endless list where each example evokes a different set of economic ties. Perhaps even more than the hi-tech diasporics, this service sector labour also furnishes the essential requirements of contemporary globalizing capital. This is not at all news for a reserve army of labour which is forced to work for an ever-decreasing wage – a situation that is compelled through the increasing illegality of labour migration or the lack of enforcement of minimum wages and health and safety regulations – the infamous winding back of union gains in the workplace and of welfare state policies. The service sector diasporics were never counted as part of a brain-drain and are still not courted to any extent by their host governments. Yet these groups also play a transnational economic role, though this is more to do with protecting their families from the ravages of International Monetary Fund structural reform programmes in their homeland countries, and avoiding the harsh realities of life in those states that have, in a neo-liberal global agenda, abandoned all attempts at universal social development (see Amin 1997).

Thus, diasporic connections provide various new means for the mobilization of people and capital, and new insights into the ways in which social organizations can transcend nation-state boundaries. But do these new methods necessarily form a challenge to the current neo-liberal global order? Or, evaluating the views canvassed in this section, does the emergence of an interest in diaspora coincide with a particular phase of capitalist development? Is diaspora another tool for market penetration or a potential method for political network-building? Are these questions asking too much of the diaspora concept when maybe we should be content with the critique it offers to homogeneity and essentialism?

Diaspora on the line

In an awkward play on a political slogan used by Black activists in Britain in the 1970s ('Here to Stay, Here to Fight'), Clifford argues that '[W]hatever their eschatological longings, diaspora communities are "not-here" to stay' (1994: 311). This focus on an(other) place raises important political problems neatly summarized by Anthias:

> I have argued in fact that 'diaspora' turns the analytical gaze away from the dimensions of trans-ethnic relations informed by power hierarchies and by the cross-cutting relations of gender and class. The relationship between forms of exclusion, and indeed differentiated inclusion, and the emergence of diasporic solidarity and political projects of identity, on the one hand, and dialogue (as in hybridisation), on the other, are important foci for research. (Anthias 1998: 577)

Indeed, Anthias makes the significant point that a singular concern with diaspora can divert attention away from racialized social relations in any particular context. Clifford is mimicking and depoliticizing a slogan that was used to assert the rights of racialized groups in Britain to equal treatment and value. In a previous section of this chapter, where we compared diaspora with immigration and ethnicity, we noted how a positive aspect of diaspora was its ability to present a more nuanced understanding of migration, but this may be to the neglect of local particularities and political realities. Anthias's criticism of some diaspora analysis is that it displaces attention from material relations between the state and racialized groups as well as with other intersecting positionalities such as class and gender. However, it may be that this is more to do with a confusion over the nature of political practice and its analysis rather than an inherent occlusion of local racialized power relations. A further example will clarify this point.

Another slogan from the anti-racist campaigners of the 1970s was: 'We are here because you were there'. A complete reversal of the conventional logic of migration is presented here. In the post-colonial context, the reasons for the presence of racialized groups in Britain has to do with the colonial past. Current migration is predicated upon links developed through colonialism. Viewed in this way, diasporic memory can act as a resource for contemporary political struggles, and it can be argued that all anti-colonial struggles actively involved diasporas. The literature here is vast, and we would point to texts by Rajani Palme Dutt (1949) and, for a further gendered complication, Jayawardene (1995). The main point is that even those groups struggling for rights within the settler context drew upon transnational inspiration. It is therefore not inevitable that evoking diaspora will lead to de-politicization. Indeed, the civil rights movement in the USA in the 1960s became a model for emancipatory movements throughout the world. These inter-linkages are most clearly expressed in the politically progressive agenda developed in Paul Gilroy's *Black Atlantic* (1993a). Diaspora here takes on a progressive and transgressive hue at the same time. In both cases, the foil or target under attack is the limiting and restricting force of the nation-state. For many of those engaged in anti-racist struggle from the 1970s, the British state was one of the primary sources of racism. Ambalavaner Sivanandan (1982), in a collection of essays which brilliantly encompasses the mood of that time, states: 'The time was long gone when black people, with an eye to returning home, would put up with repression: they were settlers now. And state racism had pushed them into higher and more militant forms of resistance' (Sivanandan 1982: 20).

Sivanandan gives a direction out of the tussle between Clifford and Anthias, one which is bound by political struggle and the historical moment. Indeed, without a situated analysis of class, anyone trying to attach any progressive tinge to any diasporic formation will find the way fraught with many pitfalls. As Spivak so brilliantly highlights at the end of the 'History' chapter in her *Critique of Postcolonial Reason* (1999), an ethnic minority or post-colonial (or we could add diasporic) is not necessarily a subaltern positionality. This point is poignantly illustrated by the story of a lineage of women whom Spivak traces from 'Bhubaneshwari, who fought for national liberation', to her great-grandniece, who has recently migrated to work in senior management for a US-based multinational (1999: 310). As diaspora becomes more an object of knowledge for circulation within the academy and other circuits of symbolic consumption, the distance between diaspora-talk, material struggles and active organizing increases.

Beginning with a conventional tour of the definitions of diaspora, we have taken a journey which has attempted to evaluate the extent to which the notions of immigration and ethnicity have been influenced or changed by the diaspora concept. We have noted that while each of these terms has, to some extent, been modified or has forced changes in the kind of analysis 'applied' to certain groups, diaspora adds another dimension rather than replaces the analytical requirements of these terms. In examining how diaspora works in economic and political ways we have gained some insight into contemporary processes otherwise labelled as 'globalization' and 'transnationalism'. As a descriptive tool, diaspora draws attention to groups of people in a way that is both useful but limiting. Indeed, it is transnationalism that has come to circulate widely in the spheres of economics and politics to indicate some of the spheres previously referred to as diasporic. It is in the sphere of the cultural, to which we turn in the next chapter, that diaspora has retained its currency and has actually bloomed. But this condition will return us to the critique that motivates our interest in working through the terms of this debate, since diaspora, divorced from organized politics, is largely unable to help us in resisting the globalizing and transnational ravages of local and contemporary capitalism.

Notes

1 From Prashad, Vijay (1995) 'ROOTS: A Manifesto for Overseas South Asians', *Sanskriti*, Vol. 6, No. 1. Available at www.foil.org/resources/sanskriti/dec95/vijay.html.

2 Four million Palestinians live outside the state of Israel and the Palestinian-governed areas, and about four million within these borders.

3 As with so many contemporary conflicts in post-colonial states, the structures left in place by colonialism have much to answer for. In the Rwandan crises, the protagonists in the conflict, the Hutu and Tutsi, were distinguished by European colonists in terms of how many heads of cattle each tribe owned. These initial differentiations led to the re-enforcement of once fluid social boundaries and ultimately to one of the worst acts of genocide witnessed in Africa since the slave trade itself (see Eltringham 2004; Melvern 2004).

4 See Castles and Kosack (1973) for a Marxist analysis of labour migration.

5 East African Asians are a good example of twice migrants or of a group who have multiple homes (Bhachu 1985). They were first displaced as indentured and contracted labour to build the railroads in British East Africa in the middle of the nineteenth century, and then exiled in the 1970s to Europe and North America.

6 Indeed, this kind of detailed understanding makes Cohen's (1997) grand typology look distinctly ropey.

7 Reported in *The Times*, 21 April 1990.

8 See Ali (2002) for a detailed analysis of the political activities of the Kashmiri diaspora in Britain.

9 Since the mid-1980s Kashmiri Pandits have been expelled from the Valley of Kashmir in India as a result of the activities of Pakistani-inspired militancy. It would be a misnomer, though, to call this group exiles, as Appadurai (1990, 1996) does, or even a diasporic group because they always contained within them a strong sense of Indian nationalism as well as Kashmiriyat. It is for this reason that this is a 'weak' example of a diasporic group not making claims to territory.

10 However, some of this thinking is still seen in *Empire* by Hardt and Negri (2000).

2

Cultural Configurations of Diaspora

> They bear upon them the traces of the particular cultures, traditions, languages and histories by which they were shaped. The difference is that they are not and will never be *unified* in the old sense, because they are irrevocably the product of several interlocking histories and cultures, belong at one and the same time to several 'homes'. (Hall 1990: 310)

> Our contention is that the understanding of diaspora privileges a place of 'origin', that is of an unchanging and stable nature, whereas the term 'Transl-Asia' is intended to priortize the notion of space. (Kaur and Kalra 1996: 223)

The political and economic implications of diasporic activity revolve around, under, in-between and sometimes through an overarching structure that cannot be ignored – the nation-state. In the previous chapter, the economic and political implications of diasporic formations were often shown to be limited by the actions and determinant moves of the nation-state. The ability to hold a dual citizenship, for instance, is illustrative of how the legal and institutional frameworks of different nation-states create varying scopes for transnational connections. Typologies of diaspora are able to arraign social groups so they can be slotted into existing social structures in a manner that does not necessarily alter the ways in which the institutions of the state operate. The fact that the British National Health Service employs about a third of its doctors from minority ethnic groups does not alter its institutionally racist character.[1] It can be argued that the presence of diasporic groups has had far more impact on the way that the nation is conceptualized than on the institutional structures that make up the state. So the USA can still present itself as a 'nation of immigrants', while putting in place institutional norms that make some immigrants subject to stricter state controls than others.[2] This nation/state divide is a crude distinction and one that we shall critique towards the end of the chapter, but it does allow us to highlight questions of belonging and how diasporic formations displace the simple equation of belonging and national identity.

By viewing diaspora as a way of looking at the world which disrupts homogeneous ideas of nationality, we move away from considering diaspora in terms of a descriptive tool for categorization, as was developed in the previous chapter. People do not neatly fit into categories, as might be the case for flowers or plants. What kind of meaning can an Indian diaspora have when there are obviously stark differences between those who travelled as indentured labour to Fiji and Trinidad in the nineteenth century (see Clarke et al. 1990), and those who form a part of California's Silicon Valley IT specialists in the twenty-first century (see Kapur 2001). To collapse and conflate these different eras, reasons for migration and processes of settlement into a single Indian diaspora renders the concept sterile. More is to be gained, perhaps, if diaspora can be considered not in terms of homogeneous groups of people, but rather as a process which has an impact on the way people live and upon the society in which they are living.

When thinking about diaspora as a process, we are not considering specific groups of people, but more general ideas that may be applied across a range of groups. Thus, diaspora can denote ideas about belonging, about place and about the way in which people live their lives. When thinking about the processual condition of diaspora, we of course do need to consider the place of residence as well as intimate or material connections to other places. Diaspora in this sense first means to be *from* one place but *of* another – a point that Stuart Hall makes in the opening extract of this chapter, and which is also pithily summarized in the title of Paul Gilroy's influential article 'It ain't where you're from, it's where you're at' (1991). The 'where you are at' is a combination of roots and routes (Gilroy 1993a; Clifford 1994). Making a play on the similar pronunciation of these two words in British-English (roots, routes – and the quite different semantic and conceptual referents they invoke), the oscillation between 'where you are' and 'where you have come from' is represented in terms of the routes by which you have got somewhere, and the roots you have in a particular place. This formulation questions absolutist notions of ethnicity and nationalism which firmly place 'belonging' in the arena of territory and history: people belong to a place because they own the territory and/or have been settled in one place for a long time. In Gilroy's formulation, belonging is both about being from a place and a process of arrival. Belonging, then, is never a simple question of affiliation to a singular idea of ethnicity or nationalism, but rather about the multivocality of belongings.

This deformation of the nation has implied both defensive, xenophobic posturing as well as progressive trans-ethnic and transnational alliances. On the former, the rapid rise of far-right groups in North America and Europe, seeking a return to a mythologized pure white nation, illustrates this xenophobic stance. At the same time, inward-looking racialized-ethnicized groups clinging on to cleansed and modernized ideals of homeland cultures also represent a defensive posture towards the certitudes of national belonging. This becomes most prominent when issues of women's rights arise, as we shall see in the next chapter. In the context of xenophobic nationalism, anti-racist alliances, such as the Campaign Against Racism and Fascism in Britain, or SOS Racism across France and Spain, are examples of trans-ethnic alliances that are implicitly critical of any homogeneous idea of the nation. In recent times, the anti-war movement has seen coalitions of Socialists, peace activists and Muslim organizations producing a fraught but mass-based mobilization which has forged an important progressive trans-ethnic alliance. As ever, the extent to which developments of this kind can last beyond responding to immediate crises remains to be seen. There are no guarantees as to which way ruptures in the hold of the nation will progress, but an increase in their frequency seems inevitable.

In this chapter, the ideas of belonging, of deforming the nation and of diasporic consciousness are taken up through a discursive terrain that surveys cultural products like music, film and literature. In presenting a schematic overview of what has become a burgeoning area of academic literature across the humanities, we recognize the work that cultural products can do in facilitating moblization for popular resistance, as well as being the inspiration for social praxis. Holding on to this progressive element, but in keeping with our critical stance, we also present how the ongoing crisis of cultural production runs up against an avaricious cultural industry churning out its wares in routine fashion.

Belongings

The diasporic condition is one that is claimed to question all notions of belonging. This theme within diaspora studies is developed by a number of authors, most notably James Clifford, Stuart Hall and Avtar Brah. For Clifford, diasporic consciousness is 'entirely a product of cultures and histories in collision and dialogue' (Clifford 1994: 319). Diasporic subjects are carriers of a consciousness which provides an awareness of difference. This sense is a basic aspect of self-identity for diasporic subjects. For example, people of Chinese Hong Kong heritage, born and living in Britain, may become acutely aware, from a very early age, that the food they eat and the language they speak at home is different from that of the other children with whom they interact. This sense of difference may also arise due to gender or class markers, but, crucially, ethnic or racial difference emerges against a dominant cultural force, which challenges the diasporic subject's sense of identity. Diasporic consciousness then forms a part of what Stuart Hall (1990) calls the work of identity production and reproduction through transformation and difference. It is by recognizing difference rather than denying it in an attempt to be part of a homogeneous whole that diasporic consciousness may emerge. Here, too, the central, unavoidable, unifying cultural force *against* which diasporic consciousness emerges is the notion of the nation. The idea(l) of a cultural norm that is ascribed to or proscribed by those occupying the boundaries of the nation-state is a powerful formulation, and one that requires further unpacking.

It seems that too much has already been written about the nation and its various antecedents.[3] Our specific interest lies in the extent to which the nation creates a sense of belonging and loyalty such that flag-waving xenophobia and a willingness to die for the idea marks the history of the twentieth century (and we are concerned to see the same unthinking banner waving at sporting events (see Marquese 1996)). Arjun Appadurai (1996) labels this affiliation 'patriotism' and notes how it previously relied upon the conflation of territory with a group of people who subscribed to some specific set of cultural norms. How this affiliation works has been described by Benedict Anderson in his now seminal volume, *Imagined Communities* (1983). A simple question about how people connect to each other within a nation when they are not able to develop interpersonal bonds with more than a handful of others leads to the proposition that a sense of community develops through the consumption of similar media forms, such as books, newspapers and television. This has historical 'roots'. No longer united by religious faith, or by loyalty to a monarch, a commonality arises principally through the products of print- and televisual-capitalism and through the ability to consume (versions of) the same information (Anderson 1983). Anderson's notion of imagined communities runs in opposition to the primordialist view which proposes that essential verities like race, kinship, blood ties and land, bind peoples. Even the less biologically determinist view, which takes language, religion and culture as the source of commonality, is held in some dispute by this version of the nation.[4] The creation of commonality is the basis for explanation here, and such studies assume the idea that the nation has to be the sole and single source of loyalty for its citizens, with a requirement that its homogeneity is fundamental, despite various critiques from feminist, anti-racist and class-based perspectives.[5]

A common language and culture constitutes a powerful metaphor that can be manipulated by political forces from both the left and right. This is well exemplified in the early works of Paul Gilroy. In an analysis of 'new racism', Gilroy argues that both left and right rely on conceptions of national belonging and homogeneity which not only blur the distinction between 'race' and 'nation', but rely 'on that very ambiguity for their effect … the nation is represented in both biological and cultural terms' (Gilroy 1987: 45). The concept of race that we see in use today is different from the biological determinism of the nineteenth- and twentieth-century evolutionists in that it relies upon a conflation of race, culture and nationhood. The racist British parliamentarian, Enoch Powell, best summarized this position in the late 1960s: 'every nation is unique … it has its own pastimes … memories … language or ways of speaking, its own … culture' (cited in Gordon and Klug 1986: 16). Implicit in this quote is the idea of an immutable British tradition which both includes and excludes. Thus, black people are excluded not simply on the basis of race, but on ideas of difference which are based upon an intersection of race, culture and nationality. In Britain, this is manifested as a defence of an essentialized British culture against, on the one hand, the enemy on the outside ('Argies', 'Frogs', 'Krauts', Iraqis), and on the other, the enemies within (black communities, Muslim fundamentalists and in an earlier period, communists or striking miners, to cite a few examples) (see Back and Nayak 1993).

Diaspora cogently challenges the ideal of a homogeneous nation in a number of ways. By bringing the enemy that is on the outside and the enemy within into a single frame, and in tangible cultural forms, diaspora poses serious problems for the coherence of nations as such. The speaking of other tongues in the school playground, the smell of strange food in the street and, of course, the organization of international 'terrorism' are all examples of how the enemy from outside has come into the fold of the nation. Brian Axel (2002), in an insightful article, argues that it is not the diasporic individual or diasporic praxis that causes this problem for the nation, but rather the conceptualization of the nation itself, such that the fantasy of unity that underlines nationalism, generates within itself the pos- sibility that '*any* citizen may be a potential foe of the nation, the threat of cultural difference is not a problem of an alien element, a parasitic "other people"' (Axel 2002: 246). The problem of the nation is therefore the impossibility of fulfilling the fantasy of the 'one nation–one people' cou- plet. Diaspora exposes this facet of the nation while not being the only social formation which can generate this kind of interruption.[6]

Diaspora also questions the nation by fundamentally puncturing the notion that territorial association or land and cultural affiliation are natural sources of identification. Clifford, in the article 'Diasporas' (1994) and in the subsequent book *Routes: Travel and Translation in the Late Twentieth Century* (1997), considers the diaspora process to subvert the idea of the modern state. We have already explained how the nation congeals territory and peoples. Deterritorialization implies staking identity outside originary claims to a land. These non-territorial claims may still be about nationality but they cannot make the argument that this sense of nationality is derived from the land. Many diasporic groups can be called deterritorialized because their collective claims to an identity do not depend upon residence on a particular plot of land: the Irish diaspora in America does not derive its Irishness from currently living in the geographical territory of Ireland, nor is this simply the case with 'second-generation' Irish in London (see Nagle 2003). As we saw in the previous chapter, the long-distance nation- alisms of Kurdish and Tamil diasporas relies upon the idea of a homeland rather than on being grounded in an actual territory. This process can be seen at its virtual extreme in the new 'communities' being formed on the internet. These virtual communities have nothing to do with territory, land and kinship, yet still carry much of the rhetoric of belonging, to which nations lay claim (Shain 1999). The internet is able to promote a transna- tional model of affiliation, which is also found in universalized religious identities. Muslim or Hindu identities are not strictly tied to a territory but to a doctrine (or several doctrines). However, these reconceptualizations have led to the emergence of more perverse forms of nationalism, such as Hindutva in India and Louis Farrakhan's brand of Black Muslim national- ism in the USA.[7] It can be argued that a more radical model, where deter- ritorialization should have or could have led to non-territorial loyalties, where identity did not rely on the link between land and nation, was present in the conceptualization and practice of the communist Internationale. Here the overarching loyalty was to class affiliation and is pithily summarized in another of Marx and Engels' maxims: 'Workers of the World Unite'. In practice, however, nationalism often reinserts itself into transnational identities in more complicated and hybridized forms.

If one aspect of diaspora invites us to think about deterritorialization, then one of the implications of this is that it references another: 'that of the people who are presumed to be indigenous to a territory' (Brah 1996: 190). Brah articulates this point in a British context, noting how the term 'native' is evaluated positively when it refers to the British 'native' as opposed to the migrated British subject, and then valued negatively in colonial contexts when the native is the colonized person and the British the colonizing superior. Claims to native or indigenous status are of a different order when they are made by oppressed peoples such as Native American or indigenous Australians. Here, legitimate claims of belonging are made in the context of centuries of 'exploitation, dispossession and marginality' (Brah 1996: 196). But they very often still rely on positing an essential relationship between territory and belonging – nativism.[8] This can potentially lead to difficulties in forging political unity between those who are historically marginalized and those who face different contemporary difficulties. Relationships between African-Americans, Native Americans and recent Muslim or Korean migrants to America, all of whom face varying orders of oppression, require careful political analyses and response. Declaring a common enemy in the institutions of the state, in corporate excess and in racism offers a beginning for indigenous commonality, but ultimately this strategy requires a starting point that does not solely focus on origins in 'essentialized and natural terms' (Brah 1996: 192).

The potential for erasing ethnic and national ties is inherent within the notion of diaspora but in practice what often occurs is both syncretic cultural formation and re-enforced ethnic and nationalist ties within the same diasporic space. The formation of hyphenated identities, British-Cypriots, Greek-Australians, German-Turks, Italian-Americans can reinforce the sense of belonging to the nation-states on both sides of the divide, but this can also result in the creation of new identities which have no affiliation to the nation-state form. The creation of British-Muslims or Black-British or Asian-Americans as diasporic identifications erases one nation-state from the formula while at the same time creating new identifications. Hyphenated identities of the Irish-American type may emphasize the difference of a group by paying attention to the 'homeland' as a key way of understanding their settlement abroad. As previously noted, this may divert attention away from concrete struggles in the place of settlement. Nevertheless, it seems that the British-Muslim version of this has more potential for the creation of varied spaces for trans-ethnic alliance and offers ways towards forging international solidarities across religion and race. Our view is that the naming of these groups does not immediately close off any political space, but rather indicates the particular dialectic of an ever-changing social field, as group identification does not remain static. There are signs, for example, that the aforementioned participation of the Muslim Association of Britain in the Anti-War Coalition in the UK could remain a positive development. Certainly, the political terrain of the UK has witnessed a range of experimental and 'new' alliances. We can only welcome more of them.[9]

Showing how diaspora questions or disrupts the nation does not mean we are arguing that diaspora stands in strict opposition to the nation. As Salman Sayyid notes:

> The diaspora is not the other of the nation simply because it is constructed from the antithetical elements of a nation, it is, rather, an anti-nation since it interrupts the closure of nation. The existence of a diaspora prevents the closure of the nation, since a diaspora is by definition [also] located within another nation. (2000b: 42)

To summarize, diaspora does not pose an alternative to the nation as it still operates within the framework of nation-states. It does, however, disable the nation in its attempt at defining a homogeneous community coterminous with a territory. Diaspora, then, forms part of a much wider set of processes. Returning to Appadurai, it is transnational movement in general – in terms of media, capital and people – that actually renders patriotism redundant. The nation no longer holds the same sole power of affiliation that it once (if ever) might have had. Transnational ties and ethnic links combine to create new social formations which divert attention away from the nation.

Transnationalism

Diaspora enables the invocation of both a time before the advent of the nation-state and the possibility of discussing groups that presently avoid or circumvent the boundaries of the nation-state. But diaspora has not been able to encompass the range of activities, particularly economic and political activities, that explicitly involve nation-states transcending their own borders to tackle larger issues such as the environment or global governance, as in the case of the Bretton-Woods organizations.[10] Here is one of the reasons why the term 'transnationalism' has arisen. It is able to describe wider sets of processes that cannot comfortably fit within the diaspora rubric. Thus we talk of transnational corporations rather than diasporic corporations. The transnational also manages to avoid the group or human-centred notions that diaspora evokes. The term allows a side-stepping of the usual pattern, when discussing diaspora, of having to evoke Jewish or Greek archetypes. At the same time transnational is a more precise, if somewhat tame, description of the contemporary world of nation-states that might otherwise be called the World System, Imperialism, Empire or New World Order. The transnational describes forces that cross or work across the nation's boundaries but do not necessarily disrupt the workings of the nation-state as executive committee. This lack of disruption does, however, allude to the weakness of the term. On this point, diaspora, at least, allows the potential for us to avoid the affirmation of the nation as the natural unit of analysis.

Perhaps the greatest strength of the term 'transnational' is that it alerts us to the contemporary state of international capitalist relations. Following Vladimir Lenin's formulation of imperialism as the highest stage of capital in 1919, we can say that to a large extent the operation of transnational corporations has seen his analysis vindicated. The domination of transnational capitalism in organizing and facilitating the exchange of diasporic cultural products cannot be underestimated. It would seem strange to think of the CEOs (Chief Executive Officers) of the world's largest transnational corporations in terms of a diasporic group. Yet they share many of the features described in the previous chapter, with their only home being a storehouse for the greater accumulation of capital. Otherwise the various countries in which they set up their subsidiaries are largely seen as secondary. Although this analogy is partly tongue-in-cheek, it is also illustrative of the way in which transnationalism has become much more closely tied to economic and political processes, while diaspora, as the rest of this chapter will highlight, has remained fixated on the social and cultural. We should be careful in discussions of diaspora not to forget the political economy of capital which has changed in such a way as to facilitate the proliferation of diaspora as an idea as well as a fashionable vector for the target-marketing of commodities.

Cultural moves

In contexts where transnational economic, political and institutional ties may be seriously strained and fraught, diasporic connections can still be maintained. A good example of this is the turbulent relationship between India and Pakistan. At the height of the tension between these two states in 2002, with the threat of a nuclear conflict looming overhead and official land borders closed, groups of people were still able to cross the border through a variety of means, and on both sides of the border the consumption of popular forms of culture, such as film and music, remained constant.[11] Indeed, for much of the formerly colonized world, the role of nation-states as a key determinant of social identity and as the main mechanism for enhancing and promoting social identity is relatively weak when considered against expressive cultural ties (music, film, faith, etc.). This is, of course, not to make Eurocentric-, political science- or sociology-inflected arguments about mature democracies (read Western) and weak nations (read Third World). Nor would we entertain any academic jaunts into doctrines suggesting the dominance of pre-modern societal forms in these countries. Rather, there is a necessity to emphasize that an over-reliance on the nation-state as an explanatory concept is an aspect of Western social science that can be distracting when considering post-colonial situations insofar as culture is concerned. In these contexts, diasporas are not necessarily reliant on the nation-state as a key unit to work against, but neither is the cultural merely a pre-economic domain of ethnic expression or tradition. The culture industry matures here too. Thus, the development of Asian dance music, and the various transnational circuits within which it circulates, traces out a space that cannot simply be reduced or mapped into various national containers (as illustrated by the proposition in the opening quote of this chapter by Kaur and Kalra, to which we return below and in Chapter 4).

Rather than considering the space in which diasporized communities and diasporic cultural production operate as coterminous with the nation-state, Brah (1996) invokes a diasporic space as one which crosses nation-state boundaries and in so doing evokes transgressive potential. Recognizing the fact that you can live in a place without totally or solely subscribing to the national heritage or dominant national discourse of that place creates a space for conflict as well as creativity. In Britain, the Tebbit cricket test described in the previous chapter would be a relevant example. A culturally based preference for a sporting team writ large is a test of loyalty to the nation, rather than a question simply about individual choice or circumstantial preference. Tebbit's Tory-era loyalty test has become more formalized in the requirements of the New Labour government of the twenty-first century, where allegiance to the nation is part of the citizenship process.[12] This measure can be understood as a reactionary response to diasporic consciousness on the part of an overtly coercive nation-state unable to comprehend the openness of diaspora and the practical consequences of transnational, post-imperial movement. The suggestion we make here, of course, is that this is a site for struggle.

Diasporic consciousness is therefore potentially a site for thinking beyond the confines of the nation. As Appadurai suggests, 'we need to think ourselves beyond the nation. ... [The] role of intellectual practices is to identify the current crises of the nation and in identifying it to provide part of the apparatus of recognition for post-national social forms' (1996: 158). Appadurai goes on to state: 'We might recognize that diasporic diversity actually puts loyalty to a non-territorial transnation first. ... The question is how can a post-national politics be built around this cultural fact?' (1996: 173). For Gilroy, this kind of politics centres around the displacement of absolutist categories of ethnic and racial difference. Working beyond the nation necessitates working beyond race. Focusing on a number of critical circulations at the political and cultural level, in *The Black Atlantic: Modernity and Double Consciousness* (1993a), Gilroy argues for a diasporic space traversing Western Europe, the Caribbean, West Africa and North America as a way of understanding and explaining Black experience.

For Gilroy, it is in the musical forms of the 'Black Atlantic' that a redemptive project lies: where previously creative expressions were devalued and considered 'primitive, savage and decadent', in the post-Second World War period these are widely consumed and universally valorized. Dance-hall musical performance is Gilroy's most favoured example, but his sensitivity and support for a range of expressive cultural forms is to be applauded. This celebration conveys an indication of a movement beyond race thinking. Diasporas and their creative outputs are one of the prime sites from which a new humanism might be imagined. While clearly this is an ambitious claim, and one that has found much criticism, not least for its universal humanist agenda, we do want to support such moves. From our perspective, however, without a political organization, or even a project with which to enable the 'planetary humanism' envisioned by Gilroy, these concepts remain relatively sterile. The argument that cultural visibility is just a necessary first step in an anti-racist cultural politics surely must be recognized (Kalra and Hutnyk 2000). However, it is Gilroy who provides an acute linkage between the creativity of diaspora and implications for a political agenda.

Creativity and commodification

If the level of institutional change remains relatively untouched by diasporic mobilization, this is certainly not the case at the level of cultural production and consumption. One of the main implications of diasporic consciousness is an ability to be at the forefront of creativity, bringing, as Homi Bhabha calls it, 'newness into the world' (1994). An emphasis on the aesthetic and experiential dimensions of diaspora has made an enormous impact on cultural and literary studies. Music, film and the visual arts all benefit from an interculturalism that is deemed integral to the diaspora experience. The intermingling, interpenetration and blending of cultural traditions, in what Dick Hebdige (1987) called, borrowing from black musical culture, the 'cut "n" mix' of contemporary culture, enables the production of hybrid, syncretic and creolized cultural forms. The basic formulation is that making culture is easier when you are living through difference. The self-conscious constructed nature of living is revealed through migration processes.[13] Cultural production, therefore, makes present what is felt absent, and transforms the familiar into something profoundly strange. Yet, unlike those anthropological approaches which have marked this process as a re-creation of tradition or a reproduction of social forms in a new place,[14] Stuart Hall (1989) maintains that these innovations of culture are not and never can be simple re-creations because they are the product of new material conditions. It is this creative potential that somehow infuses the diasporic experience that is of concern in the next three sections of this chapter, which look at music, film and literature. In what is, by necessity, a cursory and partial view of the academic debates over each of these areas, we offer an indicative engagement with the vast array of commentary on these cultural products. Our intention is to examine to what extent diasporic cultural products retain the 'seeds of resistance' that have marked, and still resonate within, the experiences of diasporic populations. As a counterpoint to the commodification of diasporic cultural production, the fashionable trend for hybridity and the ability of marketing agents to render the most progressive message palatable for mass consumption constantly interrupts these narratives.

Music

Perhaps more than any other creative form, music carries the burden of being ubiquitous in both production and consumption. It is not surprising that it is in an analysis of music that Hebdige (1987) coined the term 'cut "n" mix', nor that music has been at the forefront of diasporic cultural production. The most influential theorist in this context is again Gilroy. He notes that the creative expressions immanent in 'Black music's obstinate and consistent commitment to the ideas of a better future' (Gilroy 1991: 10) mark a specific diasporic space. Music is the vehicle that 'brings Africa, America, Europe and the Caribbean seamlessly together. It was produced in Britain by the children of Caribbean and African settlers from the raw materials supplied by Black Chicago but filtered through Kingstonian sensibility' (Gilroy 1991: 15). This kind of patterning can be repeated in many other contexts as well as with other forms of cultural production. What is specific about Gilroy's stance on musical expression is the relationship forged between expressions of resistance and expressive forms. In a similar manner the routes marked by the musicians in the bands *Asian Dub Foundation* and *Fun^da^mental* produce a different diasporic space, one that takes in South Asia, the Middle East, England and North Africa but shares a common tradition of resistance through cultural praxis with those musicians described by Gilroy. This is a music that finds its material rooted in the inner-city areas of London and Birmingham, yet nevertheless draws its inspiration from a multi-locational, multi-musical set of sources and, of course, is consumed globally.

We have previously explored these cultural manifestations in a number of publications mainly concerned with the development of South Asian dance music (Kaur and Kalra 1996; Kalra and Hutnyk 1998). Our perspectives mirror the debates which are present throughout this book. On the one hand, a recognition of the changing and fluid nature of cultural practices, always open to co-option, and, on the other hand, an appreciation of the potential for progressive work that music elicits. Our interventions began with the book, *Dis-Orienting Rhythms: The Politics of the New Asian Dance Music* (Sharma et al. 1996), which developed a range of critical perspectives on the relationship between music and politics. Most significantly, the intimate links between artists such as *Fun^da^mental* and *Asian Dub Foundation* to the creation of organizations that engage in cultural politics were exposed. In attending to the politics of Asian dance music, we also noted its commercialization and the volume *Critique of Exotica* (Hutnyk 2000) analyses the processes of commodification of this musical form as well as the more general category of world music. Alongside these books, two special editions of the journals *Postcolonial Studies* (Hutnyk and Kalra

1998) and *Theory, Culture and Society* (Hutnyk and Sharma 2000) also examined a range of popular cultural forms, but with a concentration on music. In all of this work, there is a recognition that music circulates as a commodity in the market place, but that this is not a postmodern shopping mall with a free-for-all consumptive range (although these tendencies are present). Indeed, Asian dance music was able to connect a specific set of spaces through the pleasure of music and the requirement for articulating episodes of injustice. The most recent intervention in the arena by Sharma (2005) notes how Asian dance music has to a large extent been reduced to the latest 'bit of flavour' for the multicultural taste buds of Western urban cosmopolitans, shorn of its relationship with an activist politics.

Diaspora is a privileged site for this kind of musical production because the ability to belong and not belong enables an insight into the endemic nature of inequalities within a society. However, this also engenders a material hierarchy that often places the diasporic group in a position of exploitation. Compare the status of South Asians in the USA with those in Britain and the importance of class as an indicator of the kinds of cultural production that mark resistance to racism and can transmute this into a trinket for consumer culture. The celebrated music star, Madonna, at one point in her career donning a *bindi* and wearing henna, stands in contrast to the these symbols, being the identifiers for racist groups to target South Asian women, as happened in New Jersey in the 1990s. White women donning *bindis* and wearing henna obviously represent a different register to South Asian women, who are identified with these consumer products in a way that often marginalizes and stereotypes their identities and can lead to racial violence. We have often been critical of the way cultural production by racialized groups can sometimes be deployed solely to achieve visibility in identity politics (Kalra and Hutnyk 1998). To 'produce' culture without politics or without an engagement with the politics inherent in the cultural industry is to acquiesce to an exoticizing and commercializing façade that leaves racial hierarchies intact. The cascade of resonant musical output, from Madonna to hip-hop star Missy Elliot, that has incorporated some aspect of the sitar and tabla sound, illustrates the process by which commodification can certainly enhance visibility, but only in the market place. Indeed, all creative output can then be cannabilized and commodified by the record industry, shearing it of any organic connectivity it may have had with racialized or exploited groups. As Tony Brennan clearly notes:

> Every popular art (one thinks especially of punk in this regard) is always *en route* to commodification, always in the process of becoming a commercial. But for its first two decades or so, no form more than rap was so thematically concerned with demonstrating its resistance to the market and its desire to be in it but not of it. (2001: 14)

But even rap, once described as the 'CNN for Black folks',[15] is now a global phenomenon and one of the foundations for sustaining the profit margins of transnational record companies (four of which control 80 per cent of worldwide sales of music). This process of thrusting cultural products that may come from a process of resistance to racist domination or exclusion into neatly packaged units for mass consumption is repeated in the worlds of fashion and other material cultural forms. Of course, the work of Theodor Adorno (1991) is most useful in outlining the complicity between mass culture and commodification. It is possible to apply Adorno to contemporary diasporic music cultures:

> A critique of standardization, as Adorno presented it 50 years ago, would need to take into account differential production processes and short production runs, just-in-time delivery systems and niche marketing strategies, so that the standardization of everything that Adorno feared could now be recast in terms of difference and specialization. (Hutnyk 2000: 47)

The change from mass production to niche marketing has seen the emergence of diasporic cultural products from small ethnic markets into the mainstream. Asian dance music has certainly undergone this transformation. The entry into the UK pop music charts in 2003 of the song 'Bach ke rahe' by the British Bhangra industry-based artist Punjabi MC tracks a process of commoditization. This tune was first produced by Punjabi MC, a Midlands-based DJ and record producer, in 1998 on a small diasporic record label. It is remixed by a Californian dance music specialist, and then re-released on a dance music label (owned by one of the major record houses) only to enter the charts five years on from its humble beginnings. Such trajectories show how the path of diaspora also sometimes shamelessly moves from the street to the superstore.

Film

A similar process, although in less pronounced manner, can also be seen when looking at film productions. Stuart Hall, in the influential article 'New Ethnicities' (1989), gives the example of Black films such as *Handsworth Songs* (dir. Akofamrah 1986) and *The Passion of Remembrance* (dir. Sankofa Film Workshop 1986) to illustrate how diasporic film production is always criss-crossed by multiplicities of gender, class and ethnicity and how, in turn, this provides both a critique of the normative dominant cultural form and the black homogeneous essentialized subject. Both films, alongside the early work of Gurinder Chadha, such as *I'm British, But* (1990), play some role in articulating the complexity of the lives of racialized groups in Britain. *Handsworth Songs*, in particular, emerges out of the 1985 uprisings against the police and racial injustice in Handsworth, a multiracial area of Birmingham. The film is an example of diasporic cultural production with an urgent and acute linkage to politics. Chadha's short offering, *I'm British, But*, documents young British Asians, reflecting upon their identity in the context of racism.

Film's significance for diaspora studies is in its ability to provide a narrative for academic consumption. A circuit of reviews of films such as *My Beautiful Laundrette* (dir. Stephen Frears 1985) and *Sammy and Rosie Get Laid* (dir. Stephen Frears 1987) have become a staple for talking about diasporic difference (between the USA and Europe [Spivak 1993]), but are also a means with which to contrast the politics of race between these two places (hooks 1990). The author of the books from which these films derive, Hanif Kureshi, becomes a key resource for understanding how the British Asian diaspora is 'Becoming Black/Asian-British' (Bromley 2000: 121). What is remarkable about this level of critical appraisal is the fact that more has probably been written about the significance of British diasporic cinema than there have been films produced. For this reason, perhaps, these films carry excessive expectations and an unnecessary burden of representation: as there are so few films, each one is expected to say something serious or at least relevant about the population being depicted as a whole. Chadha's second and well-publicized feature film, *Bhaji on the Beach* (1994), is particularly guilty here, dealing as it does with the entire spectrum of 'multicultural' clichés: arranged marriages, runaway daughters, inter-communal racism, sexual fantasy and dissonance due to second-generation culture clash.

The 1990s witnessed the beginning of a relative explosion of diasporic film production from Britain, which follows a long tradition of production in the USA. Almost mimicking musical production, many of these films have been overtly commercial, providing easily digestible caricatures. The 1980s, however, produced films such as *Handsworth Songs* (dir. John Akomfrah), which explored the origins of the uprisings by black communities in Handsworth, with themes of race, memory, ideology and Britain's colonial past. In contrast, the production *Babymother* (dir. Julian Henriques 2000), tells the individual story of a woman trying to break into the music scene. While both *Babymother* and *Handsworth Songs* were made by independent film-makers and were relatively marginal to the mainstream of British film-making, the former indicates the influence of a trend in Black American film which has moved away from overt social and political content.

To some extent the films analysed thus far can also be described within the confines of 'ethnic' or 'migrant' film, given their emphasis on settlement and its related concerns. In the book, *An Accented Cinema* (2001), Hamid Naficy broadens the canvas by introducing the concept of cinema 'with an accent' to describe the works of exilic, diasporic and ethnic film-makers in the West. In a mimesis of contemporary cultural theory, accented films are hybrid in style and deploy a double consciousness. 'From the cinematic traditions they acquire one set of voices, from the exilic and diasporic conditions they acquire another' (Naficy 2001: 22). This, then, enables a definition of accented cinema: 'The cinema discussed here derives its accent from its artisanal and collective production modes and from the film-maker's audience's deterritorialized locations' (2001: 23). The broad scope of this definition allows for an analysis of a wide range of film texts, but it does not take into account the extent to which national film traditions utilize diasporic themes to enhance their market capacity. Indian (Bollywood) film has shamelessly developed themes to promote its consumption in the diaspora. Another application of diasporic understanding is offered by

Christina Klein (2004) in her analysis of the film *Crouching Tiger, Hidden Dragon* (dir. Ang Lee 2000). This blockbusting martial arts love drama, set in China, drew reviews that, on the one hand, likened it to an authentic cinema of China in the traditions of Nationalist versus Hollywood mode and, on the other, was criticized as an inauthentic Hollywoodization of the martial arts genre. Klein draws upon diaspora theory to question these polarities and locate the film somewhere between 'a triangulated set of transnational relationships: Ang Lee's ties to his Chinese homeland, to other members of the Chinese diaspora, and to the culture of his American hostland' (2004: 21). Klein's analysis is no doubt a better development on those offered by the debates about authenticity that the film also provoked, but her analysis avoids the premise upon which the movie becomes transnational, that is the money involved in its production. While the sets, the narrative and the actors draw upon a Chinese diaspora, the funding of the film is firmly located within the major transnational film giants (Sony and Colombia in this case). Here the diasporic product is made visible by the intervention of transnational capital and the film moves out of the Hong Kong–Taiwan–Singapore triad of Kung Fu consumption on to the stage of globalized consumption.

The practicalities of living with difference may lend creative practitioners a greater capacity to produce cultural 'newness', but this is no guarantee against co-option. As Hall pointedly remarks:

> This latest phase of capitalist globalization, with its brutal compressions and reorderings across time and space, has not necessarily resulted in the destruction of those specific structures and particularistic attachments and identifications which go with the more localized communities which a homogenizing modernity was supposed to replace. ... The so-called 'logic of capital' has operated as much *through* difference – preserving and transforming difference (including sexual difference) – not by undermining it. (Hall 1992a: 353)

It is often wrongly assumed that diasporic cultural products are inherently progressive solely because they expose and question the boundaries of the nation or of other normative social forms such as the nuclear family. Even where this is the case, and conventional norms are transgressed, cultural products are always open to appropriation, repackaging and sale by the market. The style associated with the cut 'n' mix cultural products has been rapidly absorbed in the avaricious machinery of consumer capitalism. As Hall points out in the quote above, this process is not in any way new, but it is an important aspect of the latest phase of capitalist globalization. In the age of colonialism, the Paisley design was a nineteenth-century unacknowledged borrowing of the Ambi print from North India. Today, the patenting and control of cultural property continues. Transnational mechanisms such as the World Trade Organization appropriate and maintain rights of exploitation in place of the old mercantile plunder routines of the colonial era.[16]

Cultural commodification is a process that is intensifying, co-option begins almost before there is any chance of resistance. This is closely connected to the importance of technological change that is often discussed with reference to diaspora and global technology. Clifford's article on diaspora recites, on almost every page, the importance of 'a discourse that is travelling or hybridising in new global conditions' (Clifford 1994: 306). Diaspora relies on 'transnational connections', 'telephone circuits', 'technologies of transport, communication, and labour migration', 'airplanes, telephones, tape cassettes, camcorders', 'business circuits and travel trajectories' (Clifford 1994: 304, 305–28). This presumption of a relationship between the formation of diasporas and new information technologies points to the imbricated relationship of communication and information technologies with late phases of capitalist development. Too often, discursive frameworks ignore the role of economic factors in the circulation of diasporic cultural products.

Literature

Music and film production and their circulation certainly attract a great deal of attention from those studying diaspora, but the development of a cogent theoretical terrain for the impact of diasporic consciousness on cultural production lies not in these expressive media but in the world of literature. Diaspora has become a central motif for defining a range of new writings and criticism in the broader arena of what has come to be called Postcolonial Studies. If there is to be a direct contrast to the typologies of diaspora as presented by Cohen in the previous chapter, then the works of literary critics with a deconstruction tool kit probably constitute the most likely candidates. In the field of literary theory, the term 'diaspora' has emerged with the most prominence and force as part of a much wider range of projects that desire the undoing of Orientalism, the exposure of Eurocentrism, and work to undermine the centrality of the male figure as agent.[17]

The technique of reading cultural products as texts open to (re)interpretation is one of the reasons why literary theory has become so important in the study of diasporic cultural formations. Central to any intercultural interaction is the tension that arises when two languages clash. Here, language does not refer only to spoken formal language, but to the metaphorical basis of communication. This is central to Homi Bhabha's approach to the importance of diaspora: 'This liminality of migrant experience is no less a transitional phenomenon than a translational one; there is no resolution to it because the two conditions are ambivalently enjoined in the "survival" of migrant life' (Bhabha 1994: 224). One of the central processes enunciated in the colonial encounter which comes to the imperial centres in the creation of diasporic spaces is that of translation. The problem of cultural difference is, then, that which cannot be translated. Bhabha, quoting Walter Benjamin, notes:

> The subject of cultural difference becomes a problem that Walter Benjamin has described as the irresolution, or liminality of 'translation', the *element of resistance* in the process of transformation, 'that element in a translation which does not lend itself to translation'. (Benjamin 1968: 75, in Bhabha 1994: 224)

For Bhabha, the interstices at which cultural difference is translated are sites of radical and dangerous possibility. The idiomatic scene of translation as an impossible but necessary exchange is somehow beyond the pale of both integrationist dreams (the melting pot) and racist invocations (the pure white nation), and has the potential for the development of a post-national environment in which, in Bhabha's (1994) world, we can 'emerge as ourselves'. The site of this transgression is called the 'third space'. The ambition to take the third space as a space of radical politics has been recently refuted by Bhabha, who has reduced it from its large claims to the modest space of potential negotiation.[18] There is another genealogy of the concept of a Third Way that can be discerned, beginning with the deployment of the concept by newly independent former colonies in the Non-Aligned Movement in their attempts to carve out a space between the forces of the USA and the Soviet Union. More recently, the pragmatists of the democratic parties of America and Europe have captured the progressive elements of the Third Way concept as a means of asserting a centre-right agenda, ostensibly against the polarized positions of socialism and capitalism.[19]

To some extent, Bhabha's work represents a shift from a relationship between material and cultural forms to a mode of textual analysis legitimated within its own framework rather than with reference to other social actions and activities (see Hutnyk 2004 for a detailed analysis of this aspect of Bhabha's work). Technical analysis of novels and cinematic aesthetic analysis of films can therefore be removed from any mention of the social axes of class, gender or race. This is not to say that this avoidance is not a routine part of academic production, but we do want to point to the contrast between the supposedly 'inherently' transgressive nature of the diasporic cultural product and much of the analysis that is done under that name. Diasporic cultural products are not sufficiently transgressive so as to be always able to alter frames of reference. An example of this can be found in the recent volume entitled *Narratives for a New Belonging* (2000), where the author, Roger Bromley, outlines an agenda for the usefulness of textual narratives:

> Almost all the fictions are by, and concern themselves with, those for whom categories of belonging and the present have been made unstable as a consequence of the displacement enforced by post-colonial and or migrant circumstances. Language, home, memory and marginalization are recurring problems. ... The fictions speak of, from and across migrant identities and develop narratives of plurality, fluidity and always emergent becoming. (Bromley 2000: 1–2)

Reading a series of novels and short stories from America, Canada and Britain in the company of Clifford, Hall, Said and Spivak, the centrality of textual production serves to produce a world in which, despite the ramifications of 'racism, brutal police oppression, under-development, gender discrimination', 'narrative can become a fundamental resource ... in disconnecting and fracturing hegemonic relationship by giving shape to utterances which are outside the sentences of power and control' (Bromley 2000: 16).

These are noble sentiments and no doubt some of the motivation behind the expansion in studies of diasporic/post-colonial literatures. But the question of whether a book about books and films and their critique of inequality is sufficient to engender social justice remains unspoken. What kind of social activism might a reading of a diasporic fiction engender?

It is the reaction to *The Satanic Verses*, by Salman Rushdie, which perhaps most forcefully exhibits the power of the written word and the reactionary nature of much of the literary establishment.[20] At the broadest level, the so-called 'Rushdie Affair' is illustrative of the fragile relationship between the social aspects of diasporic groups, which in the British context are marred by racism and poor living conditions, and the literary worlds of representation in which no boundaries are sacred. This is not to say one does not comment or impinge upon the other, but Rushdie's diasporic space is not the same as that of the South Asian Muslims who campaigned against *The Satanic Verses* for its alleged blasphemous content. Rushdie's diaspora is populated by writers (at that time in England, but now in the USA, where no doubt other literati would join this list): 'Swift, Conrad, Marx are as much our literary forebears as Tagore or Ram Mohan Roy' (Rushdie 1992: 20). Rajagopalan Radhakrishnan (1996) provides a reading of the Rushdie Affair that provides further insights into this contradictory relationship. He states: 'ironically the *fatwa* (horrendous as it is) is in fact the protest symbol of the weak and much maligned-exploited-stereotyped-racialized-othered East trying to stand up to the unquestioned global jurisdiction of Western secular interpretive norms' (1996: 160–161). Yet, it is these norms that are supposedly questioned by diasporic writing. The literary establishment that comes to defend Rushdie does so in contrast to the manner in which much of his earlier, staunchly anti-racist and anti-imperialist commentary was greeted. Citing Radhakrishnan again: 'it was much easier [for liberal literary figures] to value his stand against Islamic clerisy, but not so much his many critiques of the racism and ethnocentrism "within"' (1996: 161). The resonance of the 'Affair' with the other foreign office diplomat and espionage scandals (the Profumo Affair, Foreign Affairs) also indicates the state-level political terrain upon which this ostensibly literary event was played out. In a further twist, Rushdie goes on to become an American citizen and an apologist for any type of US intervention in the Muslim world, coming out in favour of the attack on Iraq, fuelled by his anger towards European sentiments against America.[21]

Rushdie is also at the forefront of the commodification of diasporic literature. The latest flavour of the month becomes the diasporic or exiled writer, either (brilliantly) deforming the English language or providing insights into new areas of experience hitherto not savoured by the majority English-reading public. The big Indian novel really made it big in English with *A Suitable Boy* (1994), by Vikram Seth, and now every year at least one writer of this hybrid pedigree is required by the major fiction publishers. It is perhaps useful to draw a distinction between diasporic writers in English and Indian writers in English, and contrast this to those (few) translated into English (many more are, of course, not translated). It could be argued that those writing in English in India have a diasporic consciousness forged either through internal migration to the metropolis or by being multilingual. An example of one such author is Arundhati Roy, whose debut novel *The God of Small Things* won the literary establishment's Booker Prize in 1997 (incidentally, the prize was also won by Rushdie in 1981, and in 1993 he was awarded the Booker of Bookers prize). Roy was heralded by the literary establishment: 'The quality of Ms Roy's narration is so extraordinary, at once so morally strenuous and so imaginatively supple, that the reader remains enthralled all the way through' (Dinnage 1997: 14). But her responses to recent world events have been almost opposite to those of Rushdie. Not a diasporic writer but rather one that uses her ambivalent position as a Delhi-based Indian writer of English with an ability to publish in the Western press, she stridently and consistently uses her position to promote opposition to the Narmada Dam[22] and to speak out against nuclearization of South Asia and the re-colonization of Iraq.

This point of the privileged space of the diasporic is taken up again via the work of Spivak in Chapters 4 and 5, but here we want to highlight debate about the extent to which diasporic cultural production becomes important in the context of the cultural industry's desire for new-ness, a requirement to maintain and extend markets in the ever-expanding circuits of capitalism. Even in its most progressive mode, how do critiques of the nation influence the deployment of the state's army? A Muslim diaspora opposed to the war in Iraq contributed to the largest demonstration in Britain and perhaps the largest worldwide co-ordinated opposition to a war. The marching of almost 10 million people on the streets of the world's capitals is a mobilization which certainly utilized the technologies and networks that diaspora invokes, but was not sufficient to stop British and American tanks from rolling into Iraq in 2003.

Culture wars

Diasporas may hold the potential for thinking beyond absolutist notions of identity and critiquing hegemonic national cultures, but is this sufficient for an adequate challenge to the structure of exploitation? Class location and gender dynamics both cross-cut and undermine any diasporic potential for organizing outside the nation-state. There is also the potential for diasporas to promote reactionary political and cultural programmes. The support of Hindus in America for far-right and xenophobic nationalist formations in India has been well-documented (see Bhatt and Mukta 2000). This diasporic politics does not visualize a post-national formation but rather a pure national form under which all difference is erased rather than recognized and valued.

Diasporas are certainly involved in the questioning of the cultural identity of the nation. Yet, despite much cultural studies' rhetoric about their resistive potential, diasporic formations are now at the forefront of producing new cultural products, fit and ready for consumption, and ready to demonstrate the end of the nation. In a powerful critique, San Juan begins by pointing out how: 'Contemporary cultural studies posit the demise of the nation as an unquestioned assumption, almost a doctrinal point of departure' (2001: 52). However, the context for the assertion of state power has sharpened since 2001, a matter we will explore in more detail in the final chapter of this book. We note there is much to be said for the diasporic as a site of struggle – cultural and political – but there is a wide array of options left aside, ignored or never explicitly connected to diaspora in practical terms. We look to anti-racist, anti-imperialist, internationalist or single-issue campaigns (deaths in custody, troops out of Northern Ireland, Guantanamo Solidarity or Wages for Housework) and note that questions of how to organize actively across diaspora and hybridity often seem beyond the ken of those in the scholarly enclaves. This we must read as a symptomatic lacuna, even as we acknowledge that many academics and students are increasingly involved in social movements, debating difference, confronting oppression. In this book we point out the ways curricula staples, habits of theorizing and key concepts are debated in a restricted way and how engagement that may do something with the terms seems still to be left aside. With San Juan, we note the promise of diaspora as able to produce a world that could 'embody a peculiar sensibility enacting a caring and compassionate agenda for the whole species that thrives on cultural difference' (2001: 60), but we also posit that this promise is countered by the poorly paid employment and substandard conditions which mark the presence of, for example, Filipina domestic labour in the capitals of the over-developed world, and so many other cases.[23] The main critique for San Juan is the location of diaspora as a site which can afford the space for the reinvention of identities free from naturalized categories but not from 'borders, state apparatuses, and other worldly imperatives' (2001: 60). San Juan's work takes seriously Appadurai's note that:

> There is a disturbing tendency in the Western academy today to divorce study of discursive forms from the study of other institutional forms and the study of literary discourses from the mundane discourses of bureaucracies, armies, private corporations and non-state social organizations. (Appadurai 1996: 159)

Ultimately, these studies of diaspora,

> [L]acking any dialectical materialist analysis of the dynamics of colonialism and imperialism that connect the Philippines [Third World] and its peoples with the United States [centers of Imperialism] and the rest of the world ... are all scholastic games, at best disingenuous exercises in chauvinist or white-supremacist apologetics. (San Juan 2001: 62)

The way in which diasporic studies have spawned into almost every field of the humanities and social sciences, with predominance in the field of literature and arts, is shorn up in San Juan's strident critique. Free of a political relationship to those who might be called diasporic, and lacking a materialist critique, much of these studies fall into the discourse of liberal multiculturalism, so roundly discredited by Spivak. Here, diaspora only serves to alert us to those 'who have stayed in place for more than thirty thousand years' (Spivak 1999: 402). These are those native peoples of the world for whom diaspora has meant uprooting from ancestral lands for the demagogues of modernity – colonial powers drawing lines on maps and postcolonial dam-building projects, etc. What can be learnt from the destruction of the diverse cultures of native peoples, of the Aboriginals of Australia and the indigenous peoples of the Americas, is that in these places culture is destroyed only to be remade by liberal multiculturalism – as exotic enter-tainment and cultural curio, on the one hand, and continued decimation, illness and poverty on the other (hidden) hand. There is also a trace of this process in what Spivak (1999) calls 'multicultural diasporists': those who are able to communicate with the diaspora because of a shared language of the dominant, where no effort or attention is paid to the necessity of transnational literacy, or to a critique of the fundamentals of capitalist rela-tions and how to dismantle them. Diaspora becomes the easy mechanism for engaging with other cultures in a seemingly benign multiculturalism.[24] In this sense, the consumption of music, film and literature produced by the diaspora becomes the quintessential act of the cosmopolitan multicultural-ist which then enables ignorance of the places that make possible the nam-ing of diaspora. These are those places that are being bombed and crippled by the actions of imperialism resurfaced. But perhaps we run ahead of our-selves and should pay, in the next chapters, closer attention to the mixing up of our terms.

Notes

1 The infamous example of this is given by Dr Anees Esmail, who sent out identical appli-cations for jobs as a medical doctor to various places using both English and South Asian-sounding names. The success rates of the Asian-sounding applications was much lower than that for the English (see Esmail et al. 1998).

2 The requirement for registration of nationals from certain countries in the post-September 11 legislation has targeted people from Arab and Muslim countries. This has led to deportations and a general climate of fear among certain populations (see Howell and Shryock 2003).

3 There is a vast array of literature on nations and nationalism. For our present purposes, the most useful texts are Bhabha (1990), Anderson (1983), Gellner (1983) and Chatterjee (1995).

4 For the classic modernist text on the significance of the nation, see Gellner (1983), who argues that 'homogeneity, literacy and anonymity' are key traits of the modern nation.

5 In the colonial context, Anne McClintock's work (1996) has been seminal in relating a critique of gender to nationalism. Similar arguments for contemporary Britain are found in Anthias and Yuval-Davis (1989). Marhsall (1994) provides a useful feminist critique of the nation from a Western viewpoint.

6 Axel (2002) would not agree with this role for diaspora, but this is a flaw in his model.

7 Hindutva literally means Hindu-ness and refers to right-wing Hindu nationalism in India. Louis Farrakhan is the leader of a right-wing movement among Black Muslims in America.

8 However, this is not the only criteria for the political mobilization of these groups.

9 Commentary on the various Party-building initiatives in the wake of the two million-strong anti-war demonstration of February 2003 can be found in the *Weekly Worker*, available online at www.cpgb.co.uk.

10 The World Trade Organization, the World Bank and the International Monetary Fund are organizations which have their origin in a meeting at Bretton Woods in the USA after the Second World War. They were designed to provide order to global capitalism, though they have been rightly subject to a great deal of critique (see Klein 2000).

11 One diasporic group that pays almost no attention to borders of the nation-state of South Asia are the Ismailis. The followers of the Aga Khan operate in Asia and the West through an intricate network of social contacts, with a common language of communication (Urdu/Hindustani) and a common Islamic faith to bind them. An Ismaili family with close ties to Gujarat in India but now settled in Sweden came to that country in the early 1970s as refugees from Uganda, a country which they had gone to in the late nineteenth century. The families of three brothers in their everyday lives have no connection with the contemporary borders that make up the nation-states of South Asia. The elder brother was married to a woman from Bangladesh (indeed, the disputed border zone of Chittagong), the middle brother to a woman from Pakistan (Karachi) and the third to a woman from Mumbai (India). This is not an arbitrary example.

12 Indeed, the oath of allegiance that is being demanded of those applying for British citizenship actually focuses this allegiance on the monarch: 'I, [name], swear by Almighty God that, on becoming a British citizen, I will be faithful and bear true allegiance to Her Majesty Queen Elizabeth the Second, Her Heirs and Successors according to law' (Nationality, Immigration and Asylum Act 2002, Schedule I, Home Office, 2003).

13 Diaspora privileges migration as the disruption that evokes the recognition of the constructed nature of reality. However, this is akin to the disruptions wrought by industrial decline on working-class communities in the West. Indeed, the emergence of the idea of a white diaspora (see Chapter 6) is predicated on the notion of whiteness, which is associated with de-industrialization in America and the resulting construction: 'white trash' to describe a newly formed class fraction. This idea of disruption has also been more recently taken up in queer theory with the problematizing of home that diaspora offers through the lens of a non-normative sexuality (see Chapter 3 for more details on this aspect).

14 As noted in Chapter 1, one of the academic strands that has focused on home and away has been British-based Ethnic Studies. A group of authors, beginning with Watson (1977) but followed primarily by anthropologists, pathologized the idea of racialized, British-born young people caught 'between two cultures' as people who are in identity crises due to the process of migration. These negative connotations, while now fairly scant in the Euro-American academic literature, were to some extent central to the working of policy-makers and journalism. A central cause given by education practitioners for the poor educational achievements of Pakistani- and Bangladeshi-heritage young people in Britain is the fact that the 'home culture' is different from the 'school culture'. Again there are parallels to the way in which working-class children were treated in Britain with the advent of universal secondary education (see Willis 1977).

15 The rap group, *Public Enemy*, called themselves 'CNN for Black folks' on a series of posters used to advertise their song 'Black Steel in the hour of chaos' (1994).

16 The two pieces of significant legislation in the cultural field are the TRIPS and TRIMS agreements. The more insidious TRIPS agreement refers to patenting rights and has led to many indigenous crops being patented in the USA. Consequently, farmers in the Third World are asked to pay a royalty for the use of indigenous seeds. The most contentious case thus far has been the patenting of Indian basmati rice by a Texas company which has renamed it as Texmati. The Indian government has refused to recognize the patent.

17 For a critical text in the field, see Barkan and Shelton (1998). More recently, diaspora has become a marketing tool for new writing, for example, the recent collection of new writing from London entitled *Diaspora City*, edited by McDowell (2003).

18 From the discussion between Stuart Hall and Homi Bhabha: 'Stuart Hall and Homi Bhabha in Conversation', Monday 11 December 2000, University of Westminster.

19 Robert Young (2001) provides a useful history of how the idea of the Third Way was developed by the non-aligned movement, which was essentially to make a distinction between the West and the Soviet Union for many Third World countries. Anthony Giddens is best known as the architect of the Third Way in Britain.

20 Our concern here is with the relationship between different types of diasporic cultural producer. The earliest public academic text on this debate we know of was collected in the journal *Criticism, Heresy and Interpretation* in 1989.

21 'Fight the good fight', Salman Rushdie, Saturday 2 November 2002, *The Guardian*.

22 The construction of large dams on the River Narmada in central India and its impact on millions of people living in the river valley has become one of the most important social issues in contemporary India. Roy has been a campaigner against the construction of the dam in *The Cost of Living* (1999).

23 Filipinas constitute what might be called a new diaspora, which consists in large part of domestic labour, or slave labour as San Juan prefers. This female workforce exists in a state of constant oppression emblematic of the 'new world disorder' and late capitalist relations, which render the Philippines structured to produce a surplus for 1 per cent of the population. In the search for the micronarratives of ambivalence which mark these women's lives, certain ethnographers have focused on their consumption patterns to highlight their agency' (San Juan 2001: 60). See Chapter 3 for a more elaborate take.

24 The obsession of the British state and policy-makers, following the 2001 riots by Asian Muslim males in the north of England, with the teaching of the English language is an example of language being used as a way of not understanding a culture. Almost all the young men engaged in the riots knew English only too well, but this did not mean that their actions were translatable.

3

Sexual Limits of Diaspora

What about sex? We can build here upon the theoretical and empirical arguments of Chapters 1 and 2 to address issues of gender and sexuality within diaspora. It is our argument that it is not sufficient to talk about categories such as the Jewish or African-Caribbean diaspora or the metropolitan post-colonial hybrid without paying attention to how (the lack of) movement and mixture impinge differentially on the lives of women and men, girls and boys. We need to ask whether diaspora and hybridity helps constitute a subject beyond the traditional divide of gender, or whether these terms can contribute to the emancipation of women (and indeed men) from cultural orthodoxy? In foregrounding gender, we must also take on board the idea that (wo)man does not constitute an homogeneous category of analysis. 'Third World' and post-colonial feminists such as Inderpal Grewal, Norma Alarcon, Chandra Talpade Mohanty, Valerie Smith, Hortense Spillers and Gayatri Chakravorty Spivak have challenged the values of heterosexual and patriarchal convention, which more often than not are buttressed by the state, by highlighting 'the centrality of racial and class formations in the constitution of gender itself' (Butler 1994: 5). In this chapter, we look to what may be described as the 'significant minutiae' of diasporas within dynamics relating to gender, ethnicity/race, class, life-stage and sexuality.

Linking diaspora to the scattering of seed, and therefore to masculinist constructions of the nation, could render the concept forever beyond the pale of feminist reconstruction, but this might be taking the etymology of words too far. Rather, a more relevant concern is the extent to which studies of diaspora manage to alert us to the gendered dimensions of the social. In this regard, there are many critiques of a gender-neutral diaspora (Clifford 1994; Brah 1996) and, more recently, Floya Anthias (1998) outlines an agenda for gendering diaspora which includes, among others, two aspects which are of particular significance for the orientation of this chapter: first, the extent to which diasporic groups are subject to two sets of gender relations, that of the host country and that of the ethnic community. Secondly, the way in which women become the carriers of the cultural symbolism that marks out the boundaries of the diasporic group. Our attention develops these areas as well as posing the requirement for thinking about those groups who do not often feature under the rubric of diaspora, such as women trafficked in the international sex trade. More fundamentally, we take the outcomes of gender-sensitive studies of diaspora to include a focus on masculinity – and its demonization in the Black and Asian/Middle Eastern male – and use these 'complexities' to challenge heterosexual norms and paranoias.

We begin with an assessment of the gendered dimensions of migration and the symbolic imagery that is deployed, distinguishing men and women in the migration and settlement process. In this process, women become both the creators of the ties that bind as well as the carriers of culture. Does this represent a burden or a sense of empowerment to the women in question? As we shall explore in detail, one aspect of the formation of diaspora relies on a gender division that construes women as vessels of culture and men as vehicles of labour power. This is further complicated by noting differential gender roles in the 'home' and the wider society. In several cases, we find that diasporic men are most empowered in the household due to patriarchal norms, yet they are disempowered in the wider society due to competitive antagonisms and widespread paranoia about non-white masculinity (Alexander 2002; Banerjea 2002). Women might be disempowered in the household for a variety of reasons, but *potentially* empowered in the wider society where discourses of 'rescuing' vulnerable and oppressed female members of diasporic community run rife. This is an example in the metropolitan sphere of what Gayatri Spivak, on the subject of colonial India, has called 'white men saving brown women from brown men' (Spivak 1999: 285). We will see this operative in the politics of sex work as well as in international campaigns about women's 'rights'.

Due to several complex structural factors, it is increasingly women who tend to migrate in the modern era – a phenomenon that has been described as 'the feminization of global migration streams' (Andall 1999: 241). As Alison Murray further observes:

> There are now many more women involved in the largest mass migration in human history. The majority are employed on a contractual basis as foreign domestic workers (the 'maid trade') in situations which often involve debts, exploitations and sexual abuse. (Murray 1998: 58–59)

There is little in the diaspora literature that acknowledges this shift from male to female labour power. Indeed, these absences provide much of the rationale for considering gender in a separate chapter and with a range of specific nuances.

Masculinity on the move

It appears that much of the literature on diaspora and gender attends more to the circumstances of women than it does to those of men. This is a predicament that has blighted many earlier studies on gender, with their myopic lens focused on the lives and circumstances of women alone. If men are addressed in the literature on diaspora, it is done so through a generalized lens on aspects of immigration, labour, kinship, religion, ethnicity, race – that is, gender dynamics as they apply to issues of masculinity are not made conspicuous as it is assumed that these discourses are implicitly about male universes, male discourses being considered the norm. A brief re-reading of migration processes and diasporic formation indicates how both women and men are marked in gendered ways.

Male labour was, in the industrial era, valued by virtue of its perceived superior physical strength and thus labour migration, rural to urban and international, was most often first carried out by men, thus paving the way for women to join them afterwards. However, there were exceptions to this general trend and women did play a significant part in the decision for men to move overseas. In Britain, the migration of female nurses from the Caribbean in the 1950s and 1960s exemplifies how it is the requirements of certain types of labour that is a factor in deciding which gender migrates.

The contemporary post-industrial demand for labour with 'soft' skills often results in females migrating first and, as we shall see later, trafficking for the sex trade is almost exclusively female. Nevertheless, most international migration historically involved the movement of men. The fact that there were not many wives, mothers or sisters present in the community of the labouring diaspora played a considerable part in the experience of early settlement. One prominent example that resonates with our later discussion on hybridity concerns the mainly male South Asian Punjabi diasporas of the early twentieth century in North America. Between 1913 and 1948 when anti-miscegenation laws were abrogated, 80 per cent of South Asian men in California ended up marrying Hispanic women. This was a response to the fact that they could not bring Indian women with them to work in agriculture in California's San Joaquin and Imperial valleys, nor could they legitimately marry across 'races'. Instead, the men found that

> country clerks would issue marriage licenses to people of different 'races' so long as they had a similar skin colour. This softness in the application of the law soon led to marriages between Punjabis and Mexicans, who had been crossing the border in large numbers since the Mexican Revolution of 1911. (Nash 1999: 15)[1]

Lisa Lowe reports that 'the administration of [US] citizenship was simultaneously a "technology" of racialization and gendering' (1996: 11). In 1870, it was men of African descent who could become naturalized, as was the case for white men, but the bar to citizenship remained for Asian men until the repeal acts of 1943–52. In all these cases, it was the men who were afforded legal citizenship; related women became citizens only by extension.

Similarly, despite the demand for nurses from the Caribbean, it was still mostly males who migrated from that region to Britain. When we examine the log books of the much discussed *Windrush* passenger ship which ferried the first large group of African-Caribbeans to Britain in 1948, women were very much in the minority. In the Caribbean, it was elder women in particular who ruled the roost in family units or small communities. When migration to Britain began, there were approximately two men to every woman – a pattern that was to even out only in the late 1950s. As Mike and Trevor Phillips point out, the scarcity of African-Caribbean women 'left a large pool of unattached young men, more or less free of all the social limits which had previously constrained their behaviour' (Phillips and Phillips 1999: 118). Long hours, poor pay and poor housing conditions, notwithstanding, men were free to pursue their own leisure activities, uninhibited by their female relatives.

Whereas race and ethnicity were the overriding factors of asserting difference, gendered identities also carried a qualitatively different set of images for host societies. These perceptions have their roots in colonial framings – the lazy native, dangerous other, decadent or effeminate men – and continue to manifest themselves today in views about migrants, asylum-seekers and 'terrorists'. With the onset of mass migration to Britain, for instance, Black men were perceived differently from Black women. This played a part in the kinds of encounter forged between local men and women. As the African-Caribbean Alfred 'King Dick' Harvey reminisces of his time in Britain from the late 1940s:

> If it was pure men here a lot of us would go back home, 'cos the men hated us. The women, they seem to fancy us, so I would say white women let us stay in Britain. Yeah, they are the main cause for a lot of us, especially boys from my syndicate. (cited in Phillips and Phillips 1999: 117)

The syndicates involved a group of men who managed a number of clubs and gambling joints and pursued bohemian lifestyles that were seductive to 'swingers' of the post-war era. African-Caribbean men played up to the Eurocentric 'myth' of the oversexed and well-endowed Black man, having various transient sexual encounters with local women. This image led to the representation of African-Caribbean men as dangerous to the moral fabric of the country and subsequently subject to extreme forms of police control (Hall and Jefferson 1974).

These images of dangerous, racialized males have been almost continuous with the settlement of male labour from Britain's former colonies. Claire Alexander, in *The Asian Gang* (2000), focuses on what is glibly described as the 'Muslim underclass' in south-east London. She reflects on racialized representations, perpetuated by the media, of Asian men reinforced in the notion of the 'gang'. These images became particularly pervasive after the murder of the white youth, Richard Everitt, in 1994 in London and the riots in Bradford in 1995. Alexander demonstrates how unconnected, small-scale clashes become congealed and narrativized as gang warfare in the reactions of representatives from school, the police and the media. As a result, working-class Asian male youth are repeatedly demonized. Similarly, Koushik Banerjea (2002) further elaborates on the contexts in which South Asian or Middle Eastern men are pathologized. He asserts:

> The 'swarthy foe' has never seemed so real, his gendered presence never so unequivocal. In an atmosphere already poisoned by the spasms of racial violence across northern English towns in 2001, the catastrophic attacks on New York and Washington in September and subsequent 'war on terrorism', launched by America and its allies, have merely intensified the gloom. If there

was already a concern about 'the other' and 'his' corrosive presence within the western metropolis, then this rapidly attained critical status after 11 September 2001. (Banerjea 2002: 575)

These 'characters' are caricaturized as 'toxic strangers' and 'fake civilians' who are apparently lurking in our midst. Effectively, such ideas heighten regimes of insecurity and paranoia in and around civic space, a space in which 'the only certitude, sadly, is of further violence; precisely against an imprecise enemy, variously turbaned, clean-shaven, bearded, (un)employed, (non) Muslim and (not really) here' (Banerjea 2002: 575). Such studies remind us that it is not only women that need a unique address when it comes to studies in diaspora and gender, but also men in an approach which does not take their gendered identities for granted.

Representing difference

Despite a history of demonization, masculinity is frequently ignored in representations of diaspora, whereas images of women are often central to the making of diasporic difference. Eurocentric discourse affects non-white women differently from those of men. Whereas Black African-Caribbean women were seen as 'female castrators' – feared yet desired – South Asian women were largely deemed as passive or subordinate. Avtar Brah identifies three primary objectifications of South Asian women in Britain. These observations may just as well apply to diasporic Asian women located anywhere in the West and include:

1 the 'exotic oriental woman – sensuous, seductive, full of Eastern promise' typically portrayed by airline advertisements showcasing compliant hostesses;
2 the 'dirty, ugly, oily-haired' South Asian woman; and
3 the 'sexually licentious' South Asian woman-on-the-rampage. (Brah 1996: 78–79; see also Parmar 1982: 259)

While men were seen as the more threatening or predatory, women were either to be desired or pitied for living in what is often parodied as misogynist and undemocratic 'traditional' communities. Further to Brah's typology on stereotypes of South Asian women, there is also the additional view of Asian – specifically Muslim – women being seen through the lens of:

problem areas like arranged marriages, clitoridectomy, and the veil. This in turn fixes these women as 'naturally' passive because their modes of resistance are not understood within the economic, political, social, and ideological structures that shape their lives within Britain. (Puar 1995: 25)

Impressionistic understandings of the wearing of the veil, the custom of arranged marriages, generational conflicts and bodily mutilations were used as an indictment of non-Western lifestyles. Indeed, it is women's bodies that become the marker for cultural difference and therefore diasporic connectivity. Men in the public sphere are, no doubt, also racialized by reference to colonial imagery, but this is not necessarily a basis of community formation. It is here that gender is central to the enunciation of diaspora, for it is those things that are viewed as tradition that become the cement for forming at least an idealized notion of a cohesive diaspora. This double bind becomes more conspicuous for those women born and brought up in the place of settlement. Young women were constructed as what might be described as 'twice victim', subjected to the (apparent) persecution of:

> this time not only of her oppressive, patriarchal, backward culture and 'extended' family but also of her supposed longings to assimilate into white society and the racism she faces within it. She is seen to crave all that the West has to offer, but according to dominant white gazes, her culture holds her back, and only the 'rebels' succeed. (Puar 1995: 25–26)

This is another instance of how children of diaspora are often seen as confused and disoriented, positioned 'between cultures' (Watson 1977; Anwar 1979, 1998) – that of tradition-bound and static Asian cultures, and a progressive and liberal West – a problematic assumption where culture is seen in an overly rigid and formulaic manner.[2]

The objectification of Asian women as lacking agency in their diasporic communities is the residue of a colonial discourse that emphasized simplistic characterization of tradition and modernity and built up a relationship that determines not just the historical connections between Britain and India, but also much of the former colonized parts of Asia and Western countries.[3] This objectification is a formidably resilient phenomenon that has attached itself in specific forms to most Asian female populations, no matter where they reside. In the USA, for instance, South Asian women are also construed as docile and lacking agency as compared to the liberated and emancipated Western woman, a feminist model of the Western bourgeois subject (Koshy 1994). Chinese women living in the USA carry similar associations, as do women from the Philippino and Vietnamese diasporas (Chow 1993; Lowe 1996). In all of these cases, women are perceived as repositories of a culture that is seen as holding them back. In this way, an overwhelmingly negative picture is painted, and only modernity (from a Eurocentric perspective) is deemed to save them.

Women as 'carriers' of culture?

Since at least the 1960s, debate has raged among feminists and their detractors about whether women are the main transmitters of culture, particularly when it comes to their purportedly 'natural' roles as mothers rearing their children (MacCormack and Strathern 1981). This debate becomes more acute when diasporic communities are considered, where the pressures to rear children in 'their' culture and language in what may appear to be alien surroundings are so much more intensive. In these cases, women do often take on the role of 'culture carriers', but this is not naturally determined. Men also contribute to the process of cultural education, and organizations, usually male-controlled – both in the public and private sectors – have emerged to deal with issues about cultural and linguistic competence of the young. However, the central pressure, especially in the domestic context, is on women to perform this role of cultural transmitter. Anthias (1992) observes that it is mainly women, in the British Greek Cypriot diaspora, who are the more prominent 'carriers of culture'. Not only are they the main building stones of Cypriot entrepreneurship, where female skill in sewing and cooking formed the basis for their strength in the clothing, catering and retailing businesses, but also they become transmitters of the 'cultural stuff' of ethnicity with their forte in child-rearing, as controllers of female sexuality, and as mediators between patriarchs and children (Anthias 1992: 90–91).[4] This role as 'cultural bearer' can be both a limitation and a strength. It is a limitation when it oppresses those women who wish to challenge this role: when doing so, they are denounced as 'misguided' or 'inauthentic'. On the other hand, this role is a strength when it enables women to develop positions of community authority, as noted by Aparna Rayapol, who observes that women are particularly important in running the local temple in the South Indian community in Pittsburgh, USA. She claims: 'Women seemed to be in charge, controlling and managing almost everything' (Rayaprol 1997: vii).[5] As we shall see in the next section, this is a fragile and contingent relationship when it comes to political practice.

There is a deeper assumption in the role of women as 'cultural carriers' – that of cultural homogeneity between men and women, and therefore a perception of a shared common culture which is to be transmitted. Our previous example of the liaisons between Punjabi men and Mexican women in the USA in the early twentieth century disrupts any easy cultural symmetry across gender. Punjabi-Mexican-American communities formed along gender lines on the basis of shared experiences as migrants in California. The Punjabi men, who were previously shipmates or part of the same work crew, tended to remain confined to their own social group. Rather than sharing their own cultural spaces, their Mexican or Mexican-American wives 'built their own networks that, although initially based on kinship ties, [were] later extended through local affiliations and the *compadrazgo* system (ritual kinship ties such as godparent relationships) to other Mexican and Mexican-American women married to Punjabis' (Mankekar 1994: 353). Culturally and linguistically, men had more to share with each other than the majority of women, and vice versa. This aside, it was the mother's cultural backgrounds that filtered more strongly down to their offspring. Purnima Mankekar (1994) remarks:

The descendants of these early Punjabi immigrants were usually socialized into the cultures of their mothers; at the same time, however, they retained links with the Punjab through the memories they inherited from their fathers. They thus created a hybrid, uniquely Punjabi-Mexican-American culture that enabled them to straddle the worlds of both parents. (Mankekar 1994: 352)

This type of formation occurs in the context of both parties being racialized and marginalized in relation to a white dominant other. As we will note in Chapters 4 and 5, liaisons between those considered to be of different 'races' have not resulted in a 'happy hybridity', but rather have provoked extreme forms of racial violence. Women's bodies again become the site for these kinds of attack. Nevertheless, diasporic women caught between stereotypic visions, by host and community, of their role within culture have not capitulated.

The question of resistance

Diasporic contexts provide fertile, if fraught, sites from which to resist practices that oppress women. In Britain, organizations such as Women Against Fundamentalism, the Organization of Women of African and Asian Descent and various local Black Sisters groups, the most prominent and long-lasting of which is Southall Black Sisters, have fought against community cultural orthodoxy and mainstream prejudice.[6] The issues at stake are also wide-ranging, from domestic violence to sex selection (Purewal 2003), but of paramount concern is the need to resist the refrain that locates women as victim to 'barbaric' and misogynist cultural traditions, while trying to change the often horrific situations in which these women find themselves.

The example of genital mutilation (infibulation, female circumcision) provides a strong and instructive case study with which to address the issues that arise when diasporic women's groups engage in mobilization. Muslim women, particularly those from Africa, are invariably associated with genital mutilation in the Eurocentric imaginary. But where this practice is evidenced, we cannot assume that they are simply victims as such. Albeit a issue of importance, women themselves have taken this concern on for themselves and have resisted their more extreme manifestations. They are placed in a situation where they have to negotiate the parameters of their role as minority people *and* of being women. This is often accompanied by the vexed question of how much to 'expose' inequities within minority communities to the wider society. Should one remain silent and accept oppressive treatment or should one 'cry out', so to speak, at the cost of validating stereotypical prejudices about their respective 'communities'? As an academic question, this poses all sorts of problem, but in political practice women's organizations negotiate these kinds of situation on a day-to-day basis.

The British-based African Women's Welfare Group (AWWG) is a group campaigning to raise awareness about genital mutilation, both among host societies and within diasporic populations. They have been placed in the awkward position of needing to speak out against what they see as an 'injustice' against circumcised women, and yet also trying to circumnavigate the ignorant (and often voyeuristic) tendencies of mainstream society. The AWWG's concerted efforts are towards the 'education' of women and the wider society. Hadiyah Ahmed, a Somali-British woman from the AWWG, asserts:

> One of the demands of the campaign against [infibulation] is ... to inform and train health workers to safeguard the health and well-being of those women who have already been subjected to this practice as children. Of equal importance, however, is the education of African women themselves about the health risks and psychological scarring of 'circumcision' as it is traditionally called. (Hadiyah Ahmed, cited in Ruge 1992: 7)

But such practices need not spell an indictment of the cultures of which women see themselves as part. One can be critical of patriarchal structures without necessarily condemning the culture of which they are a part. Ahmed declares:

> I love my culture, but this part of it has to be abolished! I can't sit here and let men who are not affected, or who even think it is alright and done for their pleasure, persuade me to be in favour of it, to tell me that it is our culture when I know it means our oppression and torture. And more and more women think like that now. (Hadiyah Ahmed, cited in Ruge 1992: 7)

Often, to raise such problems is at the cost of risking the wrath of conventional patriarchal structures, which may well involve elderly women as well as men in the control of young women. Women who are seen to challenge traditional practices are often denounced as being too 'Westernized', even 'trecherous' for informing others about intimate practices, and thus opening the community up to criticism by the wider society. Thinking of a similar instance with diasporic South Asian populations, Thiara argues:

> women have often been seen as damaging the interests of the ethnic groups because they engage in an internal critique that is seen to be detrimental to the group project, as reflected in the promulgation of leaders that violence against women is not a problem within South Asian communities. Moreover, discussions about ethnic mobilization always focuses on benefiting the group, rather than also contesting and attempting to transform inequalities within as well as without. (Thiara 2003: 142)

The attention to lifting the status of minority groups as a whole has mitigated against the airing of, or critique of, any negative practices among their members. However, to suppress the diversity of members' views is also to go against the irrepressible gains of change. In a curious manner, mainstream, left-leaning and liberal groups who wish to 'protect' minorities from racism at large also end up converging with the discourse of 'fundamentalists' when they too caution against airing the internal problems of minority communities. It is difficult to accept that the suppression of problematic issues cannot be at huge cost. Ahmed continues:

> They think we simply open our community to criticism from the white community, which is always looking for faults in our culture anyway. They tell us we can't do this because in a racist society it will weaken our position. (Hadiyah Ahmed, cited in Ruge 1992: 8)

How much to 'spill the beans' and risk being ostracized by members of one's community and the wider society has been of critical concern in this context, more often for women than for men. This is largely because in more orthodox sectors, women's experiences are seen as relegated to the domestic or 'private sphere', not for wider dissemination. These tensions are vividly brought up in another incident when an ultra-orthodox Jewish woman in London was ostracized for alleging publicly that her children had been sexually abused by another member of her community. Demonstrations were held outside her house and she was accused of being an 'informer'. Fear of anti-Semitism lay behind their reasoning for the protest. The entry of debate about problematic issues such as domestic/sexual abuse has raised sometimes intractable concerns which can be a bane for diasporic women having to contend with questions such as how far can one talk about these issues in the public eye. Should these matters be resolved within the communities themselves? Can we draw boundaries to what is 'in' and what is 'out' of the concerns of diasporic communities? We may be placed in a double-bind: to air problems risks condemning the respective cultures, placing them in a bad light in a society where there is little under-standing of cultures seen as 'other'. Yet, to ignore the internal problems is to acquiesce to oppression.

Groups campaigning for the interests of diasporic communities also have an interest in justice for all of their members and thus have had to deploy a bifocal lens in their operations and strategies – one eye turned towards inter-community concerns, the other focused on wider societal pressures and prejudices. Such views highlight the fact that cultures (or, indeed, com-munities for that matter) cannot be seen as homogeneous sites, but highly contested ones where the frames of identity and conduct are constantly worked and reworked, both internal and external to the blurred contours of particular diasporic cultures. Returning to the example of genital muti-lation, the BBC documentary, *Female Circumcision and a Cruel Ritual* (1990), produced by Louise Panton, was the subject of a heated debate between the AWWG, the film producer and the Somali community of Cardiff. Ahmed recounts:

> Louise Panton was aggressively told that she, as a white British person, had no business making such a film and should not meddle with 'our affairs'. One woman asked me: 'Why are you saying all this in public?' And I answered: 'Because I am Somali. And we have to face the truth'. And the men then started to make noise and to shout at me. They sensed the danger that would follow from women talking between themselves. (cited in Ruge 1992: 7)

The above example illustrates the tensions between loyalty to one's own 'community' and to one's rights as a woman. But it is the context of a docu-mentary that will be overwhelmingly viewed by a population which already negatively stereotypes the 'community' in question, that gives urgency to the debate.

Perhaps, still the most powerful example of a political situation in which women's rights conflict with those of the community is found in the so-called 'Rushdie Affair' that we discussed earlier in Chapter 2. To adopt another take on this affair, we can say that the *fatwa* on Salman Rushdie announced by the Ayatollah Khomeini in 1989, over what was seen as the blasphemous book, *The Satanic Verses*, raised key issues where feminists of colour had to deploy bifocal (or even, multifocal) strategies:

> As a militant section of Britain's Asian community took to the streets, demonstrating, burning copies of *The Satanic Verses*, 'marching under the banner of Islam rather than of anti-racism' the traditional defenders of freedom of speech were faced with a problem. Should they support the book-burners' right to express their own culture as they defined it, even if that meant validating death threats? Or should they side with the racists, all too evident throughout the media, who had leapt at the chance to characterise black people as barbarian adherents of primitive religions? Some jumped one way, some the other, and as the argument raged a group of women from a variety of backgrounds started to organise against fundamentalism both in Britain and internationally, at the same time taking a clear position against racism. (Bard 1992/93: 3)[7]

The rise of community fundamentalism relies crucially on diasporic links and there is a burgeoning literature that documents links between these groups internationally (see Bhatt 1997; and Bhatt and Mukta 2000). Both in South Asia and in Britain, women are crucially impacted upon by this turn to religious modernism – that is, the resurgence of traditionalist religious ideologies in the face of modernity. This has had several effects on the experience of women who faced the twin yoke of racism and sexism. Women's groups, such as Women Against Fundamentalism and Southall Black Sisters, have sought to redress this balance. On the one hand, they have been mindful of mainstream prejudice. On the other, they have had to deal with fundamentalists and anti-racists alike, who accuse the women's groups of 'dividing the struggle against racism' and of 'playing into the hands of the racist media'. It is only in the process of political struggle that these various political positions can be negotiated and, contingently, resolved.

Diaspora spaces and their impact upon women's liberation/oppression certainly operate in the political practices we have discussed. However, much of the organizational logic, and certainly the practice of the aforementioned women's groups, is rooted in Britain. Indeed, there is a certainty that the political space to be challenged is singular and materially based in the country of settlement. In this sense, these groups are taking seriously the criticism outlined in Chapter 1, made by Anthias (1998), that diaspora may deflect attention away from the relationship between the state and racialized/gendered groups. Even where it is clear that the issues of concern, such as sex preference, genital mutilation and domestic violence, are produced and exaggerated in diasporic spaces, the political practice required to challenge these oppressions remains rooted in the nation-state.

Coming/going out

If issues that impinge on women's bodies evoke a crisis in the boundaries of what is 'in and out' of any particular diasporic space, then issues of sexuality cause seismic eruptions. Notwithstanding the theoretical uses made of diaspora in queer theory, which are briefly reviewed at the end of this section, the focus on women, as 'carriers of culture', within accounts of diaspora, are sustained by a normative heterosexuality. In her bid against the stranglehold of monolithic identities based on gender alone – men versus women – Inderpal Grewal (1994) reminds us of the hazards of insisting upon binaries and insider–outsider oppositions. She insists that:

> There are many narratives by women of color around the world that propose and enact new forms of locating themselves within societies. These forms are both oppositional and non-essentialist, and confront and fracture the self–other opposition in the name of inclusions, multiple identities and diasporic subject positions. (Grewal 1994: 234)

Grewal adopts Gloria Anzaldúa's (1987) observations on heterogeneous subjectivity in her work on 'mestiza consciousness' – an entity that is 'not unitary or concrete, for it is always in the process of becoming' (Grewal 1994: 250).[8] Heterogeneous subjectivity is useful for considering the various inter-dynamics between themes of gender and sexuality. Such an investigation serves two primary roles: first, heterosexual or patriarchal assumptions about diasporic contexts need to be challenged, both for members' and hosts' expectations. Secondly, an enquiry that foregrounds the particularities of race/ethnicity undermines the generalizing assumptions of Eurocentric feminism, which posit that gender and sexuality are the main overture. An instructive example is provided by a debate on lesbianism and US Chicana/Latina identity between Sarah Hoagland (1988) and Linda Tessman (1995). Hoagland suggests the need for lesbian separatism – that is, refusing to subscribe to heterosexual 'camps'. She proposes the notion of the 'generic lesbian'. However, Linda Tessman argues for the specificities of race/ethnicity which impinge upon such a universalizing gesture. Tessman elaborates:

> The claim that Black women are affected by every major system of oppression – sexism, racism, economic oppression, etc. – may be true, but because these systems of oppression operate variously on, say, people racialized in different ways, fighting the particular oppressions that affect Black women will not necessarily address the particular forms of oppression that affect, say, Latinas. (Tessman 1995: 81)

This is a view that is also in sympathy with Maria Lugones's critique of Hoagland (Lugones 1991). The notion of 'generic lesbians' requires that Lugones leaves her community of colour, namely US Chicanos. But within this community, Lugones sees herself as a critical cultural participant against racism. If she were to leave it, she would also abandon the vital role she plays as an agent for change and survival for the diaspora. Lugones asserts that while she came to the lesbian community as a marked cultural individual ('my culture on my back'), still, it did not provide the space for struggling Hispanic rights. She contends that there is a need to engage within Chicana and Latina cultures as well as to join arms with feminists from elsewhere. Otherwise, cultures can never change in a progressive light.[9]

In addition to the state, religious authorities, even in avowedly secular countries, can have a major influence on the ideological regimes of family and community. Lesbian identity is a rupture to the morality brigade attached to conservative agendas. When coupled with the issue of race/ethnicity, further tensions are made evident. On one occasion, for instance, the British-based Jewish Lesbian and Gay Helpline was told that it could not join the Chief Rabbi's high-profile Jewish Walkabout in London's Hyde Park because it was not an organization that 'promotes family values'. Bard elaborates:

> In the Jewish community, too, this has particular implications for women, whose primary role, it is clearly stated, is to bear and raise children, and transmit the culture of the group to future generations. If their individual choices about sexuality and reproduction conflict with that stated communal need – in other words if they are not heterosexual or do not want children or, indeed, offer their children a different version of Jewish identity – they are told that they have no place in the community. Those who question either the problem or the solution are silenced by the claim that they are giving Hitler a posthumous victory. (Bard 1992/93: 4)

Strong words from a community that sees itself as beleaguered historically and yet in the present is able to sing the chorus of 'preservation' to ostracize others. The recourse to binding ideas of preservation and posterity is a repeat of those that we witnessed earlier against women struggling for change within their communities. Sexuality, however, generates a hostility of a different degree. To be seen to go against family (writ large, community) values is to raise the wrath of those who see salvation only in a conventional solidarity. Evelynn Hamon, for instance, notes how heterosexual Black women cast Black lesbians as 'proverbial traitors to the race' (Hamon 1994: 137).

However, the hostility towards homosexuality has not stopped diasporic groups from organizing along these lines. Groups such as the NAZ project based in London have express aims to promote and develop 'a strong South Asian gay community'. Their objectives are: 'To promote greater understanding of the diversity that exists within our communities in terms of sexuality and sexual behaviour' (*Rasanah Khaberie* 2000: 2). Linked with the same named organization based in New Delhi, NAZ works through diasporic networks to tackle the issue of HIV/Aids.

At an academic level, diaspora studies have had an impact on the emergence of queer theory. Queer theory is, simply, a means of discussing the above topics without positing that homosexuality is the necessary opposite to normalized heterosexuality. This school of thinking also developed as a critique of the oppositions assumed in the distinction between gay and lesbian studies. In terms of connections to diaspora studies, there are two levels at work. First, the extent to which diaspora resonates with the experiences of queers fundamentally questions the idea of settled and normative notions of home. For the diasporic individual, home is an unsettled category due to migration; for the queer, home is unsettled because of normative heterosexual expectations (see Fortier 2003). The second level relates to the transnationalization of queer movements and cultures. In particular, the research and writings of Jasbir K. Puar are worth noting. Puar (2002) expresses a concern with privileging queer diasporas' travel and tourist practices though the 'return to homeland' trip which is not just about visiting family, but more significantly connecting/rediscovering a queer tradition in the 'homeland'. For Puar (2002), the privileging of this form of travel ignores neo-colonial antecedents and throws into question the distinction that can be made, if any, between heterosexual and white gay capital.

Puar's work indicates, once again, that it is not possible to provide an overarching singular identity to encompass the practices of diasporic queers. Instructive views are offered in Homi Bhabha's comments on the intersections of class and gender:

> ... the transformational value of change lies in the rearticulation, or translation, of elements that are *neither the One* (unitary working class) *nor the Other* (the politics of gender) *but something else besides*, which contests the terms and territories of both. There is a negotiation between gender and class, where each formation encounters the displaced, differentiated boundaries of its group representation and enunciative sites in which the limits and limitations of social power are encountered in an agonistic relation. (Bhabha 1994: 28, original emphasis)

Negotiation, of course, requires organization and we can take these observations further. We note how, in all of the above case studies, we do not have a coming together of bounded senses of particular gender with particular ethnicities, sexualities or classes which then combine again to make hybrid mixtures, but rather we see these as sites for activists and group intervention. Each of these categories is but an abbreviation for much more complex dynamics – situations where one is often neither one nor the other, but 'something else besides' and engagement is enacted by actually existing groups. It is at times of crisis and in campaigns that identities congeal around various banners, such as those of gay rights, women's rights or of the class struggles involved in factory strikes.[10] It may often be that just as quickly as they form, they disperse, only to re-coagulate again. Perhaps they are less 'a function of knowledge than performance, or, in Foucauldian terms, less a matter of final discovery than perpetual reinvention' (Fuss 1991: 6–7). But diasporic identities do become part of a chain of endless influence where factors of race/ethnicity, gender, sexuality, life-stages and class, in their variable interconnections, become prominent in political struggle. Theory is not capable of making the prediction about which identity becomes the most cogent and effective in any particular context, but it should alert us to the potential of emancipative possibilities.

Diasporic or dystopic

Whereas we have previously focused on the relationship of diaspora to gender and sexuality, for the final section of this chapter we turn to an area of analysis where diaspora studies has made few interventions. Contemporary global movements of labour includes the (often illegal) trafficking of women for domestic servitude and the sex trade. Tackling the rigid boundaries of migration studies, we articulated the benefits that a diasporic perspective brings in Chapter 1. These are a focus on process rather than static events and a recognition of ongoing relations between home and abroad. Yet, domestic labour and those trafficked into the sex industry remains beyond the scope of a diasporic perspective. Is it because it is mainly women and children who are caught up in this migration that warrants this occlusion? Or is it that the exploited plight of these subjects renders them beyond the often celebratory tone that much cultural studies of diaspora evoke? As we have asked in other parts of this book, for us the crucial question is whether diaspora is a useful tool for enabling some semblance of redress for these exploited subjects (Murray 1998: 58). Undocumented or illegal labour, asylum-seekers or, even more pointedly, sex workers and child labour in foreign territories rarely attract the label diasporic. Perhaps to name them in this way undermines the dystopic present that their status indicates. This is not our intention. Rather, it is to reverse the contingent and unstable nature of these constructs, to assert diaspora as a place of belonging for these groups just as much as it is for more settled populations and perhaps also a route from which to gain legitimation when other avenues for this process are blocked. It is in the interstices of the international movement of women for domestic labour and the sex trade that there emerges a need to pay attention to what might be called 'diasporas in the making'.

Alongside economic oppression, female-only migration has become the site of all kinds of racial and sexual abuse. Indeed, in some cases, contracting for work as a domestic labourer can be a foil for more nefarious activities to do with the international sex trade. Countries in the economic peripheries and those that are in political turmoil are hotbeds for the often forced 'picking' of young women and children for work in the overseas sex market. This is in addition to those people who have been beguiled into thinking that they are paying their way to asylum sanctuaries in the West, only to find themselves destined for a life in the 'underworld'. As Chris Ryan and Michael Hall observe:

> Many women are trafficked to work in brothels; about half are trafficked into bonded sweatshop labour or domestic servitude. Once in the United States, the women who work in brothels typically are rotated from city to city to evade law enforcement, keep the women disoriented and give clients fresh faces. (Ryan and Hall 2001: 120)

Regan E. Ralph, the Executive Director of the Women's Rights Division in Human Rights Watch, explains further:

> In a typical case, a woman is recruited with promises of a good job in another country or province, and lacking better options at home, she agrees to migrate. There are also cases in which women are lured with false marriage offers or vacation invitations, in which children are bartered by their parents for a cash

advance and/or promises of future earnings, or in which victims are abducted outright. Next, an agent makes arrangements for the women's travel and job placement, obtaining the necessary travel documentation, contacting employers or job brokers, and hiring an escort to accompany the woman on her trip. The woman has no control over the nature or place of work, or the terms or conditions of her employment. Many women learn that they have been deceived about the nature of the work they will do, most have been lied to about the financial arrangements and conditions of their employment, and all find themselves in coercive and abusive situations from which escape is both difficult and dangerous. (cited in Ryan and Hall 2001: 120)

Being designated as unlawful citizens means that these women do not tend to speak out against the treatment meted out to them. They constitute what can be described as silent or silenced diasporas consisting of individuals who are not even permitted to ask for their human dignity for fear of persecution from the industry operators and/or deportation courtesy of the state. In the case of US immigration law, for instance:

Anyone who has worked [in the sex industry] within ten years of applying, whether legally or illegally, arrested or not, can be barred from entry, denied a visa or residence permit, or deported. With other crimes, migrants can be excluded only if they were convicted of an offence, either within the previous five years or repeatedly. (Alexander 1997: 91)[11]

Ralph observes that even when trafficked women are freed from their employers, they face further mistreatment at the hands of the authorities. Officials prefer to:

focus on violations of their immigration regulations and anti-prostitution laws, rather than on violations of the trafficking victims' human rights. Thus, the women are targeted as undocumented migrants and/or prostitutes, and the traffickers either escape entirely, or else face minor penalties for their involvement in illegal migration or businesses of prostitution. (cited in Ryan and Hall 2001: 121–122)

Some feminists have begun to argue that, rather than controlling it, laws restricting migration and prostitution in fact end up encouraging trafficking. They point out that if prostitution was an 'above-ground occupation', it would be much easier to regulate and thus change women's working conditions for the better (Alexander 1997: 91). Trafficking is generally of the poor and vulnerable into richer and relatively politically stable countries. According to Human Rights Watch, thousands of Thai and Filipina women are trafficked into forced labour in Japan each year, often with the involvement of Japanese-organized crime syndicates (*yakuza*). Since the end of the war in Bosnia and Herzegovina in 1999, many women have also been trafficked to the West, for forced bonded prostitution, from this area (Ryan and Hall 2001: 122–126).

This perspective is further developed by Alison Murray (1998). Basing her evidence on the Australian context, Murray argues that there is a lot of sensationalism and emotive rhetoric built into reports about the international trafficking of women and children. Figures for trafficking are speculative, yet they form the basis of several scholarly texts, helping them 'to become accepted fact through the repetition of the rhetoric' (Murray 1998: 55). Murray argues that anti-trafficking campaigns actually have a detrimental effect on workers. The women's conditions vary greatly and many of them enter their contracts willingly, knowing what is expected of them. Some of them even go on to become recruiters or brothel managers themselves. Recalling the typology of stereotypes about Asian women above, Murray proposes that the campaigns end up presenting women as victims and may in fact increase discrimination as they perpetuate the stereotype of Asian workers as passive and diseased:

> Clients are encouraged to think of Asian workers as helpless victims who are unable to resist, so they may be more likely to violate the rights of these workers. The campaigns also encourage racism towards Asian workers within the industry (where Australian workers accuse them of undercutting and not using condoms) and in the general community where Asian workers form an ostracized new 'underclass' without equal rights. (Murray 1998: 58)

Murray's thesis is to move away from thinking of Asian woman in the 'erotic-pathetic' double-bind (Murray 1998: 60). She contends that:

> Logically there is no difference between 'debt-bonded' Asian workers and Australian workers choosing to work for Hong Kong triads for more money than they can get in Sydney: it is racism which says that the former are victims and the latter agents. Even the East European workers now being chronically exploited all over the world are rarely constructed as victims in the same way. (Murray 1998: 60)

Murray articulates a powerful argument for taking note of class as well as gender and 'race' when looking at the issue of sex workers. Yet, there is an absence of the ties that may bind Asian women together. San Juan provides a relatively balanced corrective to studies that concentrate simply on the negative aspects of the migration of Filipina women in the domestic/sex trade. San Juan notes the extent to which Filipina women behave as a diasporic group when they are able to make contact with each other. They are becoming cosmopolitans, and empower themselves by 'devious tactics of evasion, accommodation, and making-do' in a bid to send remittances back 'home'.[12] However, the fact remains that they are also in danger of returning 'home' in a coffin due to the maltreatment they receive at the hands of ruthless employers: in fact, the rate is about five or six coffins a day (San Juan 2001: 54). The selling and buying of bodies in trafficking represents capitalism at its most ruthless. This phenomenon seems to mitigate against the recomposition of cultural coherency in diasporic circumstances, but racism at large is a major factor which leads to these women coming together with some degree of commonality. Similarities in backgrounds, present locales, occupations and aspirations among these migrated women sow the seeds with which to cohere in the face of hostile circumstances. Diaspora becomes a tool for at least providing the basis for mobilizing against their oppression, not in the mode of cultural consciousness, but rather at the intersection of class, gender and racial politics.

Does the dissection of diaspora in terms of gender and sexuality render it redundant for the analysis of transnational formations and links? The practice of groups such as Women Against Fundamentalism tend to oscillate between a concern for diasporic issues that become politically articulated and organized in a local context and cultural traditions that have their provenance elsewhere. We have also seen how certain gay groups, such as NAZ, have begun to develop practice at an international level, making use of diasporic links to enhance their work. Even in the case of the modern domestic slave trade, diaspora provides a base for providing at least a moment of solace in otherwise difficult lives. But in each of these cases, we have moved far from the cultural celebration of diaspora that was illustrated in Chapter 2. A critical engagement with the various stratifications that can be applied to diaspora necessarily involves this kind of shift. Once engaged with social structures and formations, diasporic cultural effervescence loses much of its fizz. The next two chapters continue with this method of identifying cultural effects and examining them in the light of the requirements of social justice. But our concern shifts from diaspora to hybridity, which is often represented as one of the outcomes of diasporic interaction.

Notes

1 Since the immigration law of 1965, the population of Asian Indians grew from a few thousand to over 100 000, accompanying a revitalized sense of Punjabi culture. Eventually, tensions arose between new Punjabis and Hispanic-Punjabis in San Joaquin Valley cities (see Leonard 1992; Nash 1999: 16).

2 This paradigm is still almost exclusively applied to second- or third-generation South Asians rather than those of African-Caribbean backgrounds, the latter being seen as less problematically British. Alexander notes:

> Where black/African-Caribbean identities have become defined as fluid, fragmented, negotiated and creative, Asian identities have been defined – in opposition – as static, bounded, internally homogenous and externally impenetrable [...]. 'Difference' in this case, then, is imagined in cultural absolutes and oppositions, less an engagement with the other than the reification of irreducible and antipathetic 'Others'. The dilemmas of these two versions of 'difference' are most clearly apparent in relation to youth: where African-Caribbean youth cultures are seen as moving outwards, into mainstream cultures, transforming and transgressing ideas of integral British cultural identity, Asian youth cultures, if acknowledged any existence outside the black hole of 'community' identity, are seen as mysterious, incomprehensible to 'outsiders' and exclusive. (Alexander 2002: 558)

See also our discussion on Third Culture Kids in Chapter 6 as an instructive comparison to diasporic second-generation children.

3 The latter is a subject that we shall return to in our discussions on international 'domestic servants' and the sex trade.

4 Their role as definers of ethnic boundaries culturally is also supported legalistically. Britain's Nationality Bill, 1983, constitutes those women who are defined within the new national boundary as having 'an independent right to transmit to their children British nationality. ... At the same time it excludes particular categories of women who reside in Britain from reproducing the national collectivity' (cited in Anthias 1992: 93).

5 Celia Rothenberg's (1999) study on women in Palestinian diaspora communities located in Jordan and Canada notes how it is women who are primarily responsible for cultural connectivity, not just between generations but also across continents. She concentrates on the experience of 'closeness' – both a term of social geography and one of kinship – with people they have left behind in the West Bank and to others within their adopted communities. This feeling did not deplete with movement from the West Bank, but persisted among communities, propelled by the women, in places as far afield as Kuwait, Jordan and Canada.

6 On the Organization of Women of African and Asian Descent, see Brah (1996). On Southall Black Sisters, see Gupta (2004).

7 For more on the debates raised by *The Satanic Verses*, see also Malaise Ruthven's *A Satanic Affair* (1991), Tariq Modood's *Not Easy Being British* (1992), Paul Gilroy's *Small Acts* (1993b) and Stuart Hall's 'New Ethnicities' (1989).

8 As we shall explore in greater detail in Chapter 4, the *mestiza* is the mixture that occurs from Spanish and Indian interaction in the colonial conquest of the Americas. For Anzaldúa (1987), the use of mestiza is a recovery of the term to indicate an in-between or hybrid state.

9 Whereas above we have singled out debates on diasporic lesbian identities, we also need to be wary of proposing too reified a field. Evelynn Hamon points out the need to deconstruct normative assumptions articulate in what she calls:

> The consistently exclusionary practices of lesbian and gay studies in general. ... [T]he canonical terms and categories of the field: 'lesbian', 'gay', 'butch', 'femme', 'sexuality', and 'subjectivity' are stripped of context in the works of those theorizing about these very categories, identities and subject positions. Each of these terms is defined with white as the normative state of existence. (Hamon 1994: 127–128)

10 See also Kaur and Banerjea (2000) on the relations between crises and musical identities and associations and the congealing of musical identities and associations.

11 In even less repressive countries such as the Netherlands, a proposed law would permit residents of the new European Community and possibly Eastern Europe – that is, mostly white women – to work legally in regulated brothels. But this is not extended to those women from outside the EC – mainly, Africa, Asia and Latin America. (Alexander 1997: 92).

12 The annual remittance of billions of dollars by Filipino workers abroad suffices to keep the Philippine economy afloat: 'Throughout the nineties, the average total of migrant workers is about a million a year; they remit over five percent of the national GNP, not to mention the millions of pesos collected by the Philippine government in myriad taxes and fees' (San Juan 2001: 55).

4

Hybrid Connections

Hybridity and diaspora

It is by now established that authors writing on diaspora very often engage with the mixed notion of hybridity. We will see that this term also offers much for debate, and that this debate in turn offers material that elaborates, and may further complicate, the cultures and politics of diaspora. This chapter explores this uneven terrain and presents a topographical survey of the uses and misuses of hybridity, and its synonyms.

In its most recent descriptive and realist usage, hybridity appears as a convenient category at 'the edge' or contact point of diaspora, describing cultural mixture where the diasporized meets the host in the scene of migration. Nikos Papastergiadis makes this link at the start of his book, *The Turbulence of Migration: Globalization, Deterritorialization and Hybridity*, where he mentions the 'twin processes of globalization and migration' (2000: 3). He outlines a development which moves from the assimilation and integration of migrants into the host society of the nation state towards something more complex in the metropolitan societies of today. Speaking primarily of Europe, the Americas and Australia, Papastergiadis argues that as some members of migrant communities came to prominence 'within the cultural and political circles of the dominant society' they 'began to argue in favour of new models of representing the process of cultural interaction, and to demonstrate the negative consequences of insisting upon the denial of the emergent forms of cultural identity' (Papastergiadis 2000: 3). Hybridity has been a key part of this new modelling, and so it is logically entwined within the co-ordinates of migrant identity and difference, same or not same, host and guest.

The career of the term 'hybridity' as a new cultural politics in the context of diaspora should be examined carefully. The cultural here points to the claim that hybridity has been rescued – or has it? – from a convoluted past to do duty for an articulation of rights and assertions of autonomy against the force of essential identities. The hybrid is a usefully slippery category, purposefully contested and deployed to claim change. With such loose boundaries, it is curious that the term can be so productive: from its origins in biology and botany, its interlude as syncretism, to its reclamation in work on diaspora by authors as different as Paul Gilroy, Stuart Hall, Iain Chambers, Homi Bhabha, and James Clifford. It is in the dialogue between these works especially that hybridity has come to mean all sorts of things to do with mixing and combination in the moment of cultural exchange. Gilroy, for example, finds it helpful in the field of cultural production, where he notes that 'the musical components of hip hop are a *hybrid* form nurtured by the social relations of the South Bronx where Jamaican sound system culture was transplanted during the 1970s' (Gilroy 1993a: 33). Hall, as we will see in more detail presently, suggests hybridity is transforming British life (Hall 1995: 18), while Chambers finds talk of tradition displaced by 'traffic' in the 'sights, sounds and languages of *hybridity*' (Chambers 1994: 82). As we have previously noted, Bhabha uses hybridity as an 'in-between' term, referring to a 'third space', and to ambivalence and mimicry especially in the context of what might, uneasily, be called the colonial–cultural interface (more on this in the next chapter). Clifford uses the word to describe 'a discourse that is travelling or *hybridising* in new global condi-tions' and he stresses 'travel trajectories' and 'flow' (Clifford 1994: 304–306, emphasis added). Worrying that assertions of identity and difference are celebrated too quickly as resistance, in either the nostalgic form of 'tradi-tional survivals' or mixed in a 'new world of hybrid forms' (Clifford 2000: 103), he sets up an opposition (tradition/hybrid) that will become central to our critique of the terms.

There is much more that hybridity seems to contain: 'A quick glance at the history of hybridity reveals a bizarre array of ideas' (Papastergiadis 2000: 169). In addition to the general positions set out above, hybridity is an evocative term for the formation of identity; it is used to describe inno-vations of language (creole, patois, pidgin, travellers' argot etc.); it is code for creativity and for translation. In Bhabha's terms, 'hybridity is camou-flage' (Bhabha 1994: 193) and, provocatively, he offers 'hybridity as heresy' (Bhabha 1994: 226), as a disruptive and productive category. It is 'how newness enters the world' (Bhabha 1994: 227) and it is bound up with a 'process of translating and transvaluing cultural differences' (Bhabha 1994: 252). For others, hybridity is the key organizing feature of the cyborg, the wo-man/machine interface (Haraway 1997). It invokes mixed technologi-cal innovations, multiple trackings of influence, and is acclaimed as the origin of creative expression in culture industry production. With relation to diaspora, the most conventional accounts assert hybridity as the process of cultural mixing where the diasporic arrivals adopt aspects of the host cul-ture and rework, reform and reconfigure this in production of a new hybrid culture or 'hybrid identities' (Chambers 1996: 50). Whether talk of such identities is coherent or not, hybridity is better conceived of as a process rather than a description. Kobena Mercer writes of 'the hybridized terrain of diasporic culture' (Mercer 1994: 254) and of how even the older termi-nologies of syncretism and mixture evoke the movement of 'hybridization' rather than stress fixed identity. Finally, a turn-of-the-millennium volume, *Hybridity and its Discontents*, is able to describe hybridity as: 'a term for a wide range of social and cultural phenomena involving "mixing", [it] has become a key concept within cultural criticism and post-colonial theory' (Brah and Coombs 2000: cover).

Hybridity and the anterior pure

The idea of borrowing is sometimes taken to imply a weakening of a supposedly once pure culture. It is this myth of purity that belongs to the essentialist nationalisms and chauvinisms that are arraigned against the hybrid, diasporic and the migrant. It is to combat this rationale that so many writers insist that affirmations of hybridity are useful in the arena of cultural politics. Such affirmations are proclaimed precisely because the varieties of cultural borrowing that are thereby entertained undermine the case of a pure culture. These claims may be more important than the philosophical incoherence of the terms, but this incoherence has to be considered. A key question would be: to what degree does the assertion of hybridity rely on the positing of an anterior 'pure' that precedes mixture? Even as a process in translation or in formation, the idea of 'hybrid identities' (Chambers 1996: 50) relies upon the proposition of non-hybridity or some kind of normative insurance. This problem is taken up again in the next chapter, but our interest here is the specific manner in which notions of purity are related to the biological antecedents of hybridity. Hybridity theorists have had to grapple with this problem and have done so with a revealing degree of agitation. Gilroy, for example, has moved away from an allegiance to hybridity and declared:

> Who the fuck wants purity? ... The idea of hybridity, of intermixture, presupposes two anterior purities. ... I think there isn't any purity; there isn't any anterior purity ... that's why I try not to use the word hybrid. ... Cultural production is not like mixing cocktails. (Gilroy 1994: 54–5)

The latitudes of sexuality fester in the earthy connotations of this quote as Gilroy knowingly references the less reputable anxieties at stake. It was probably work like that of Robert Young's *Colonial Desire: Hybridity in Theory, Culture and Race* (1995) which provoked the outburst. Numerous scholars have examined the botanical and biological parameters of hybridity, but the matter is perhaps best exemplified in Young's historical investigation, which traced the provenance of the term 'hybridity' in the racialized discourse of nineteenth-century evolutionism. The Latin roots of the word are revealed as referring to the progeny of a tame sow and a wild boar (Young 1995: 6). Is this old usage relevant to the diversity of cultural hybridities claimed today? In the sciences of agriculture and horticulture, hybridity is used with little alarm, the best-known hybrid being the mule, a mixture of a horse and donkey, though significantly this is a sterile or non-productive mix. In the world of plants, hybrid combinations are productively made by grafting one plant or fruit to another. Although in this field such graftings may seem legitimate, only a mildly imprudent jump is needed to move from notions of horticulture and biology to discussions of human 'races' as distinct species that, upon mixing, produce hybrids.

Both Gilroy and Hall have made efforts to distinguish their use of hybridity from its dubious biological precedents. Gilroy clearly recognizes the problem of purity when he laments 'the lack of a means of adequately describing, let alone theorizing, intermixture, fusion and syncretism without suggesting the existence of anterior "uncontaminated" purities' (Gilroy 2000: 250). He is correct that the descriptive use of hybridity evokes, counter-factually, a stable and prior non-mixed position, to which 'presumably it might one day be possible to return' (Gilroy 2000: 250). Who wants to return is a good question (which we discuss further in Chapter 6). But equally, can a focusing and tightening of descriptive terminology, or the even further off 'theorizing', be adequate to the redress that is required? Does it disentangle the range of sexual, cultural and economic anxieties race mixture provokes? Gilroy continues, this time with the arguments of Young firmly in his sights:

> Whether the process of mixture is presented as fatal or redemptive, we must be prepared to give up the illusion that cultural and ethnic purity has ever existed, let alone provided a foundation for civil society. The absence of an adequate conceptual and critical language is undermined and complicated by the absurd charge that attempts to employ the concept of hybridity are com-pletely undone by the active residues of that term's articulation within the tech-nical vocabularies of nineteenth-century racial science. (Gilroy 2000: 250–251)

It is difficult to agree with the view that scholarship should avoid examin-ing the antecedents of emergent critical terminologies (we will see in the next chapter that certain other terms are not used). Hall also reacts, naming Young, admittedly in defence against an even more sweeping condemna-tion of post-colonial theory, yet significantly with the penultimate words of a volume entitled *The Post-colonial Question*, where he writes:

> a very similar line of argument is to be found ... [in] the inexplicably simplis-tic charge in Robert Young's *Colonial Desire* ...that the post-colonial critics are 'complicit' with Victorian racial theory *because both sets of writers deploy the same term – hybridity – in their discourse!* (Hall 1996: 259, original emphasis)

It is absolutely imperative that the uses and usefulness of hybridity as a descriptive term, as political diagnostic and as strategy be evaluated with-out recourse to petty common-room squabbles. That the use of a term can be condemned because of one sort of association or another remains prob-lematic unless the consequences of that association can be demonstrated to have unacceptable consequences. As hybridity appears in several guises, it is important to look at what it achieves, what contexts its use might obscure and what it leaves aside.

Contact zones

As a process with a long pedigree, hybridity evokes all manner of creative engagements in cultural exchange. Some works stress the developmental temperament of the migrant encounter, starting with – this is a some-what arbitrary 'origin' – anthropological studies of syncretism of the 1940s. Ethnographic field researches, such as those concerned with migrant work communities in the 'copper belt' of what is now Zambia, were carried out under the colonial auspices of the Rhodes Livingston Institute and the

Manchester University Anthropology School (see Schumaker 2001). 'Syncretism' was the word recruited to describe the formation of new cultural practices in the urban work towns set up near the colonial copper mines. Anthropologists had previously only been interested, in a diminutive, salvage kind of way, with the 'loss' of cultural forms under 'contact' and acculturation. Salvage anthropology was concerned with documenting 'disappearing worlds' and lost customs, survivals and traditions, and it was only in belated recognition of the resilience of indigenous communities that they began to think in terms other than decline and fade.

The studies of mining communities initiated by the Manchester School (Gluckman et al. 1955) were instrumental in the first effervescence of 'syncreticism-talk' in the post-Second World War period, but later South American examples of creative communal response to mining colonialism were prominent. Michael Taussig's study among tin mine workers in South America supplements economist readings of commodity fetishism with cultural contextualization. It shows how local ideas about Christianity (itself problematically local and global), and especially the idea of the devil, produced specific understandings of money's malevolent force (Taussig 1980). Fusions here provide a cogent yet unorganized take on 'mixed' economic conditions (see Nugent 1994 on transition). Yet, other modes of developmental syncretism were not so explicitly culturalist. Consider, for example, the Green Revolution adoption of new seed technologies, ostensibly to feed the Third World, but in reality leading to massive environmental devastation. This could not so easily be described as cultural hybridity, without deep irony. The same today applies to those with specific commercial interests who are involved in genetic patenting overwriting diversity in the agricultural sector (see Visvanathan 1997).[1]

Investigations into and descriptions of the acculturation process had been governed by what can only be characterized as a period of anthropological prejudice and single-minded ethnocentrism – the whole discourse about Westernization and diffusionism suggests an obsessive fear about identity and with maintaining and even extending the cultural hegemony of the dominant culture. In settler societies, such as Australia and South Africa, this took on the racist appearance of first extermination programmes, and then more insidious forms of 'ethno-cide'. Institutions such as the farcically mis-named Aborigines Protection Society in Australia, in the first part of the twentieth century, were engaged in the allegedly benevolent 'smoothing of the dying pillow'. This idea of easing the pains of the violent destruction of the Aboriginal peoples, was an unforgivable companion to the white Australia policy. Here, atrocities such as the forced removal of 'mixed' and 'half-caste' children from the care of their aboriginal parents in favour of fostering (and domestic slavery) in white missions and with white families have long caused concern. As documented in the film *Lousy Little Sixpence* (dir. Alec Morgan and Gerry Bostock 1982 – sixpence was the compensation Aboriginal parents were offered) and fictionalized in *Rabbit-Proof Fence* (dir. Phillip Noyce 2002 – the rabbit fence was an Australia-wide divide erected to secure farmland from breeding bunnies), the 'stolen generations' remain a running sore in race relations in Australia.[2] Remembering that the dispossession of Australia's original inhabitants had as much to do with mineral and agricultural capitalism, it is not necessary to stress that the notion of 'culture clash' also betrayed significant pathologies on the part of the self-proclaimed 'masters'.

Interestingly, the analysis of the clash of cultures as adopted by anthropologists, even where critical of colonialism (Worsley 1964: 51), often took on a culturalist bent, paving the way for concerns less to do with political redress than with the management of colonial relations. The very idea of cultural survival through fusion, mixture, miscegenation, creolization, etc., provoked apoplexy among the great and the good of colonial rule, and much academic energy has subsequently been expended attempting to unravel the violent consequences of a paranoid 'first contact'. It remains an open question as to what degree fears of cultural mix were governed by base economic interests and how far psycho-social categories must be contextualized.

Another field where the notion of hybridity has a distinct history focused on preservation is in linguistics. The concept of creolization and the idea of a linguistic continuum both evolve from the study of interactions, such as that between African and European peoples in the Caribbean. Out of the violence of slavery there emerged a number of new languages which were classified in a derogatory mode called pidgin and, more locally, patois. French patois (Haiti) or English patois (Jamaica) provided for the development of the idea of hybrid languages, which consisted crudely of one language's vocabulary imposed on the grammar of another. It is important to remember that the process of slavery also produced an amalgamation of various African languages. There are other examples, such as the ways colonialism in the Pacific spawned a range of idiomatic 'tongues', and entailed a separate but similar history of violence, acculturation, missionary activity, 'black birding' (meaning the kidnap of islanders to work on Queensland sugar plantations) and ongoing underdevelopment. The resulting creolized languages offered fruitful material for linguistic research, but these researches were often undertaken in isolation from, and even blissful neglect of, socio-political contexts. Some examples of a political linguistics can be found (e.g., Newmeyer 1986). However, among linguistics scholars there is often a good deal of resentment of the way a technical term 'creole' has been appropriated metaphorically to do work in culturalist discourse.[3] The precious anxieties of scholarly terminology often inhibit clarity and analysis. Although outside linguistics, the cultural translation model for creolization is popular and often invoked.

Translation is loosely regarded as a metaphor for method in many disciplines and has thrived in cultural studies and social theorizing inspired by writing from Clifford Geertz to Jacques Derrida and beyond. Geertz presented the idea of the anthropologist as interpreter, providing 'thick descriptions' (Geertz 1973) while observing 'over the shoulder' of his

Balinese informants. With *The Interpretation of Cultures* and later with *Works and Lives* (1988), Geertz set off a cascading debate on the propriety of translation and interpreted/translated texts of culture in the hands of institutionally resourced academics. The translator is a broker between cultural forms or documents, and is thereby in a powerful position, not always evenly 'in-between'. The question of who translates and why has been broached several times, for example recently by Virinder Kalra (2000) in relation to the analysis of Bhangra lyrics in the seemingly hybrid musical cultures of British-Asian creativity. The argument is that in making the hybrid the focus of attention, intended and explicit political content falls away in translation. This is due to, variously, the idiomatic and/or institutional situation of the translator (see Spivak 1999; Kalra 2000).

Another interesting, yet still problematic, commentator on this set of issues has been Derrida, who wrote that '[i]n a sense, nothing is untranslatable; but in another sense, everything is untranslatable; translation is another name for the impossible' (Derrida 1996/1998: 56–57). His argument is that language and cultural experience must be understood as idiomatic and therefore the idea of a perfect translation is misguided, and yet, attempts to translate are necessarily made, however quixotic. If there is no 'pure' access, from outside, to the idiom of a language or culture, there can be no absolute equivalence of translation. This idea undermines the sanctity of the scene of translation in ways now recognized by many, but not all. The self-appointed ventriloquists of culture still prevail and the metaphor of translation as a code word for ethnographic studies of 'otherness' has not been displaced. Derrida also identifies the translator as a 'rebel against patriotism' (Derrida 1996/1998: 57) and translation as an art enabling a side-stepping of a singular, homogeneous frame of understanding.

Thus, in many formulations, the hybridizing moment is a communication across incommensurable polarities, with or without peculiarities of idiom or grammar (often left without). At an abstract level this translation syntax implies the possibility of a calculus of difference, although it is reliant upon an idealized and perfect assumption that translation across difference can actually occur. Oftentimes translation is assumed by those who can enforce their way, those who have the power and resources to engage in (sanctioned) translation, and so the translated text becomes an appropriation of (cultural) ownership and even of creativity without attention to contexts. Terminological ambiguity in this contact zone complex means we should perhaps take seriously the possibility that a discussion of hybridity can open up crucial issues of power and control, such as who translates and why. This is not the same as saying hybridity can be effective despite, or even because of, its problematic conceptual difficulties. But neither would we deny the usefulness of a technical term that potentially allowed questions to be asked as to the political context and investments engaged in the scene of translation or in 'contact' itself. Whether it does so, however, is a bigger problem. In these circumstances, the impossible governs a politics of translation where the only plausible response is to engage a constant critique of the process. At the end of the next chapter we offer the dialectics of exchange as a more interesting way to make sense of this.

Cyborgs (or the sexual life of savage machines)

It is plausible, then, to consider another valorization of mixture, if only to indicate again the dangerous absence of attention to questions of inequality – across notions of race, culture contact and, in Gayatri Spivak's preferred term, the international division of labour. In studies of science and technology it has been possible to present hybridity as the central co-ordinate of contemporary capitalist relations, and sometimes as an unmitigated boon. If anthropologists were concerned with saving culture and linguists with the specificity of language, then science studies personnel have been obsessed with human and industrial hardware. The cyborg is the 'hybridization of human and machine' in the work of Michael Hardt and Antonio Negri (Hardt and Negri 2000: 405), although they do note that the cyborg is a fable and that hybridity, like mobility and difference, is not libratory in itself (Hardt and Negri 2000: 154).

Other presentations of the cyborg are altogether more upbeat, postulating an advanced fantasy multicultural future similar to the blind uniformity of the television space-age sitcom *Star Trek*. Geordi (Levar Burton), the black engineer with prosthetic eyewear in the *New Generation* series, and Seven of Nine (Jeri Ryan), the technologically enhanced Borg poster girl in the *Voyager* series, are classic examples of the type (we can ignore the android Data as just a robot, an inferior point of view character for pre-teens). Famed for its forays into racial politics, with the first cross-race screen kiss in the original 1960s series, no one less than Martin Luther King thought it worthwhile to congratulate director Gene Rodenberry and visit the set.[4] Yet, the prime directive of *Star Trek's* Federation (a kind of intergalactic US Empire) exhibits the same anxiety about racial mixture that its key character roles seem designed to deflect. The prime directive counsels against interaction with 'pre-warp' cultures (meaning: underdeveloped planets), although more often than not the plot requires this directive be breached. The overt text is about the volatile dangers of unrestricted technological advance (meaning: against technology transfer), but in nearly every case the transgression of the rule takes on a voluptuous cross-species sexual charge. Up above, in the starship, purity is secured, Geordi and Seven are integrated into the Starfleet crew.[5] The cyborg of science fiction is significantly the moment of erasure of cultural difference under the efficiency of the machine–human interface, eradicating or compensating for structural defects (Geordi's blindness, Seven's sense of collective responsibility as one of the technology-fixated Borg).

Californian 'History of Consciousness Programme' theorist, Donna Haraway, has a more serious take on the figure of the cyborg, and is, on the whole, enthusiastic. For her, a 'cyborg anthropology attempts to reconfigure provocatively the border relations among specific humans, other organisms, and machines' (Haraway 1997: 52). Her concern ranges from prosthetic devices (these could be as different as eyeglasses) to the internet as a global prosthesis, and her studies of science offer considerable scope for speculations about hybridity. To restrict this discussion to one of her specific examples, like the especially-bred-for-cancer-testing Oncomouse™, might seem to be a reduction as her text deserves separate reading: there is, in fact, substantial work available on these themes in the emergent discipline of social studies of science and technology (Nader 1996; Bowker and Star 1999). But using the insight that 'informatics hybridizes with biology in the New World Order' (Haraway 1997: 129), the parameters of this work can be elaborated insofar as it pertains to diaspora and hybridity, specifically the occlusion of difference under the sign of technological advance. Again, think of the character of Geordi in *Star Trek* with his eyewear (let alone the Borg themselves as paradigmatic cybernetic human–machine interface in space) and consider how marginality is relegated to the deviant and abnormal, only to receive a technological fix in the phantasmagorical 'modernity' of this fiction.

The cyborg, like the gene map, is more often than not blind to the sociopolitical components of race in its enthusiasm to eliminate difference by magical intervention. A critique of the erasure of race and inequality in the cyborg might address the failures of a discursive critique of gender too (see Chapter 3). If the cyborg is a woman, what achievements in terms of liberation can be claimed – so much for Oncomouse™, who though dedicated to cancer therapy, comes from a line of rodents whose experimental activity has had to do less with practical prosthetics than with the fashion industry and cosmetics. The trademark is a family resemblance. Cyborgs abound. We might also invoke the science fiction of the writer William Burroughs – part novelist, part junkie – and his education at the Los Alamos school, which was to become the site for the development of the atomic bomb. Los Alamos evokes images of the old Wild West. To then suggest that the internet generation can be conceived as cyborg humanity is hardly remarkable – the code of language itself was thought by Burroughs as alien, 'as a virus from outer space'. Language as a cyborg hybridization provokes more effectively in Burroughs than in the staged hybridity of *Star Trek*.[6] Language certainly has landed the human animal into considerable trouble, though it is, of course, the instigator of, and precursor for, pleasure, sex and travel, and fantasy writing. And in such writing the fertility obsession of the white race, which so often descends upon sexuality and accusations that the mixed, mongrel, mulatto and half-caste are degenerate impurities, can be worked through in the safety of the speculative imagination.

Avatars of a technology–humanity interface paranoia are the end-time outcomes of an eschatology that runs from nature to human to machine. The middle phase was the nature–human mix. Avtar Brah and Annie Coombs report that it was in the eighteenth century that 'the concept of hybridity was expanded to incorporate humans' (Brah and Coombs 2000: 3). There can be no doubt that what are nowadays catalogued as human hybrids have a very long gestation; we could think of the goat-men, winged feet, angels and mermaids of Western mythology.[7] It is probably somewhat impolite, but certainly correct, to note that the human has long been a promiscuous boundary jockey. The mythological nature–human hybrid then gave way to less imaginative concerns in the evolutionary development and civilizational programming paradigms of white supremacy. In myriad examples, salacious carnal mixing has been a favourite theme. What deserves study is the motley inventive terminology of mulatto, mestizo, cross race, mixed blood, half-caste, quadroon and octaroon, all manner of mixed miscegenation, in marriage and heterogeneous alliances, in several shades of adulteration. These diverse nominations of interbreeding betray a disproportionate fervour and zeal for classification.

Ann Phoenix and Charlie Owen conceptualize the issue of race mixture as a terminological confusion with worrying consequences:

> Although people with one black and one white parent have historically been categorized as black, they have, simultaneously (and contradictorily) been identified as separate from both black and white people. The specific terms commonly used to describe people of mixed parentage, and sexual unions between black and white people, tend to pathologize those who cannot easily be fitted into the taken-for-granted racialized binary opposition. Thus 'half-caste', 'mixed-race', 'bi-racial', 'maroon', 'mulatto' (from mule), and 'metis' (French for mongrel dog) all demonstrate essentialism and bipolar thinking. (Phoenix and Owen 2000: 74)

Why was it that British colonial purity, after initially open and later covert mixings galore, sought so often to limit intercourse between hosts and guests? Anthropologist Ann Laura Stoler writes extensively of this in an essay in the Brah and Coombs (2000) volume as well as in her book engaging with miscegenation, sexuality and colonialism in the context of colonial education practices (Stoler 1995). The context here is primarily an anxiety and ambivalence about desire, sex, intermarriage and hegemonies of bloodstock. The fear is not of winged goat-men but of black people claiming white privileges through the spurious accident of 'paternity'. Ruling-class elements of the white 'race' wanted to keep the lines of descent clear. In this regard, attention to the sexual urge in race mixture resonates with Young's difficulties with hybridity as a category in contemporary theory insofar as it focuses attention on the dependant relationship to 'purity'. Thus the historical legacy of slavery, apartheid and 'Aboriginal Protection' is predicated on notions of the distinct 'races' that colonial administration and race law long wanted to keep separate. And they wanted this separation to protect from fear of a 'contamination' that was always already well underway.

That issues of sexual border-crossing still exercise anxieties today is revealed in everything from excessive additional attention paid by immigration officials and other public service personnel to 'mixed' couples, through to the calculated provocative image-morphing advertisement campaigns of Benetton, or the 'coffee coloured people by the score' pop song jingle of the 1960s.[8] The entire problematic of mixed parentage and mixed relationships depends upon the fiction of racial difference in blood and genetics. This fiction persists despite the extensive statistical indications of both gene mapping, which show we are all mostly the same, and history, which shows that, for example, 70–80 per cent of black people in the USA have some white ancestry (Zack 1993). The history of slavery and colonialism certainly accounts for a greater intermixture of peoples than is generally accepted (Phoenix and Owen 2000: 75), but this matter is distinct from the domain of cultural exchange – we could note that legal impediments against mixed-race marriage were not lifted in the USA until 1967, just as the 'White Australia' policy, restricting non-white migration to that country, with racial purity as its unwritten but obvious goal, prevailed until 1973 (Sykes 1989: 23).

Radical purity, and race as danger, is the suppressed dark aspect of the far side of the human–machine or cyborg interface – that of the robot. In Bhabha's terminology of colonial mimicry, the robot might be thought of as kin to colonial overlord Macauley's not quite white class of Westernized Indians. Jean Baudrillard has pushed this towards the slavery-sexuality register, recognizing that 'the robot is a slave' and that the 'theme of the robot that goes off the rails and destroys itself is … closely akin to the theme of the robot in revolt' (Baudrillard 1968/1996: 122). The robot-slave is diabolical technology and must be controlled, must be forced – by a technological fix – into the always friendly 'docile body' that disciplines itself (Foucault 1975/1982). This is clear in Isaac Asimov's 'first law of robotics', where the robot-slave must not harm the master and must have self-limiting mechanisms to ensure this. Baudrillard is eloquent here:

> The robot … good as captive force; perfidious as a force that may break its chains. … It is in fact [humanity's] own sexuality … once liberated, unchained and in revolt [that] becomes man's [sic] mortal enemy. This is the lesson of the frequent and unpredictable revolts of robots, of the maleficent mutations that affect them, and even merely of the disquieting, ever-present threat of such brutal conversions occurring. (Baudrillard 1968/1996: 121)

It is the sexually threatening subordinate that spells danger for the privileged position of white middle-class complacency. Anxiety is signalled but denied in the innocent fascination of the robot and cyborg, and displaced from race and class into space and mechanics/technology, or on to 'alien' terrain.

Another scene redolent with the paranoid-fear-world-conqueror complex, and dripping with sexual and miscegenation cyborg and technological anxieties, is acted out in the *Alien* movie series. The all-American heroic WASP heroine, Ripley, battles to preserve a prophylactic exclusion of another life form – sporting a metallic vagina dentate aggression instinct (Creed 1993) – which only wants to live, albeit at the expense of its host. That this can be read as a right-wing Reaganite parable of immigration and miscegenation fears has been amply demonstrated by Pamela Church Gibson, who points out that a joke at the expense of a Hispanic crew member of the spaceship in *Aliens* (dir. James Cameron 1986) plays on the terminology of 'ILLEGAL Aliens' (Gibson 2001: 40). The alien is not an innocent monster and it is the Black American, the Hispanic and the welfare mother who are all symbolically killed off in the films. Ripley herself appeared as the perfect Reaganite woman – militarist paternalism – before she became sexually active in *Alien 3* (dir. David Fincher 1992). When Ripley is impregnated by the Alien, species distinctions are blurred at the same time that racial stereotypes are foregrounded but overlooked. Gibson writes:

> Perhaps there is more work to be done around issues of ethnicity in these films. However, it should be remembered that racial and ethnic differences between the human characters are perhaps minimized when the Alien looms among them as the sign of a difference that threatens them all. (Gibson 2001: 47)

In *Alien Resurrection* (dir. Jean-Pierre Jeunet 1997), it is the Winona Ryder character who saves the day, an android that one crew member wanted to have sex with, much to his dismay when he finds out her true 'nature'. The most advanced example of human-technological mixture, however, is Ripley's resurrection – religious metaphor not without significance – as the product of DNA cloning. The Alien also mutates, and from Ripley gains a womb, so that rather than nesting, she gives birth to a new monster baby, which Ripley of course kills, knowing full well, without words, that the spawn of the human–Alien mix is a greater danger, thus reasserting the message of race politics by displacement.

Creativity

It is not so strange, then, that the dynamic of exchange and mixture in the work of contemporary 'hybridity theorists' is intended as a critique of the negative complex of assimilation and integration that is so prevalent in dominant popular culture. Such work insistently affirms the creativity and effervescence of cultural pluralization. This is conceived as a theoretico-political intervention by some major theorists, although it is, of course, never presented uncritically. For example, in Hall's discussion of what he sees as very welcome changes in British cultural life, the term 'hybridization' is used to describe the confluence of black style and the market. With a certain mischievous tone, he notes a displacement where 'some sectors of the mobile (and mobile-phoned) black youth' have taken advantage of Thatcherism and the enterprise culture of 1990s Britain as part of a general trend towards 'the racial and ethnic pluralisation of British culture and social life'. This process is 'going on, unevenly, everywhere' and through television and other media the 'unwelcome message of cultural hybridization' is being brought into 'the domestic sanctuaries of British living rooms' (Hall 1995: 16–18). While this is good news, it is not unequivocally progressive. The same process can also be seen going on in youth culture where 'black street styles are the cutting edge of the generational style wars' (Hall

1995: 22). The question that should be put here has to do not with the evaluation of this diversity, but with the ways its advent leads either to new possibilities in a diasporized polity or, as seems just as likely, to the increasing incorporation of the mobile-phoned youth into the 'host' society, the culture industry, and more generally into a hybridized mode of capitalism. What is significant here is that the hybrid creativity of Black style is affirmed (as it is affirmed by the market and ultimately by the entrepreneurs who want to cash in), and expressions of enthusiasm for this creative change are obvious.

In the book *Dis-Orienting Rhythms: The Politics of the New Asian Dance Music* (Sharma et al. 1996), Sanjay Sharma notes the 'hybridization and syncretism' of South Asian cultural production in the UK in terms very similar to Hall, engaging in much more detail with the Asian dance scene as it was in the mid-1990s (S. Sharma 1996: 33).[9] *Dis-Orienting Rhythms* was a more committed consideration of South Asian popular culture than that of Marie Gillespie in her study of Punjabi teenagers in Southall, but she too refers to the transcultural experiences from which 'pluralist, hybrid cultural forms of expression are being wrought' (Gillespie 1995: 6). South Asian hybridity in the UK is again singled out, in passing, by Paul Gilroy:

> In reinventing their own ethnicity, some of Britain's Asian settlers have also borrowed the sound system culture of the Caribbean and the soul and hip hop styles of black America, as well as techniques like mixing, scratching, and sampling as part of their invention of a new mode of cultural production and with an identity to match. The popularity of Apache Indian and Bally Sagoo's attempts to fuse Punjabi music and language with reggae music and raggamuffin style raised debates about the authenticity of these hybrid cultural forms to an unprecedented pitch. (Gilroy 1993a: 82)

In a clear celebration of processes of transcultural dynamism, Gilroy is for the 'legitimate value of mutation, hybridity, and intermixture' which 'keep the unstable, profane categories of black political culture open' (Gilroy 1993a: 223).[10] In an important reminder for Black activists, he insists on this in preference to any reifying cultural or ethnic absolutism, which he says must be rejected, even in the musical forms he might otherwise approve. Though he wants to avoid the term if it implies purity: 'The hybridity which is formally intrinsic to hip hop has not been able to prevent that style from being used as an especially potent sign and symbol of racial authenticity' (Gilroy 1993a: 107).

In later work, Gilroy affirms the carnivalesque intermixing that polyglot space can sometimes achieve – he mentions specifically the Rock Against Racism movement of the late 1970s that was an early and formative influence for him – and this may certainly, as he says, project a 'rebel solidarity'. Such solidarity, which has its pastoral moments, enacts a 'universal humanity powerful enough to make race and ethnicity suddenly meaningless' (Gilroy 2000: 249). The trouble is that to sustain these exemplary and creative moments amidst the mundane hierarchies of really existing capitalism in Britain requires recognition, exactly like that at the heart of Rock

Against Racism, that injustice on the basis of race has to be fought so that a universal humanity can be gained. This does not mean that the Rock Against Racism carnival is important because it is mixed, but that (the sometimes pastoral nostalgia of) affirmations of the carnivalesque offer an opportunity to extend a politics of unity across differences. The singularity that is the carnival requires more than goodwill to transcend the festival moment and extend its hybridizing mutating process more generously. Creative production is all too easily commercialized. And so the call must be for organization of the activists and punters who attend, mobilizations must be built and campaigns take work before they can ignite support and solidarity. The ambivalence and cautions of both Hall and Gilroy raise the problem of indecisiveness exactly at that point where they recognize that hybridity as process is not enough.

The trouble with a discussion of hybridity in music, or in cultural production more generally, is that it remains open to co-option so long as the hybrid registers only at the level of commodities, or commodified identities. Where hybridity has been less helpful in explanation might be just where the most interesting political mixings have been offered. Music used as a mobilizing tool joins politics with creativity more urgently than can be readily absorbed by surface culturalist and formal calculus. Of course the use of political grandstanding as a vehicle to cultural market profile is also well known, but hybridity neither hinders or helps at this level.[11] One of the most interesting aspects of political–musical crossover in the work of *Asian Dub Foundation*, for example, is not so much their blending of musical influences, since all music does this, but rather the educational work their music achieves. In their lyrics and practice they bring issues and campaigns around racism and imperialism, such as the case of Satpal Ram or the War on Terror, to youth who might otherwise not be so well informed (ill-served as they are by mainstream journalism and televisual news).[12] The ADFED project which sees the band commit resources to conscious politics and community organizing is a case in point.[13]

And yet...

Given the convoluted and multiple histories of the hybrid, it is no surprise that authors such as Ella Shohat and Robert Stam, for example, complain of a failure to elaborate the 'diverse modalities of hybridity'. By this they mean to draw attention to things as varied as 'colonial imposition, obligatory assimilation, political co-optation, cultural mimicry, and so forth'. They warn that we should not forget that hybridity is 'power-laden and asymmetrical' (Shohat and Stam 1994: 43). The examples of the Manchester School anthropologists, bio-botanical antecedents, resource industry related culturalism, Australia's Aboriginal policy, cyborg futures and the complexities of linguistic and commercial usage show at least one thing clearly: that a more rigorous attention to the trajectory and career of the terms 'syncretism', 'diffusion', 'creole' and the 'hybrid' indicates where a political critique and organizational effort must extend understanding and forward emancipatory struggle. One author calling for a more nuanced typology of the hybrid is Amitava Kumar. He maintains that it is still 'surprising to see that "hybridity", as an abstract concept, remains a mantra of postcolonial identity' and continues by pointing out the need 'to distinguish among different forms of hybridity and mixing' (Kumar 2002: 56). Kumar adds a paean to the work of Arundhati Roy, who refuses the hybrid hyphenation of the designations she is allocated when she says, for example, that to describe her as a writer-activist sounds a little like the mixed terminology of words like sofa-bed. Roy makes a crucial comparison, in the context of a critique of the co-existence of neo-liberalism and fundamentalism in India, where she equates 'a dubious hybridity and an equally suspect cultural nationalism' (Kumar 2002: 57; see also Roy 2001).

What must be cleared away are the conservative notions of the hybrid. Hybridity conceived as national or cultural 'identity' is in part a response to the earlier problems of acculturation and diffusionism. Papastergiadis writes: 'The interpretation of identity as hybrid is a direct challenge to earlier quasi-scientific claims that hybrids were sterile, physically weak, mentally inferior and morally confused' (2000: 15). This colonizing fantasy of white supremacy is to be displaced in an affirmation of the figure of the hybrid as a 'bridging person' offering a 'new synthesis'. How? Papastergiadis points out a number of limitations in stressing hybridity's positive achievements. These include blurring the very differences that hybridity ought to highlight in a hybrid reconciliation between differences; a rush to promote hybridity as such as a new form of 'global identity'; and a failure to attend to 'the deeper logic of accumulation and consumption that frames modern identity'. Additionally, the foreshortening of the notion of hybridity reduces the concept to the banality of 'the occasional experience of exotic commodities which can be repackaged to sustain the insatiable trade in new forms of cultural identity' (Papastergiadis 2000: 15). On the whole the assessment is that the notion is useful but easily bowdlerized in the rush to name and fix otherwise oscillating positions and perspectives. The trouble is that in the turbulence and complexity identified in the object under discussion – migration, hybridity, globalization – the specificity of hybridity is left somehow hazy. Surely there should be no condensation into mere typology if explanatory insights are sought?

As an always already compromised category, it is not insignificant that hybridity extends its contradictions to adjacent terms. It undermines the fixity of the 'pure', of identity and the centre as soon as its status is examined: there is nothing that is not hybrid. If everything is hybrid, there is nothing gained by knowing this, so the coherence of other agreed terms begins to fade. The centre is also co-constituted with the periphery; the pure is muddied more in the breach than in itself. The truth is illusion, born of classificatory agreements without solid foundation. The multifaceted character of hybridity introduces a viral destabilization to classificatory systems and language itself. Perhaps this conceptual reflex maintenance work does not in itself provide any of the programmatic solutions we may want it to suggest, but that a politics of interpretation founded on hybridization might be plausible should at least be considered. This latter trajectory can be explored if we take up some of the questions asked by Garcia Calclini. His effort to distinguish between hybridity as a descriptive noun and 'hybridization' as a process is useful if we consider that diversity and heterogeneity are not the same as, and do not in themselves account for, mixing. Garcia Calclini has no qualms about reclaiming the term from biology (2000: 42). His question is only that which we should also ask: does it help to explain things better (2000: 43)? We could go further and ask if better explanations are all that are required. The points Geert Lovink makes in his *Dark Fiber* (2002) about hybridity deserve attention in this context. He is perhaps right to note that those who adopt hybridity as an ideology have 'no way back'. Where he is probably wrong is in retaining hybridity as a descriptive term when its role as displacement – especially in a tactical politics – is one that leaves more radical and necessary questions unaddressed (Lovink 2002: 272). There are problems built into the idea of a new model for explaining social interaction utilizing the terms 'hybridity' or 'hybridization'. The problems have to do with the validity of projecting unstable terminologies on to processes that might better be engaged within the language the processes generate themselves, or, if this is deemed impossible, in terms of an explicit political project rather than a documentary one – with all the distance and observationalism that documentation entails. Garcia Calclini's question can be rephrased: does a helpful 'explanation' help politically? We should carefully evaluate any tactical or strategic use of hybrid positioning that engages a politics of assertion against establishment hegemonies of order. We need to do this so as not to throw out potentially useful options in the all too heady rush to critique. But then we should also be alert to the ways in which the 'same old, same old' manages to reassert itself in the dialectics of co-option.

Notes

1 For those interested in resource politics, Shiv Visvanathan's work is essential reading (Visvanathan 1997), but see also the organizations Minewatch and Partizans for the development of a global anti-mining activism (see Moody 1990).

2 Old news for some, the history of this period cannot be contained under the sign of mixed racism as the later duplicities of the Office of Aboriginal Affairs continue up to the present with betrayals of the Land Rights and Reconciliation movements by the Australian courts and the refusal of Prime Minister John Howard to acknowledge Aboriginal grievances continuing up to the time of writing (2003).

3 We owe thanks to Steve Nugent for this point and for alerting us to Newmeyer.

4 Captain Kirk [William Shatner] and Communications Officer Uhura [Nichelle Nichols] were under the influence of mysterious interplanetary drugs, thus the kiss broke class boundaries of Captain and Officer as well as racial boundaries between white and African-American, but it could be explained away with reference to alien narcotic mischief – a malevolent form of intergalactic drug/date rape.

5 For a contrasting space fantasy meditation on purity, see the genetic drama *Gattica* (dir. Andrew Niccol 1997), starring the improbably less than perfect Uma Thurman attempting to bypass screening tests so as to escape the bonds of earth.

6 But see also Constance Penley's *Nasa/Trek* (1997). Burroughs became a counter-culture and publishing industry darling in the 1980s, as he ever was. See his music–performance crossover work with Laurie Anderson (*Home of the Brave* 1986) and with the Disposable Heroes of Hip-hoprisy (*Spare-Ass Annie* 1993), as well as cameos in films like *Drugstore Cowboy* (dir. Gus Van Sant 1989) and *Decoder* (dir. Muscha/Maeck 1984). I am grateful to Megan Legault's excellent final film in the Goldsmiths MA Visual Anthropology for this last reference, *Encoding/Decoding* (dir. Legault 2000).

7 The riddle of the Sphinx – it was Sigmund Freud, with a symptomatic curiosity himself, who suggested that the riddle of the Sphinx was 'probably a distortion of the great riddle that faces all children – where do babies come from?' (as glossed by Barbara Creed 1993: 18). It should not go unnoticed that the Sphinx is a hybrid creature – lion's body, woman's face – and Creed's linking of this with the primal scene of much science fiction indicates again how the themes of correct sexual congress are played out in the fantastic.

8 For discussion of 'mixed couples' in the UK based on census data, see Phoenix and Owen (2000); for an anti-racist morphing project in the art world, see www.mongrel.org.

9 For discussion of the convolutions of the South Asian dance scene and the exoticizing Asian-ification of the post-colonial metropolis of London, see Chapter 2.

10 This is somewhat of a different position from the 'Who the fuck wants purity?' line quoted earlier (Gilroy 1994: 54–55), the point being that Gilroy keeps the debate alive. The notions are slippery, difficult, contested and not necessarily internally coherent.

11 The posturing of Bob Geldolf and Bono from *U2*, meeting Vladamir Putin and Tony Blair inside the summit at Genoa, while Carlo Guiliani died outside under police fire is one sorry example (see Indymedia discussion at http://uktest.indymedia.de/en/2001/07/8214.html).

12 See Hutnyk (2000) for a more detailed discussion of music's uses and the work of *Asian Dub Foundation* in particular. Satpal Ram was unjustly imprisoned for 14 years for defending himself against a racist attack. Campaign work by ADF and others was instrumental in securing his eventual release.

13 For the ADFED project, see http://www.asiandubfoundation.com/adfed.php.

5

Hybridity and Openness
(or, Whose Side Are You On?)

The nation

Business as usual, or chaos? In a so-called post-national world, as we have seen, organized and obedient allegiance to the nation, or to any fixed identity, could perhaps become more difficult. Many are tempted to agree with proclamations of the end of grand narrative and the dissolution of all certitude. The nation, however, is resilient in many spheres – there can be few doubts about the military capabilities of the armed state, and the framework of governance and national boundary maintenance still takes quite orthodox forms. It might be a good test of the extent to which diaspora and hybridization have or have not undermined totalizing thought to ask what hybrid or diasporized forms of governance or border control might look like? Examples could be assembled, imagined, projected, but just who claims hybridity, and why, should be our questions when we again approach writing on the twin juggernauts of identity and the nation-state.

Everyone seems to accept that questions of the nation, and assertions of national identity, seem fraught today in the face of globalization-inspired uncertainty. The idea of the national is threatened by the consequences of a serious consideration of diaspora and hybridity. In its mainstream forms, it is 'place of birth' and nationalism – allegiance to the homeland – that are at stake when hybridity (or diaspora) is valorized as the postmodern or post-colonial condition. The idea of some primordial grounding in place is questionable as soon as it becomes a criterion for denial and exclusion of others. The idea of hybrid identity in diaspora as an anchor has its advocates. Paul Gilroy once suggested diaspora as an alternative to 'the stern discipline of kinship and rooted belonging' (Gilroy 2000: 123) – it delinks location and identity and it disrupts bounded notions of culture and racialized bodily attribution. The possibility of rethinking the contingency of commemoration and shared memory is not the only benefit here. Hybridity can become both a positive eventuality for some, and a constructed anchoring device for others (nautical metaphor intended).

Yet while hybridity is not proffered as the answer in every instance, its valorization proceeds apace in avowedly political circles. Kobena Mercer was among those to suggest that 'emerging cultures of hybridity' might offer something of importance. Although including some caveats, his context is an urgent Black politics that will challenge the bounded national polity of Britain, and he writes, quoting Gramsci:

> It would be preposterous to claim that Black British culture offers a 'solution' to the crisis of authority that will take us into the twenty-first century, but nevertheless I suggest that the emerging culture of hybridity, forged among the overlapping African, Asian and Caribbean diasporas, that constitute our common home, must be seen as crucial and vital efforts to answer the 'possibility and necessity of creating a new culture' so that you can live. (Mercer 1994: 3–4)

New cultural hybridity becomes the panacea for uncertain times, and in conditions of diasporic hybridization, without the certainty of the nation-state or class-identity for comfort, we may usefully and chaotically affirm promiscuity at every turn. In this conception, hybridity is a contender for a 'new model' of social possibility that will assert 'uncertainty' as its political guide.

Home

The polarization implied in the terminology of hybridity (a mix of cultures; of here and there) is most dubious when generalized in the diasporic context under the sanctity of the 'home' (or home culture; think 'home counties' or 'homeland security' here).[1] As we will see, the dynamic of hybridity as process is beset by several problems, even in its most progressive forms. The first and foremost of these, as detailed in the previous chapter, is the tendency to reaffirm, even in process, ideas of fixed and prior 'cultures' which enter into the exchange of hybridity – the hybrid is either compromised already or left twisting in emergent suspension between two more coherent wholes. It is here that the problematic of so-called postmodernity can be rethought as the malaise of muddled hybridity thinking – the mix of old and new, of different styles, the pastiche of elements that reaffirms the old. The question of novelty emerges, often in discussion of post-colonial identities, as the character of self in the contemporary globalized metropolis, yet the post-colonial always remains new, an arrivee from 'over there'.

Here and there, the host and the visitor; as with all ascribed positions, these entail degrees of implied uniformity that oftentimes congeal into hardened categories. The very idea of a 'host' and an 'arrivee' culture assumes a degree of non-hybridity which is difficult to sustain unless there is an insistence on an unbridgeable difference between the here and the there. The co-constitution of locations under global imperialism is denied, in effect, with calculated intent. The idea of the host is a property claim, a claim to ownership, homeland, right, authority. The idea of the host as 'not hybrid' resident of a homeland takes its most spurious forms in white supremacy and nationalist chauvinism. This is paralleled, with less violent consequences no doubt, in ideas of musical ownership, where proprietary rights to sounds are claimed and types of music are ascribed to national and cultural groups, as in Indian music, Chinese music, African-Caribbean music etc. As we will see in Chapter 6, the absent designation here is 'whiteness' – never ascribed, thus granting assumed centrality and coherence.

Against cultural ascription, critics of essentialism point out that simply investigating the diasporic, historically mixed, culturally diverse origins of even the most 'Aryan' assertions of origin and purity will reveal hybridity in all cases – the Anglo-Saxon is as much the hyphen as Hindus are the peoples on the other side of the Indus river (we have already seen that there are problems with the claim that everyone is already hybrid, already diasporic).[2] In *Dis-Orienting Rhythms*, Raminder Kaur and Virinder Kalra used the hyphenated and inventively ironic term 'Br-Asian' to point out the 'hybridity inherent in all identifications' (Kaur and Kalra 1996: 230). Papastergiadis wants to affirm the power of the hyphen in hybridity, 'the energy that comes from conjunction and juxtaposition' (Papastergiadis 2000: 143). In Chapter 2, we noted how certain hyphenated identities can re-enforce national identification, such as British-Indian, but that diasporic spaces also evoke new hyphenated formations, such as Asian-Muslim. In such cases, the terms either side of the hyphen are not the constituent parts, but rather what might be called a co-constituting – and often unstable, in-translation, interactive – entity. Bhabha writes that 'hybrid hyphenations emphasize the incommensurable elements – the stubborn chunks – as the basis of cultural identifications' (Bhabha 1994: 219).

Reworking hybridity in this way would entail neither a triumphant synthesis nor a partial or unfinished negativity, unless it insisted on the certainty, or fixity, of the constituted whole. Anti-essentialist scholarship has continually attempted to critique this with a comprehension seeking to leave differences as different, but to recognize them as somehow always erupting, in order to move elsewhere once again, renewed. The test is to decide whether the moribund stasis of the essential, of the nation, of the Aryan in the hands of the totalitarian group, and so on, is the antithesis of this effervescent hybridity, or if hybrid identity falls prey to its own illogic by merely asserting a new same.

In the racialized landscape of urban Britain, synonyms of hybridity appear to provide for a description of geography that disguises deep-seated, entrenched inequalities. Diversity is the codeword that foregrounds the marketable aspects of neglected and run-down inner-urban areas while maintaining a hegemonic base for capital and the conventions of the old and established. This is demonstrated in the compulsive reporting of housing price inflation in the UK and the search for brown-field areas for investors. In both newspaper supplement glossy specials on prime neighborhoods and in governmental schemes for renovation and renewal, there is a denial of lived experience of differences. The needs of residents conflict with real estate profiteering where the ever-present population is excluded by means of government planning which takes form of policies for taxing the poor (the problem of class hierarchy), by reporting that is focused upon destitute asylum-seekers (problems of racial profiling) and by general neglect of those for whom the rhetoric of diversity has little meaning (the homeless, disenfranchised, unemployed). Cultural diversity stands or falls upon the stability of real estate values and suburban reputations, and while 'some' local colour is favoured, the most 'mixed' areas do not feature high on the scales of services or interest. At this juncture the rhetoric of government housing schemes as 'opportunities for all' rests upon a refusal to address already existing material hierarchy. The new opportunities are distributed 'fairly', the contracting spread across all zones. With the winding back of the welfare state, hybridity and pluralism achieve a devious sleight-of-hand, presenting the banality of equal and fair treatment as egalitarianism without reserve – with privileges for just a few. If this were not so brutal, it would be comic. We are all the same in our differences: single mothers, refugees, Anglo-Saxons and Poles. The premature insistence on equality for all ensures the permanent retention of privilege for some.[3]

So the trouble with hybridity is that it does not offer an adequate language to discuss even the mundane exchanges of cultural difference in so-called 'postmodernity', let alone come to grips with contemporary social, political and economic conditions. This is not simply to say that things are more complex, although there are reasons to entertain this notion. Nicholas Thomas offers a Pacific example when he suggests that cultural artefacts found in the context of 'colonial contact' are not always 'productively seen as hybrid objects or expressions of hybrid identity'. They may be culturally mixed – he has in mind contemporary Pacific Island art forms – but the:

> culturally 'mixed' nature of these objects does not somehow reflect or express a mixed 'identity' because it reflects no identity. If we describe these artefacts as bearers of a hybrid identity, we may be imprisoning them in a frame that is no less misleading and invidious than that of colonial ethnic typification. (Thomas 2000: 199)

A similar lack of adequacy is identified by Lola Young, who makes the useful point that Black is not about melanin content, it 'may be thought of as always already "hybrid" and any attempt to use it as a homogeneous, self-contained category is contingent on a political interpretation' (Young 2000: 166). Against the cultural essentialisms of interest groups, a political alliance under the term 'Black' as an anti-racist category remains viable for some.[4] Such Black alliance does not explicitly feature in the trajectory Young follows, but her dismissal of melanin grading is of course welcome. For others, hybridity is of little use to a Black politics. Salman Sayyid offers the point that 'at the same time as making possible the weakening of hegemonic formation, cultural hybridity makes it impossible to displace the hegemonic formation' (Sayyid 2000a: 267). This is because, as Sayyid has it, subaltern cultural formations are unsustainable in the face of a critique of absolutism or essentialism, and strategic essentialism is a reactive and thereby restricted response. The adoption of essentialism in circumstances which excuse an indentitarian mobilization may appear to work in some circumstances, but it often proceeds in unexamined ways and with dubious consequences we want to keep in mind.[5] Throughout this book we have presented an uneasy oscillation between the progressive possibilities (as expressed by Mercer) and the limitations of terms such as 'hybridity' and 'diaspora'. The positions of Young and Sayyid again evoke the differing viewpoints. But, we would also suggest that hybridity as politics seldom addresses how capitalism forces an equivalence in which all differences can be made similar by the market; various and fragmented yes, but always up for sale.

Racial absolutism

The discursive replication of hybridity-talk deserves the critical attention it receives, if only to make explicit what is not being said. Gilroy calls for us to find 'an adequate language for comprehending mixture outside of jeopardy and catastrophe' (Gilroy 2000: 217). More than descriptive capacity is needed. Gilroy is correct, but for slightly skewed reasons when he declares his hand:

> We do not have to be content with the halfway house provided by the idea of plural cultures. A theory of relational cultures and of culture as relation represents a more worthwhile resting place. That possibility is currently blocked by banal invocations of hybridity in which everything becomes equally and continuously intermixed' (Gilroy 2000: 275)

As the culture industry makes all differences equivalent, the dilemma is that any 'resting place' is a kind of complicity internal to the problem – capitalist encroachment upon all aspects and varieties of life – mixed or stable, it does not matter which. Like descriptive and theoretical competency, 'resting' means nothing if unable to examine and work past complicity in its own subsumption and suppression. The plurality of cultures, or the truism that everything is hybrid, surely leads to the torturous reasoning of 'if so, so what?' – that is, stasis.

Maybe it is the mongrel, interfering, mix that undermines racialist absolutism, and it is the corrosive friction of intercourse and exchange that destabilizes purity and property by right. But is it also perhaps the message of hybridity that reassigns fixed identity into what becomes merely the jamboree of pluralism and multiplicity? So what then for adequacy and the necessary struggle? Paul Gilroy's risky venture of arguing his way 'beyond' race can be followed in a trajectory that also moves to a kind of beyond of hybridity. He wants a 'new idiom' for discussion of the transcultural in a way that can comprehend mixture in ways that are not stuck in 'jeopardy and catastrophe':

> Finding this valuable new idiom does not require merely inverting the polarity of hybridity's internal circuits so that what was previously seen as loss, dilution, and weakness becomes valuable instead and offers an opportunity to celebrate the vigorous cosmopolitanism endowed in modernity by transgressive and creative contacts with different people. ... Perhaps ... we might begin to comprehend ... 'transcultural mixture', and the assumptions about alterity that it promotes, as phenomena without any necessary or fixed value at all. (Gilroy 2000: 217)

The aim is to push through to a position where 'viable notions of civic reciprocity' make obsolete any registration of 'the forms of otherness signified by that narrow band of phenotypical variations that produces racialized difference' (Gilroy 2000: 217). The problem, of course, with these 'modest aspirations' that would allow (constructed, projected, essentialized) racial difference to pale into insignificance is that [civic] 'reciprocity' – or gift exchange – is well known in anthropology and philosophy as a kind of trick or gamble, bound up indeed with an economy of debt and obligation, as well as theft and extortion. Jacques Derrida has discussed this in terms of Immanuel Kant and the impossibility of legislating for hospitality (you cannot be forced to offer a 'welcome') and again like translation, the extreme of purity is shown not to exist (Derrida 2001). This is the key to explaining the refusal of the Australian government to welcome migrants (despite a tri-century history of 99 per cent migration) and to characterize those in detention camps as uninvited queue-jumpers (MacCullum 2002). Hospitality is political; there are no altruistic gifts and the ideal world of exact reciprocity cannot be conjured into place without massive redress of already established disequilibria (Bataille 1988; Derrida 1992). The drive to define and fix definitions is just what makes useless the categories of so much social science: caught in stasis, the closed character of analysis can only replicate itself, unable to attend to dynamic and contradictory processes in capitalism and social life as lived.

Allegiance to fixed categories, or their uncategorical rejection, is a deranged form of (not) thinking that settles on concepts or fetishizes them as objects (for or against) rather than using them to open up analysis and understandings to be challenged. However attractive the idea, however fragile the concept, it is not yet time to disregard (the effects of) 'race' as a criteria for assessing the extent of redress and reparation for crimes committed on the basis of racism. Similarly, hybridity provokes discussion and thought, clarification of ideas and action. Thus, the withering away of the category of race is also an ideal, part and parcel of a dictatorship of all oppressed peoples, united in losing their chains, different in ways that can ultimately be disregarded in economic terms. But while shared oppression mobilizes those fighting against racist attack, the terminology of racism cannot be wholly abandoned just yet – not everyone has achieved the middle-class credentials to evade the ghettoes. Even those 'cultural activists' who explicitly claim a left political orientation around a hybridity of alliances against racism are no less exempt. This is summed up neatly by Lauren Berlant and Michael Warner when they write that 'a rhetoric of alliances and hybridity can work to proliferate and coordinate different forms of identity politics, but a formalism of hybridity does not necessarily break with a consumerist relation to identity' (Berlant and Warner 1994: 112). In an important essay in *Dis-Orienting Rhythms*, Ashwani Sharma has made the point that the concept of hybridity can be incorporated into 'cultural politics' in a way that sees it 'reworked by hegemonic structures to produce new marginalized and essentialized identities, keeping in place and perpetuating the violence of "postmodern" culture' (A. Sharma 1996: 20).

Hybridity going native

Where might we find the thinking that could transmute interest in hybridity into an analysis that works? We do not want to dismiss out of hand the cultural abundance that hybridity theory seems to promise. But against celebratory-critical accounts, our contention is that interminable discussion of hybridity will usually just facilitate continued culture industry feasting upon plurality and difference. Michael Wayne criticizes 'postmodernism' for advocating 'a liberal multiculturalism or hybridity at the expense of understanding the material divisions that can exist irrespective of cultural exchanges' (Wayne 2002: 212). Rather than a politics of hybridity, what we see is a diminished hybrid market place of trinkets and emblems, sometimes writ large to avoid issues of racial and economic justice. Substantial struggles are subsumed as the cannibalizing capacity of capital is served up for all to see. Expression, creative exchange, and the possibility of political struggle are left to putrefy in the rest-stop of smorgasbord culture.

The examples can be multiplied by a consideration of what is and what is not considered hybrid, and why. We can examine explicit public moments of cultural exchange – food, music, film – and ask if hybridity helps our analysis of the culture industry. There are many culinary instances. For example, hybridity can be reduced to the curiosities of the 'curry house' where the national dish of England, 'Chicken Tikka Masala', can be consumed. This described in inimitable style by Koushik Banerjea and Jatinder Barn: wherein a 'peculiar hybrid performance' has the boozed-up white punters of Britain temporarily relinquishing 'the mantle of purity' – irony here – for the consumption of a 'gastronomically challenging Other' (Banerjea and Barn 1996: 216; Kalra 2004). There is, of course, also the equally tasty goreng mix that Chua Beng-Huat puts on the table: the *mee-goreng*, served in Singapore is known as 'Indian food' although it is made of noodles (*mee*), which are Chinese and not an Indian staple, and *goreng*, which is Malay for frying. It is served by Indian hawkers and not found in the 'imagined homeland of Singaporean Indians' (Chua 1998: 187). Chua also noted that there are Halal forms of Chinese food, and many other examples can be listed on the post-colonial menu. Food is not the only banality subjected to hybrid categorization. Conversely, there are a number of examples that are ostensibly just as equally mixed but, to date, have not been designated as hybridity: for example, backpackers, television, Maoism in Asia, Jimi Hendrix.[6] But Hendrix described merely as 'hybrid' would not capture the mischief of what Michael Franti called his 'fucking up of the star-spangled banner' (Spearhead concert, Manchester 1997) at Woodstock in 1969. The sonorously climactic, still problematically commercialized, rendition of that tune offered a fitting soundtrack to the defeat of the USA in its war on Vietnam. It prompts us to ask just why some things are foregrounded as hybrid and some not?

What matters perhaps is to ask questions about the motives behind ascriptions of mixture or hybridity in popular culture. It often seems that the mixed character of cultural product is selectively applied. British Asian women idealizing a Manchester United footballer in the film *Bend it Like Beckham* (dir. Gurinda Chadha 2002) is readily remarked, in reviews, using terms such as 'culture-clash', 'traditions versus cultural homogeneity', and even 'hybridity at play'.[7] The film earns awards and box-office dollars. Whereas the player in question, David Beckham's misspelled Hindi tattoo running up his left arm, his wife's band's name, his first and second sons' names or his move to Real Madrid are not deemed by necessity to be described as hybrid.

Keeping to the world of film, Richard 'Cheech' Marin, starring in *Born in East L.A.* (dir. Richard Marin 1987) is described as hybrid, to the exclusion of the film's insightful political critique. Addressing the issue of immigration restrictions at the US–Mexican border, Marin's 'third Generation' Chicano character is deported to Mexico even though he doesn't speak a word of Spanish (see Noriega 2001: 190). In this context, the Mariachi version of Hendrix's 'Purple Haze' in the film is also not simply 'fusion'. Nor the fact that in the film 'Indian' and 'Chinese' would-be border-crossers are played by Latinos in wigs and makeup. Marin's character teaches these stand-ins how to pass as Chicano to avoid deportation once inside the USA, knowingly invoking the Chinese Exclusion Act that was in operation from 1882 to 1943 (Noriega 2001: 197).

Would it be to go too far to think mischievously with this discussion of 'passing for a local' that hybridity might mean an openness to diversity such that we would have to redeem the old anthropological transgression of 'going native' for new times? Picking up on the idea of the translator as an impossible poet, and the trinket collector as the archivist of the global, might there somehow be an ideological reversal and restructuring to enable a context open to this as an entertaining idea? The intellectual commissars of culture remain hostile to many forms of what might readily be called hybrid if found in the 'margins' rather than as staples of dominant white privilege. Hendrix, Marin and Derrida might all enact a politics of the in-between. Yet the project of cultural diversity was first of all claimed by the elite classes, those children of the upper classes sent to view the art and culture of Europe, now transmuted into Peace Corps and NGO volunteerism by the charity-set bent on bringing democracy and decency to the downtrodden. 'Going native' persists in taking the most mundane forms, especially where gap-year university students return from their travels adorned with the flotsam and jetsam of the souvenir markets of the world. Why is this not also called hybridity? Other border-crossers from the white side are even less qualified and become traitors to the national: the soldier in Terrance Mallick's 1998 film *The Thin Red Line* goes absent-without-leave (AWOL) and lives among the indigenous people of the Solomon Islands; the beatnick, wigga, hippy and feral transgress against national belonging and the cornucopia of decency; the revolutionary communist, as much as the mystic or schizophrenic, departs from approved bourgeois identity and from the national(ist) ideal. These figures are not named as hybrids so much as loss, rebellion, deviance – the old moves of integration prevail.[8] There is good reason to consider the selective ascription of hybridity to the marginal, and not the centre, and to examine this at the crucial juncture of identity in a way that evaluates openness to difference: to what degree does the hybrid interrupt dominant identifications and reveal refusals and blockages of hegemonic nationalist order? Floya Anthias offers a pithy formulation:

> It could be argued that the acid test of hybridity lies in the response of culturally dominant groups, not only in terms of incorporating (or co-opting) cultural products of marginal or subordinate groups, but in being open to transforming and abandoning some of their own central cultural symbols and practices of hegemony. (Anthias 2001: 12)

What this leaves us with is, of course, that it is not the mere fact of openness, going native or hybrid that would satisfy the 'acid test', but what sort of hybridity and openness? A celebrated hybridity that enables an opening for the capitalist market to difference, migration and the exotic does little to challenge 'practices of hegemony'. Just as inserting a hyphen in the representation of the nation can present a sleight of hand to avoid issues of racial justice, 'going native' is possibly just another mode of commercialization of difference; the extension of commodity relations to each and every one of our exchanges.

Border exchanges

If hybridity selectively seeks out its subjects and these still form around the well-known categories of racialized difference, the exploited and the marginal, it is perhaps relevant to see whether this diversionary process is also at play in some related concepts. In particular, borders are often evoked in discussions of hybridity, but notions of population and its control by borders are not. David Morley, in a magisterial survey-like coverage of cultural studies texts, makes the point that an 'internal hybridity is the necessary correlative to a greater openness to external forms of difference, and is thus the condition of a more porous and less rigidly policed boundary around whatever is defined as the home community' (Morley 2000: 6). The burden of his book, *Home Territories: Media, Mobility and Identity*, is the need to 'move beyond the singularity of perspective that has characterised ... traditional nationalism so as to construct a sense of identity, security and stability which is more open to others, beyond its own narrow confines' (Morley 2000: 260). Could the community, or non-traditional nation, even the diaspora or the hybrid, be a matter of openness? Could such groupings become more open to others unless those others become selves? Here borders are not just opened but abolished, community becomes universal. Are we all going native? mixing? diversifying? Diversity, for others, is a fashion for cosmopolitan intellectuals unconcerned with hybridity except in their narrow localities. Openness to hybridity in the centre has not, for Gayatri Spivak, meant openness to the predicament of those not yet able to access the urban utopias. On the contrary, we can identify, at least anecdotally, a decline of interest in, knowledge about and solidarity with those on the wrong side of the imperialist divide. Spivak's withering critique of post-colonial complacency suggests we should look at how a selective openness works in hybridity talk so as to come to be presented as a political strategy (Spivak 1999). This again raises the question of what a radical openness to alterity would look like. At any rate, is it a coherent possibility, or does coherence and appearance hardly matter in a place – the planet – where difference is the condition of all? Is there a global political project in hybridity or is some other code for redistribution required? We can begin to assess such questions and search out a politics of radical openness if we start with Brah and Coombs' idea that the use of the concept of hybridity has sometimes produced 'an uncritical celebration of the traces of cultural syncretism which assumes a symbiotic relationship without paying adequate attention to economic, political and social inequalities' (Brah and Coombs 2000: 1).

The discussion of translation and the metaphoric charge of 'border theory', found in terms such as 'transgression', 'crossover' and 'fusion' should not obscure the real and brutal practical politics of borders. However much the appealing formulas of crossover might be emphasized, the material and political impact of sharp blockages to travel – immigration law, customs officers, detention camps, deportations – mean the theory seems to fall somewhat short of the line. E. San Juan Jr. suggests that notions of 'syncretism and interstituality [as code words for hybridity] might better be read as ciphers for the erasure of the record of "popular democratic" and collective resistance' (San Juan 2002: 14). In particular, he asks how a 'refinement' of 'research into diasporas, immigration, transcultural or border-crossing phenomenon [might] insure us against subordination'. He wonders if 'transcultural' or 'transmigration' studies can produce 'knowledge useful for an oppositional, not to say emancipatory, project' (San Juan 2002: 153).

The politics of crossing borders – and campaigns against the detention camps which maintain borders – in particular seem unjustly served by theoretical arabesques around the hybrid. There is little need for theory that leads to inaction. And it is difficult to see how the mixture and the cross-referenced enthusiasm of some explicitly political border-crossing events are all that usefully described as hybrid. As an example, we might consider what happened in Australia over the Easter weekend in 2002, with the liberation of detainees at the Woomera detention camp. In the remote desert 'outback', activists trespassed the security fences and surrounds of the detention camp, normally well-guarded by the Wakenhut Security Corporation, and 50 detainees awaiting forced 'repatriation' to Afghanistan and Iraq were able to escape through the razor wire fence. Many of these people were recaptured by state police, but a number of them made it to the city centres of Sydney and Melbourne to enjoy café latte and pizza. There was a very tangible sense here that something more than 'hybridity theory' had been put into practice through the diversity and creativity – and militancy – of the action.[9] But it is significant that, to date, none of the prominent border or hybridity theorists have felt inclined to comment. Indeed, upon watching the video of this event at a conference on migration in Manchester in 2003, well-known urban theorist and self-identified migrant, Saskia Sassen, raised instead questions of the legality of these trespassings. Forsaking 'others' in the desert, the Australian government continues to patrol its borders, internal (detention camps) and external (coastal, airports), to protect itself from the threat of 'alien' refugees. The detention camps in the desert are the obverse side of the hybrid metropolis. If diaspora refers to a moment of forced exile from nation, what do we make of that pain and trauma when it becomes a comfortable cultural(ist) asset that excludes newer arrivals – on the one side some are co-opted, on the other occluded, excluded and jailed? Those who are blocked from this translation can only wait for 'illegal' support.[10]

Similar ways in which the theoretical can be supplemented might readily be found. We would support a mode of activism which works through a kind of neglect of the excesses of hybridity and diaspora talk, but which stresses both internationalism and migrant politics. This is confirmed if we look at how examples of metropole-based solidarity movements are organized by diasporic people who do not only focus on the theoretical significance of their condition: 'Che-Leila' in Sussex fighting for Palestinian, Cuban and Iraqi self-determination would be one; the leaflets and posters collected to document the history of the Asian Youth Movements in Britain would be another.[11] It is rare to find these movements describing themselves as post-colonial, let alone hybrid, but there is no question that the interests they pursue come out of the same field of struggle that hybridity theorists pertain to address. The problem with theorizing here is that it sometimes clouds the issues, and opportunism born of conceptual sophistication can overwrite the urgency of politics.

Urbanization-causes-hybridity?

The excess of border theory provides an apt example of the way that syncretism and hybridity, as academic conceptual tools, provide an alibi for lack of attention to politics. Where Gilroy calls 'syncretism ... that dry anthropological word' (Gilroy 1994: 54) there might be reason to be suspicious of the ways previous scholarly attention has focused on movements of mixture. The old explanatory routine of population pressure and subsequent urbanization as the root of all ills for contemporary society was much discussed in the syncretism literature of anthropology. These themes should feature prominently in critical discussions of hybridity. Where Papastergiadis writes approvingly of the 'teeming hybridity of the postcolonial city' (Papastergiadis 1998: 175), there might be an opportunity for an incursion that remembers all those excluded from that city and trying to get in. Garcia Calclini also offers a typical example:

> Undoubtedly urban expansion is one of the causes that intensified cultural hybridization. What does it mean for Latin American cultures that countries that had about 10 percent of their population in cities at the beginning of the century now concentrate 60 to 70 percent in urban agglomerations? (Garcia Calclini 1995: 207)

Surely, the rural population remains part of any demographic, especially where its movement is blocked (see the essays on the limits to travel theory in Kaur and Hutnyk 1999), and this in turn raises questions about who can and who cannot be considered hybrid or open to hybridity. Scare stories about over-population in the Third World, with subsequent campaigns for fertility control and the tightening of immigration restrictions, intractable asylum law and reduction of refugee programmes, should all be questioned as the nether side of an hierarchical prejudice and exclusion. In his book *Population and Development*, Frank Furedi offers a cogent critique of the way population 'paranoia' and 'the goal of population stabilization' and control 'took precedence over that of development' (Furedi 1997: 73, 80–84). In an equally crucial commentary, Gargi Bhattacharyya, John Gabriel and Stephen Small (2002) foreground 'population scare' as a metonym for a range of anxieties about the degradation of racial privilege. Closures abound.

Many of those who had the good sense, relative fortune, or circumstantial luck to escape agricultural slavery (under feudal lords or under industrialized farming) by means of migration to the rich metropolis find themselves still to be afflicted by an international division of labour remapped across multiple zones. In the cities of the West as much as in the peripheral metropoles, the newly industrialized enclaves and the re-pauperized *barios*, there continues a comprehensive demarcation. It should be clear that those who escaped the peasant predicament only to exchange landlords for racists and institutional discrimination are probably marginally, materially, better off than their excluded brethren, still caught at the sharp end of IMF and World Bank agricultural policy. Those who remain in the theatre of that peasantry now find the emigration option replaced by sweatshop micro-production, service subservience or street-corner begging (perhaps just a few can avail themselves of new romantic tribal ethnicities so as to attend liberal colloquia on first peoples, but at best it is more likely they will be found hawking trinkets to backpackers). This does not mean they are the problem; equally, they are not to be romanticized. We should certainly salute the attempt of those workers who refuse slavery, and those who struggle under the wire (or risk asphyxiation on a channel tunnel crossing wedged underneath a lorry, or the danger of drowning on a makeshift raft in the Florida Keys), but we cannot pretend that running away is the revolution. On the whole, prospects seem slim for those who want to escape the immiseration of their situations. The issue is not over-population, and to use this as criteria for limiting redistribution is the ideological programme excused by the urbanization-causes-hybridity thesis. What must be analysed as more than a descriptive condition are the turbulent effects of population migration that, glossed as diaspora and settlement, has rearranged the necessities of struggle and life. Whether it be the settler colonialists in Australia, Southern Africa or the Americas, the Chinese in Malaysia and Indonesia, Tamils and Bangladeshis in the Gulf or Punjabis in Britain – and so many more examples – an openness fostered by hybridity does little to undo exploitation and inequality.

The generalized fear of hybridity is also played out in science fiction urbanization scenarios where the cities of the future are imagined as dystopias of ethnic mixture – urbanization leads to the Asian hybrid future of *Bladerunner* (dir. Ridley Scott 1982) in Los Angeles 2019 or the Islam-inflected megalopolis of the twenty-fifth century in *The Fifth Element* (dir. Luc Besson 1997). Like sexual mixture, urban crowding is fantasized as a problem to be worked through by agents of law: as with any number of (white, Western) sci-fi heroes, Decker in *Bladerunner* and Korben Dallas in *The Fifth Element* both fight to preserve the purity of the earth from non-human invasion. The Federation of *Star Trek* police space with patrols to manage threatening, endlessly multiplying, differences. It was German National Socialism that wanted *Lebensraum* – room to live – and tried to expand the borders of Germany. The Japanese imperial government of the 1930s went in for the co-prosperity sphere, which is akin more to economic imperialism than settler colonization. More recently, US imperialism marches to war in Afghanistan and Iraq in the interests of corporate building contracts and resource extraction. All these modes of expansion are figured in the off-world adventures of *Bladerunner*, *The Fifth Element*, *Star Trek* and many other films where planetary expansion involves 'terra-firming' and conquest or pacification before acclimatization. The task of adapting Mars to human habitation (*Mission to Mars, Red Planet*, dir. Anthony Hoffman 2000; dir. Brian de Palma 2000) is a well-worked variant of the *Lebensraum* ambition and is motivated by the same failures to deal justly with the here and now. By displacing thought about life problems 'here' today on to fantasies of the future 'there', what do we avoid?

On this planet it is the local 'aliens' who are a terminological problem for sociological classification as much as for state administration. Talk of urbanization processes reveals the ways descriptions congeal into a conceptual refusal to recognize settlement, opting instead for models of arrivals, second generations, immigrants, hybrids – as if these categories were ever stable and could be applied to really existing groups of people. As always from elsewhere, the lived-in formation of the centre is made subservient to an assumed but unchallenged, template – as if there were original rightful inhabitants. Londoners, in this example, are not those who live in London, but rather the 'residue' of the white 'east-enders' whose brethren mostly decamped to the almost suburban Essex in 'white flight'. The racist cartography of urbanization is clear and can then be mapped on to the class position of advocates of hybridity-talk. Of course then the east-end lads image becomes passé as hybridity is recruited to remake London as the multicultural capital, dining out on its mixed cuisine (expensive venues, underpaid and undocumented service staff) and its multiracial vibe (hints of danger, licentious scenes). It is in the interests of those invested in a certain version of multiculturalism to honour integrated 'ethnic' fractions and well-meaning white people alike in the polite society of the suburban milieu, with excellent services and shopping malls galore. In an indulgent inner-urban ghetto-exotica an economically privileged fantasy cosmopolitanism can risk a dark inner-city evening out. Of course any political assessment that might carve up the surplus in a more equitable way, locally or globally, is left unconsidered.

Just as in the previous chapter we often found anxiety about cross-racial sexuality behind discussions of cultural survival, syncretism, hybridity and mixture, at least historically, in the contemporary period a similar invest-ment provokes concern about urbanization. These 'scourges' of cultural homogeneity are seen to operate alongside a hybridity-talk that is unable and unwilling to defend against exclusionary attacks – the champions of hybridity appear complicit in the middle-class comforts that their own cosmopolitan lives afford, while denying the same to others left to languish in the 'Third World' and rural extraction zones. It is an 'unrestful' conclusion that the tranquil discussions of cultural hybridization, diaspora and mixture do little more than confirm middle-class securities and draw others into the hegemony of a fabricated, and commercialized, diversity. This is, indeed, the 'tranquillizing hybridization' (Garcia Calclini 2000: 48) that the culture industry develops as panacea for putting up with socio-economic disparities. Hybridity lulls us to sleep.

Lessons of Hybridity?

To wake us up: this might, finally, be the place to ask again if the use of a term like 'hybridity', in the social sciences, offers understandings hitherto unavailable, and do these understandings then form any sort of basis for political consciousness and a project of emancipation? Or is it merely the case that hybridity offers up no more than festivals of difference in an equalization of cultures that would confirm Adorno's worst fears of a market that sells 'fictitiously individual nuances' (Adorno 1991: 35) in a standard-ized world, where each product must claim to be 'irreplaceably unique' (Adorno 1991: 68)? Garcia Calclini is alert to this when he writes:

> When hybridization is the mixing of elements from many diverse societies whose peoples are seen as sets of potential consumers of a global product, the process that in music is called equalization tends to be applied to the differ-ences between cultures. (Garcia Calclini 2000: 47)

The charge is that a flattening of differences is secured at the very moment that celebrates difference and the creative productivity of new mixings. This flattening has infected the terms of scholarship to the core. In a provocative volume, *Ethics After Idealism* (1998), Rey Chow suggests that the popularized concepts of hybridity, diversity and pluralism may be grouped with others such as heteroglossia, dialogism, heterogeneity and multiplicity, as well as with notions of the post-colonial and cosmopolitan. Her point is that these concepts all serve to 'obliterate' questions of politics and histories of inequality, thereby occluding 'the legacy of colonialism understood from the viewpoint of the colonized' and so able to 'ignore the experiences of poverty, dependency, subalterneity that persist well beyond the achievement of national independence' (Chow 1998: 155). Chow continues in a way that takes to task the metropolitan celebrant of the hybrid: 'The enormous seductiveness of the postmodern hybridite's discourse lies ... in its invitation to join the power of global capitalism by flattening out past injustices' in a way that accepts the extant relations of power and where 'the recitation of past injustices seems tedious and unnecessary' (Chow 1998: 156).

The same distraction might be discerned in enthusiasm for the figure of the cyborg in Haraway, and science fiction. This is not to say that this erasure of past injustice happens in the same way, but the cyborg as a kind of robot ignores the politics of race by displacing the not quite (not white) human into a future scenario rather than recall the registers of difference, racism and slavery. As was discussed in the previous chapter, Baudrillard linked the theme of slavery with that of revolt, and it is not innocent coincidence that these themes must be suppressed. The dangerous sexualized underbelly of hybridity must be contained and restrained just as the robots and servant-slaves of dominant humanoids must always obey. Here the comprador and collaborative force is strong in diaspora and hybridity, where elite transnationals have a vested interest in working on both sides of the transnational connection. Ramaswami Harindranath describes 'an economic, political and cultural elite "hybrid" class' who collaborate with global capital in a reconstituted cultural imperialism (Harindranath 2003: 160). The consequence, however, is that it becomes possible to forget colonial violence, white supremacy, systematic exploitation and oppression: for those who can join the 'belonging' reserved to the compliant elite fraction of hybridizing capital, hybridity saves.

As already noted, it is Spivak who is the most critical thinker here, pointing out that attention to migrancy and hybridity reserves importance to the metropolitan sphere and leaves the zones of exploitation, as arraigned across international divisions of labour, in darkness. In several books, but most explicitly in her *Critique of Postcolonial Reason*, she repeatedly takes to task those hybridized and diasporized members of the cosmopolitan set who market themselves as representatives of the culture they call origin from the luxurious comfort they now call home (Spivak 1999: 191, 361).[12] This is 'going native' in a rather different way: brown employees of the World Bank, IMF and UN conference circuit can only politely be called hybrid. In this conception, hybridity is about the opportunism of diasporic migrants seduced by complicity and advantage. Spivak's critique centres upon the mode of 'post-colonialism' which takes the place of 'the thoroughly stratified larger theatre of the South', by displacing interest and attention to that 'South' by way of a 'migrant hybridism' so that the South 'is once again in shadow, the diasporic stands in for the native informant' (Spivak 1999: 168–169). Subalterneity is occluded or flattened (despite the problems there might be with subaltern talk) by the celebrated access of hybridity talk. This is achieved with the help of the scholarly enthusiasm for hybridity, as discussed above: 'An unexamined cultural studies internationally, joins hands with an unexamined ethnic studies ... to oil the wheels of what can only be called the ideological state apparatus ... triumphalist hybridism as well as nostalgic nativism. Business as usual' (Spivak 1999: 319n).

The 'business as usual' that remains to be studied here is the culture industry's co-option of cultural difference. The sophisticated artistic or rustic-ified ethnic performance of culture sits comfortably with an upward mobility of middle-class aspiration in the globalized ecumene. Beneficiaries of surplus while their class underlings succumb, the cultural effervescence of hybridity is indulgent insofar as it no longer contests monoculture but rather facilitates a corporate multiculture.

Perhaps the final lesson should be wrought from the work of the scholar who has inspired so much of the interest in hybridity, which these last two chapters have outlined. Bhabha writes:

> In my own work I have developed the concept of hybridity to describe the con-struction of cultural authority within conditions of political antagonism or inequity. Strategies of hybridization reveal an estranging movement in the 'authoritative', even authoritarian inscription of the cultural sign ... the hybrid strategy or discourse opens up a space of negotiation where power is unequal but its articulation may be equivocal. Such negotiation is neither assimilation nor collaboration. (Bhabha 1996: 58)

Is it unreasonable to think that the word hybridity – as a cover for so many things, an avoidance of much politics – is also a way of not saying dialec-tics? In Bhabha's discussion, the notion of dialectics is prominent.[13] He writes that for Franz Fanon, those who 'initiate the productive instability of revolutionary change are themselves the bearers of a hybrid identity' and these people become the 'very principle of dialectical reorganization, con-structing their culture from the national text translated into modern Western forms of information technology, language, dress' (Bhabha 1994: 38). Yet this process and 'commitment to theory' seems to be carefully dis-articulated from that body of theory that would think dialectics as an inter-nationalist revolutionary project. For Bhabha, 'the problematic of political judgement' cannot be represented as a 'dialectical problem' (Bhabha 1994: 24). He wants to take his 'stand' on the 'shifting margins of cultural dis-placement', and asks 'what the function of a committed theoretical per-spective might be' if the point of departure is the 'cultural and historical hybridity of the postcolonial world' (Bhabha 1994: 21). He continues: 'Hybrid agencies find their voice in a dialectic that does not seek cultural supremacy or sovereignty' (Bhabha 1996: 58). Faced with 'politics', Bhabha rhetorically asks: 'Committed to what? At this stage in the argument, I do not want to identify any specific "object" of political allegiance' (Bhabha 1994: 21). What he offers instead is an 'inter-national *culture*' based not on the 'exoticism or multiculturalism of the diversity of cultures, but on the inscription and articulation of culture's hybridity' (Bhabha 1994: 38). This has been a recurrent problem for us throughout this book – notions of 'partial culture', 'shifting sands' and 'versions of historic memory' occlude another, and possibly more radical politics. The ambivalence analysed in the hybrid threatens to incapacitate the politics of 'intervening ideologically' (Bhabha 1994: 22). When Trinh T. Minh-ha writes: 'after a while, one becomes tired of hearing concepts such as in-betweenness, border, hybridity and so on. … But we will have to go on using them so that we can continue what Mao called "the verbal struggle"' (in Trinh and Morelli 1996: 10), there might be reason to feel very hostile to notions of hybridity simply as translation. The struggle goes beyond mere word play: the effort requires us to see the term reclaimed from racist biology to do work for anti-essentialism, which itself reifies and must be countered in turn. Hybridity, then, becomes a new mode of essentializing, which is subsequently conceived as a verb – hybridization – but which further excludes and so must be questioned again. And none of this makes sense if it is not taken into organized politics, critical of going native, co-constituted here and there, and where we still think that interpretation and understanding is not yet enough. Openness to redistribution requires the mechanism of wanting to change the way things too often simply 'are'. Thus, dialectically, we would still have this coda: there is 'a world to win'.

Notes

1 This is also significant in the contexts of migration and asylum or refugee debates in the UK as well as in Australia. Under Minister Blunkett, the 'Home Office' became the arbiter of more than security; its passport bureaucracy calibrates identity in general.

2 The ascription of Hindu to a religious category belies this definition of the peoples of India. Persians used the label to describe people in geographic terms: those on the other side of the Indus river.

3 The solace provided by the realization that this situation can only further ready the population for uprising is tempered only by astonishment that they don't.

4 Sharma and Housee (1999); Sharma et al. (1996); Alexander (2002); also see the informative special issue of *Amer-Asia Journal*, Vol. 25, No. 3, 2000 for a politicizing take on the cultures of South Asian youth in America (Prashad and Mathew 1999–2000: ix).

5 The all too rapid sprinkling of tracts which alibi identity politics and entrenched positions with an automated recourse to the strategy of being essentialist – as if this was all that the critical term 'strategic essentialism' implied – misses what was important in Spivak's contextualizing use of the phrase. See the interview with her 'Subaltern Talk' in Spivak (1996).

6 Actually all of these could be called hybrid, and no doubt will be in time, and television obviously should be, as a cartoon in Marshall McLuhan's book *The Medium is the Message* (1967) quips, the conjunction of the word tele-vision, made from Latin and Greek, can never be expected to produce anything worthwhile. He meant it in jest – and not that there ever was some 'pure' *telos* corrupted by a 'pure' vision (Heraclitus notwithstanding).

7 A more appropriate and idiomatically translated title for the Japanese release of the film was *Falling in Love with Beckham* (2003), thus exposing an underlying white supremacist Aryan fantasy in the displaced racial romantic celebrity desire of Tokyo teens.

8 Neither Marlow nor Kurtz offer models for going native. Perhaps another possible reclaimed anthropology does – its fieldwork and participant observation continually in tension,

examined, evaluated; its collaborative and activist aspects foregrounded; solidarity as a watchword? Perhaps?

9 We must stress that we are not at all anti-theory, just not *only* for theory.

10 See www.noborder.org/camps/02/aus/.

11 Che-Leila is a non party-affiliated organization in Britain that will provide support to the international movements who are fighting imperialism, which is the source of poverty, hunger, destitution and humiliation in oppressed peoples' countries (see www.worldalternative. org/palestine/che_leila.htm). The documentation project organized by Anandi Ramumurthy collects artefacts from various anti-racist and anti-imperialist campaigns by Asian Youth Movements at www.tandana.org.

12 In a discussion of cultural nativism and the New World Order, Spivak teaches a reading of Gramsci that is helpful here, and it is worth reproducing one of her footnotes in full. She writes:

> Indeed, Gramsci is useful here if read freely. Necessarily without a detailed aware-ness of the rich history of African-American struggle, he was somewhat off the mark when he presented the following 'hypothesis' for verification: '1. that American expansionism should use American Negroes [*sic*] as its agents in the conquest of the African market and the extension of American civilization' [from Gramsci 1971: 21]. ... If, however, these words are applied to the new immigrant intellectuals and their countries of national origin, the words seem particularly apposite today. The partners are, of course, 'Cultural Studies', liberal multiculturalism, and post-fordist transnational capitalism. (Spivak 1993: xx).

13 It is clearly the case that the Marxist notion of dialectics relies more upon flux move-ment and flow than what the orthodox, Hegelian and tripartite presentation of thesis, antithesis and synthesis may imply.

6

Journeys of Whiteness

Idling away the narcolepsy of a London Underground tube journey, we were struck by an advertisement for international phone calls pasted above our heads. It declared cheap rate calls with a prefix of the company name followed by the region in question: X-Africa (Nigeria, Ghana, Kenya), X-South Asia (India, Pakistan, Bangladesh, Sri Lanka) and a category that was simply addressed with a suffix to the company name: 'X-max'. The latter included regions as far afield as Australia, New Zealand, Canada and the USA. There are two implications of this type of advertising. First, those who belong to the 'max' countries are not named in any way because they are the norm against which Africa and Asia can come into existence. Secondly, by naming those countries 'max' we see a hierarchy asserted. In the simple space of an advert, we have two of the prominent themes that mark studies in whiteness: invisibility and supremacy. The 'max' countries may well consist of multiracial societies, but the predominant group of people that the advert was addressed to, and the common theme that united these disparate groups, was the fact that they were essentially white people away from their 'homes' or, alternatively, what may be collectively described as white diasporas.

However, the two terms in the phrase, 'white diaspora', almost seem antithetical. This largely owes to the fact that diaspora is commonly used to address racially marked people, often viewed as a minority in the countries where they settle. In contrast, 'white' is hardly ever addressed for it is normalized in the racial hierarchies as the 'unmarked', the 'universal', beyond racial formations and, implicit to all these descriptions, the institutionally powerful with the freedom to move about. Here we see that hybridity does not describe the cultural productions, nor the urban enclaves of white diasporas (such as Earls Court in London, home to travelling Australians). In their new hostlands in the metropole, whiteness is assumed to integrate seamlessly, to present no major problems and is therefore given the status of honorary native. From Toronto to Sydney, the privilege of whiteness is maintained. When comparing public concern for the approximately four thousand annual boat arrivals into Australia and the six thousand or so Britons who are currently illegally at large in that continent, Minister for Immigration, Philip Ruddock, argued that the British overstayers posed less of a security risk than the 'new arrivals'. The status of whiteness overrides any such matters as illegality. It is an invisible marking that grants access. On the other hand, the racial marking on the bodies from Afghanistan, Iran,

Iraq and so forth are seen almost in the same light as vermin, to be, if not repelled, at least controlled.[1]

Even though there has been a recent turn in race/ethnicity studies to mark whiteness as a racially powerful and distinct regime of power (see below), this has not been cohesively applied to studies of diaspora and hybridity.[2] This chapter attempts to apply a corrective to this absence. The overriding assumption about diaspora is that it applies essentially to non-white migrant communities residing in the West. Hybridity, as we have demonstrated in detail in previous chapters, is usually restricted to discussions of the cultural output of these Asian and African-Caribbean diasporic groups. Where whiteness makes an appearance, it is often in discussions of those who do not quite fit into Anglo-Saxon ideals of acceptance and normality. So, for instance, the web advert for the journal *Diaspora* announces a dedication to:

> The multidisciplinary study of the history, culture, social structure, politics and economics of both the traditional diasporas – Armenian, Greek, and Jewish – and those transnational dispersions which in the past three decades have chosen to identify themselves as 'diasporas.' These encompass groups ranging from the African-American to the Ukrainian-Canadian, from the Caribbean-British to the new East and South Asian diasporas. (1991)

There is a notable absence here of Germans in Argentina, or Poles in Canada. Rather, those examples that are not obviously non-white, as with the Jewish, and people of the Mediterranean, can be described as those of 'secondary whiteness'. Such diasporas have not been openly welcomed into Anglo-Saxon structural supremacy – that is, their perceived ethnicity does not grant them invisibility in the metropolitan mainstream. They have historically been 'raced' in particular ways such that at certain times they too have invariably experienced racism in its many forms. Richard Dyer elaborates on these gradations of whiteness:

> Latins, the Irish and Jews, for instance, are rather less securely white than Anglos, Teutons and Nordics; indeed, if Jews are white at all, it is only Ashkenazi Jews, since the Holocaust, in a few places. (Dyer 1997: 12)

Narratives of migration are no guarantee in exposing power relations related to racial hierarchies. The USA, for instance, is often cited as a 'nation of immigrants', yet the conflation of European migrants that constitute part of its population are never termed diasporic or hybrid in the same way. There is no excuse also in the length of settlement of various groups to explain this absence of naming: the Chinese were one of the earlier settler populations on the continent, but they are still routinely referred to in diasporic terms.[3] What this chapter sets out to achieve is to view people like Columbus and his shipmates as migrants rather than 'discoverers', and the community of travellers that Davy Crocket represents as diasporic rather than as pioneers.

What would it mean to turn the lens round and consider diaspora in relation to the movement of white communities, if such entities can be said to exist? Would it be seen as a gesture of putting under the scalpel otherwise invisible and hegemonic formations of whiteness, exposing the racialized hierarchies that sustain white power? Or would this diasporic perspective be tantamount to depoliticizing what could be accurately described as neo-imperial movements, thereby invalidating the specific insights of diaspora and hybridity for already marginalized groups? It is irredeemably the case that journeys of whiteness are closely linked to supremacist discourses, whether that be (neo-)colonialism, racism, transnational capitalism, and even migration or tourism (Kaur and Hutnyk 1999). Extreme cases of neo-colonialism or neo-fascism are often dismissed as extraordinary or exceptional. Les Back notes the formation of a 'transnation' among far-right white supremacists. He looks at the use of the internet among scattered far-right sympathizers in what he describes as 'white diasporas of the New World' (Black 2002a: 128) – that is, referring to long-term European migrants in the USA, Canada, South Africa, Australia, New Zealand and parts of South America.[4] Physical diasporas are consolidated through the internet, enabling, if not a physical movement, at least the high-speed exchange of ideas and opinions which have very tangible effects in various localities of this transnation. In this case, white diasporas are ostensibly about international supremacy, even though self-perception may delude the protagonists to believe that they are racially threatened. Instances of far-right white supremacy such as this, however, are often dismissed by the not-so-extreme white diasporas as exceptional, failing to take account of the privileges bestowed upon themselves due to their common racial features.

Perhaps to combine various white groupings into one is to do disservice to the variety of histories of people across the world. More crucially, it raises the problem of demarcating essentialist groupings based on specious characteristics, which to some extent replays and reinforces the ideology of a unified white supremacist capitalist formation. To overcome this, we pursue our arguments with a variety of case studies to expose the structural and ideological contexts which uphold the privilege of whiteness. We ask whether there are any gains to be made in marking the movement of whiteness in relation to diaspora studies? We demonstrate that there is potential in such an enquiry, particularly as it permits us to highlight power relations, hierarchies and unspoken assumptions where an absence of this topic only furthers the invisibility, normalization and supremacy of whiteness across much of the world. We can begin to test the applicability of our key terms 'diaspora' and 'hybridity' to the case of whiteness, simultaneously placing all three categories under critique. However, we are cautious about an uncritical embracing of a sole focus on whiteness, to not be would reinscribe its hegemony in the process of centring it in our analysis.

A spotlight on whiteness

In the last couple of decades, studies on whiteness have developed to supplement a long-term academic interest in race and ethnicity. Much of the available literature arises out of feminism, labour history, and lesbian and gay studies (e.g., Frankenberg 1993; Dyer 1997; Rutherford 1997). Theorists began to acknowledge that the 'invisible' prevalence of whiteness also needs to be seen as a racialized category. The power of whiteness lay in the fact that it was a racialized identity that had become normalized. Whiteness is not just a facile reference to white people in a literal manner, but rather a description of *the historical legacy of colonialism and contemporary realities of structural power of the white-dominated West in virtually all spheres.* Scholars invariably agree that whiteness exercises hegemony over other racial groups in its taken-for-granted invisibility and dominance in the West. Bhabha describes the phenomenon as 'the positivity of whiteness which is at once colour and no colour' (Bhabha 1994: 76). bell hooks, preferring to describe it as 'white supremacy', declares that 'only a few have dared to make explicit those perceptions of whiteness that they think will discomfort or antagonize readers' (hooks 1997: 166). This reluctance is part of the liberal conviction that everyone is essentially the same, sharing a common humanity – another instance of the doctrine of universal subjectivity. To hear of perceptions of whiteness from the 'other side', however uncomfortable, is often dismissed, such that they 'unwittingly invest in the sense of whiteness as mystery' (hooks 1997: 168).

Like other forms of identification, whiteness has its own dynamic constituencies and differentiation. In many situations in multiracial Southall in west London,[5] for instance, it divides sharply into the provisional categories of English and Irish ethnicity.[6] As Gerd Baumann reports in *Contesting Culture*:

> To speak of a *white community* is commonplace among South Asian and Afro-Caribbean Southallians; yet it is rare among their white neighbours themselves. Their self-classification acknowledges only one internal distinction as clearly as this: that between Irish and English Southallians. (Baumann 1996: 92, original emphasis)

Baumann does not analyse the implications of this differential identification beyond the mode of anthropological field work reportage. The white neighbours' inability to speak of whiteness is clearly part of its hegemonic invisibility. Rather, when whiteness is articulated, it is done so along the lines of ethnicity (that is, according to region or nation), in this case that of the English and the Irish. Crucially, and following hooks' (1997) outline of the discomfort that arises from hearing 'whiteness' spoken from the 'other side', for Black Southall, whiteness is not an invisible category. The African-American novelist Ralph Ellison provides a further critique of what is and what is not visible in his fictional work on black lives in 1940s America, *Invisible Man* (1947). He writes:

> I am an invisible man. No, I am not a spook like those who haunted Edgar Allan Poe; nor am I one of your Hollywood movie ectoplasms. I am a man of substance, of flesh and bone, fibre and liquids – and I might even be said to possess a mind. I am invisible, understand, simply because people refuse to see me. Like the bodiless heads you see sometimes in circus side shows, it is as though I have been surrounded by mirrors of hard, distorting glass. When they

approach me they see only my surroundings, themselves, or figments of their imagination – indeed, everything and anything except me. (Ellison 1947: 7)

From Ellison's perspective, it is blackness that connotes invisibility in the sense of dehumanization.[7] Whiteness is associated with visibility because it grants ostensible rights, privileges and status. Thus, from a non-white perspective, whiteness is certainly not invisible. Whiteness is normalized to the point that it *appears* invisible to some, not that it is racially unmarked from other perspectives. In this sense, whiteness is produced as an absence which has a marked presence from a non-white perspective. At the same time in the wake of exercises in self-reflexivity and studies on whiteness, the concept must not be left unquestioned (Kaur 2003).[8]

How diasporas disappear

If whiteness enables the application of a vanishing cream, such that the movement of white peoples does not result in diasporic formations and subsequent cultural forms not labelled as hybrid, processes must be at work which mark out certain groups and leave others invisible. A key factor in this process is the political environment, and more specifically immigration policies. The political history of whiteness in the USA provides a crucial example for the way in which certain diasporas can disappear. Vron Ware summarizes three main phases in the history of US immigration policy:

> the first beginning with the naturalization law of 1790, which limited naturalized citizenship to 'free white persons' – that is, those of European heritage; the second around the time of mass settlement of immigrants from Europe from 1840s until 1924 when restrictive legislation came into force. In this period, monolithic whiteness fractured into a hierarchy of white 'subraces' dominated by Anglo-Saxon purity; and the third period of alchemical fusion of these plural and differentiated white 'races' – Jews, Greeks, Irish, Italians, Slavs, Poles, Portuguese – into a more unified Caucasian entity, brought unevenly into being by the migration of African Americans to the cities of the North and the West and ensuing struggles for civil rights. (Ware 2002a: 23)

Alchemical fusions and alliances become more pronounced in the face of groups seen as even more different from others. Attitudes towards Native Americans, Blacks and other migrants of colours played a phenomenal part in the imagination of US unity. Ali Behdad notes how:

> immigration makes the ambivalent concept of the 'nation-state' imaginable in America: while the figure of the 'alien' provides the differential signifier through which the nation defines itself as an autonomous community, the juridical and administrative regulations of immigration construe the collective sovereignty of the modern state. (Behdad 1997: 156)

As a matter of course, the American nation oscillates between tolerance and the exclusion of specific migrants. It is this ambivalence that in fact has produced concepts of the American nation.

Others contend that the USA has a much more concerted multiculturalist strategy when compared to European countries' more nation-oriented policies.

Maud S. Mandel (1995), for instance, critiques assumptions concerning the necessity and inevitability of the 'national project' in Western Europe and compares it with a 'multiculturalist' American approach to immigration, acculturation, integration and assimilation. While an instructive comparison, it must be remembered that this is in the arena of ideals rather than practice. Given that the birth of the American nation requires the genocide of the Native peoples there and the creation of an imported slave population, it is an act of great amnesia that produces the USA as a land welcoming of all immigrants. Even in the contemporary period, the US government's approach towards non-white migrants is far from an exemplary mode of multicultural democracy. Indeed, as we will demonstrate in Chapter 7, the USA leads the way on policies that exclude and demonize Muslim immigrants. As with other countries in the West, whiteness continues to signify and consolidate 'Americanness' and 'certain subjects are illegalized as "aliens"' (Socialist Collective Review 1995: 11).

Only some diasporas are permitted to 'disappear' to become an unproblematic part of a nation-space. This is not a static process: at some points a diaspora that is rendered invisible by its ability to use economic status to purchase that invisibility can, by virtue of circumstance, be thrust into the limelight. The South Asian and Arab diaspora in America is a case in point. Kamala Visweswaran (1997) notes the contradictory ways in which South Asian immigrants have positioned themselves in the USA. Many once wanted to be counted as 'white' in order to escape racism.[9] Such aspirations have been valorized in the 'model minority' status attributed to successful middle-class Asians in the USA (Prashad 2000). Others claimed racialized reclassification as minorities entitled to benefit from federal programmes. And recently, still others aligned themselves against Affirmative Action.[10] Whatever their attitudes and approaches, South Asians in the USA were effectively reclassified in the post-September 11 violence that targeted Arabs, Muslims and brown folks generally (see Puar and Rai 2002; Kalra 2004). This is an example where skin colour or melanin content plays no significant role in the rendering of invisibility but is always available for marking difference. Despite their aspirations for assimilation, South Asians in the USA were forced to form part of the 'dark diaspora' brigade.

Admittedly, skin colour often plays an ambivalent role in determining racial hierarchies. Of more import are wider structural and ideological contexts in which diasporas are formed. In her study of Greek Cypriots in Britain, Anthias notes that even though they are colonial migrants and are culturally marked as distinct and disadvantaged in the housing, employment and education arenas, Greek Cypriots 'are not generally regarded as a racialized category, and are usually left out of those discussions whose focus is racial prejudice or institutionalized racism' (Anthias 1992: 1). As with African-Caribbeans and South Asians, Greek Cypriots were part of the New Commonwealth migration of the 'long boom' in the 1950s and 1960s. Anthias's argument is to reinstate Cypriots as structurally and ideologically affected, if not racially disadvantaged. Skin colour, she argues, is too ambiguous an index of social status:

colour itself is not an empirically given dimension of social structure – while Turks in London are 'white', they are 'black' in Germany. Some Cypriots are darker than some Asians and yet they may be regarded and regard themselves as a white or European group. (Anthias 1992: 14)

Again, we return to the pervasive power of the *structures of whiteness* as a historical and institutional force to be reckoned with, rather than whiteness as a chromatic entity. It is not skin colour *per se* that we must draw attention to, but the way people are positioned in institutional structures and discursive formations, attributing greater privileges and rights to some when compared to others because of what they are deemed to represent.[11] Overwhelmingly, the closer diasporas are to Anglo-Saxon ideals and institutional whiteness, the easier it is for them to 'disappear' and settle down in new terrains in the West.

Not diasporas? Expatriates, TCKs and tourists

It is clear that 'white diasporas' are hard to envisage, as usually whiteness is seen as something that diasporas come up against, an invisible yet hegemonic presence that must be negotiated. It is incontestable that in most situations the racial economy of diasporas orients its possibility of movement and ineluctable forces impinge on the displaced. However, by way of contrast, in the case of the permanent migration of white people, it is their subjectivity and *choice* that produce the diaspora. This is not to simply say that diasporic movements of racialized peoples have no element of subjectivity. Nor, for that matter, can we say that white people are just driven by monadic choices and not affected by structural features at all. Rather, structural constraints hinder the movement of racialized peoples while enhancing and benefiting white people. Effectively, whiteness acts as a passport of privilege.

This is exemplified in the way that white diasporas are described. Terms such as 'expatriate' and, more recently, 'Third Culture Kid' are more often used than is 'diaspora'. The notion of expatriate, living outside the 'homeland' – a combination of the Latin *ex* (outside) and *patria* (motherland) – demonstrates some strains equivalent to theories of diaspora. In contradistinction, however, there is also the overtone of colonial expansion or, in Cohen's typology, 'imperial diasporas' (see Chapter 1), which sets the movement of expats aside from those diasporic populations who have shifted from countries that were politically, economically and culturally oppressed under high imperialism. The case of the Third Culture Kid or Transcultural Kid (TCK) and its 'adult' avatar, ATCK, can be used to illustrate these points. TCK was a phrase developed by Ruth Hill Useem in the 1960s, while studying Americans living and working in India, to refer to the children of these expatriates. The expats were primarily foreign service officers, missionaries, technical aid workers, businessmen, educators and media representatives who had set up their own little 'villages'. State, private and makeshift schools were also set up for the education of minor dependants, or TCKs, accompanying their parents abroad. Lest it be forgotten, it was expats and ATCKs who were historically agents of colonization (Stoler 1991).

A Third Culture Kid is defined as:

> an individual who, having spent a significant part of the developmental years in a culture other than that of their parents, develops a sense of relationship to both. These children of business executives, soldiers and sailors, diplomats and missionaries who live abroad, become 'culture-blended' persons who often contribute in unique and creative ways to society as a whole. The TCK's roots are not embedded in a place, but in people, with a sense of belonging growing out of relationships to others of similar experience. (Alma Daugherty Gordon, www.tckworld.com 1993)

A comparison with the conventional literature on diaspora raises some interesting features. Whereas the dominant trope for refugees and exiles is uprootedness, for expats it seems to be transplantation.[12] 'Transplantation', a term that implies choice and agency, connotes establishing an extension of the motherland elsewhere. Although TCKs are displaced, they still predominantly identify with their home country even if their return experience is not what they might have imagined it to be. Expats may well be dispersed but return when 'the time is right', for instance after a period of placement or on retirement. Repatriation or returning 'home' is common, but it is a period which is frequently one of the most difficult in the expatriate lifecycle. As with other studies, for the TCK, nationality of origin is experienced more intensely once abroad. But on return to the homeland, TCKs may well find that their imagining and performing of Britishness may be very distinct:

> A TCK can never change back into a monocultural person. Parents of TCKs can return 'home' to their country of origin, but the children, enriched by having shared life in their formative years with another people, will find characteristics of both cultures in their very being. Acceptance of this fact frees TCKs to be uniquely themselves. In fact, TCKs have tools to be the cultural brokers of the future. (Alma Daugherty Gordon, www.tckworld.com 1993)

It is notable that in this case, being 'between cultures' is not seen as symptomatic of a social pathology as was the thinking in early writings on children of more conventional diasporas (Watson 1977; Anwar 1998; for a critique, also see Kalra 2000). Rather, largely due to their imbrication in structures of whiteness, TCKs seem to have become investments for the future as cultural mediators. These are not troubled hybrids. Rather, the privilege of whiteness enables a standpoint from which they are seen as 'multi-skilled, enriched and talented'. However, when non-white youngsters who are placed between the specious entities of 'cultures' are considered, then they are pathologized; they are often seen as culturally confused, disoriented and even dangerous (see Alexander 2000, 2002). But of course the question of class is paramount here. The TCKs are not marked out solely in terms of being white, but rather in terms of their class status within a globalized labour market. The conceptualization of expat is implicitly about exploitation, be that in the business world or in the world of international development.

Implicit in the conceptualization of expats and TCKs is a sense of return. The first permanent settlements of Europeans abroad is to be found in the era of 'settler colonialism' (Wolfe 1999), where people from Europe ended up residing in 'far-flung corners' of the world, such as North America and Australia. In the majority of these cases, 'native' people were decimated or oppressed – effectively 'erased' – so that 'white diasporas' then became 'indigenized' as 'native' and rightful, albeit controversial, owners of the land. This is a phenomenon that Koushik Banerjea refers to as the consequence of 'propertied whiteness', where phenotype becomes 'the ontological fact of personhood' investing these people with disproportionate legal rights, land and material goods (Banerjea 1999: 19). It is with such examples that we see the erasure of the diasporic trace of white migrants, who now effectively constitute the model exemplar of the nation-state. In other examples of settler colonialism, as with the cases of Canada and New Zealand, comparatively more efforts have been made to recompense the rights and properties of indigenous natives. Still, this remains a matter of contention (Neu and Therrien 2003).

It might be argued that the term 'diaspora' should not be used in a way that includes the movement of relatively privileged people across the world. The travels of settler colonists, business migrants, tourists, political exiles and contemporary diplomats should perhaps not immediately be thought of as diasporic. If this were the case, should we discount the inclusion of rich industrialists from, for example, Nigeria and Pakistan, in our understanding of diaspora? Each diasporic configuration has its internal elites as well as people placed differentially in systems of ethno-economic power according to such factors as class, educational capital and gender. The wife of a working-class shopkeeper is obviously differently located from the concubine of a wealthy industrialist, for instance. The diasporic condition of settler whites is also differentially organized. We can argue that particular configurations of racial, ethnic, class and gender issues makes each diasporic formation a special case in point, with certain general similarities (see Chapter 2). Simultaneously, the understanding of the amoeboid term of diaspora needs also to be qualified for each and every case.

Travel and tourism provides another context in which both structural factors and agency can be explored in the specific situation where white travellers or tourists (generally from the North to the South) end up residing in the place of their former holiday destination. They often form their own (often provisional) communities of people that are not entirely at one with the host society, but neither do they see themselves as in league with foreign visitors. Europeans in contemporary India are a good example of this phenomenon. Instead of adopting the lifestyles and values of the host society, they form their own 'communities' (often described as 'hippy' by locals) which distinguish them from the more transient visits of other foreigners (Kaur 1999). Resident white people in Bangkok are not only privileged in the business sector, but also some of them use their positions there to revel in the sexual leisure industry around them (Seabrook 2001). Other examples are provided by John Hutnyk in *The Rumour of Calcutta: Tourism, Charity and the Poverty of Representation* (1996). By focusing on gossip and travellers' tales circulating among backpackers and volunteer charity workers in Calcutta, Hutnyk demonstrates how the city is framed in a discourse of decay by those who work with a Mother Teresa mindset. Rhetoric of this kind also presaged colonialism. European traders and missionaries in outposts of the East India Company from 1600 regularly reported on their surroundings in terms of 'decaying civilizations' (Dube 1999).[13] In each of these cases, the privileged economics of whiteness renders a tourist destination into a home away from home that is not called diasporic or hybrid.

Whereas the above examples required our own transposition of the notion of diaspora on to various case studies, Karen O'Reilly, in her work on the British on the Costa del Sol, specifically asks whether this movement can be seen as part of a diaspora (O'Reilly 2000: 158). With reference to William Saffran's list of features of diaspora (see Chapter 1), O'Reilly concludes that as 'this definition relies so heavily on memory of and commitment to the homeland, the British in Spain hardly warrant the label of a diaspora' (O'Reilly 2000: 159). Nor, as with later modifications of the term 'diaspora' and Khachig Tölölyan's (1996) development of the notion of 'diasporic consciousness' (see Chapter 2), can the British in the Costa del Sol be seen as part of a larger transnational community scattered around the world. Ultimately, the envisaging of white diasporas is contingent on the kind of definitions proffered for the term. O'Reilly concedes that if we were to adopt Cohen's (1997) definition of diaspora, then the term has potential for the British in the Costa del Sol. As outlined in Chapter 2, Cohen argues that diaspora should be less about 'myths of return' alone, but also allow for the memory of traumatic events and the creation of homelands in addition to trade, labour and imperial diasporas. Adopting the latter view, we could see the British Empire as a kind of diaspora where there was a dispersal of British people around the colonies, having some kind of aspiration of return, and an awareness of other dispersed Brits. This sense of the term 'diaspora', then, as O'Reilly argues, does have potential:

> The British migrants to Spain in modern times are not part of this [colonial] tradition, but are nevertheless British and are at some level very aware of their Britishness. The Britain they have left behind is one they do not identify with much, but the historical nation remains part of who they are. They do not expect to be allowed to integrate into Spanish society, and they retain a strong dependence on their home society, sometimes financially and sometimes emotionally, but always with the secure knowledge that if all else fails, they can (and do) just go home. In these ways, the British in Spain can be conceptualized as a sort of diaspora, without (as yet) a diasporic consciousness. (O'Reilly 2000: 159)

The British in Spain are an example of a white diaspora which has not led to the implementation of systematic imperial structures, but their position does reflect economic disparities between both countries. Therefore, the permanent migration of white people around the world need not constitute political formations of whiteness as absolute privilege. Instead, their circumstances could be such that, whereas, globally, white people do have a higher symbolic purchase (which might also have their local ramifications), their actual presence could entail a deep ambivalence – between positions of power internationally and of marginality nationally. This is apparent, for instance, in the widespread phenomenon of 'retirement migration', particularly from countries in northern Europe to the southern parts and elsewhere (King et al. 2000). Oftentimes, there is some kind of historical link with the countries of migration, as happens with practices of retirement in countries of their homeland's former colonization. Additionally, the decision to migrate may be motivated by aesthetic and climatic considerations, as with mainland Americans on the islands of Hawaii, the Welsh in Patagonia and Britons buying farmhouses in France. Yet, in almost all of these cases the movements rely on moving from places that are seen as relatively expensive and, for some, too overly populated with racialized migrants, to places perceived of as cheaper and whiter. In this way, there is no escaping the logic of whiteness that pursues travels and settlements of this sort. We have seen how expats, TCKs and tourists are conventionally not seen under the rubric of diaspora because they constitute powerful white formations. However, other 'white but not quite' people, such as the Irish and the Jews, have commonly been aligned with studies on diaspora.

The luck of the Irish as 'home-grown blacks'

Changing configurations of intuitional and ideological power render certain groups as racialized inferiors and others as superiors. This has less to do with melanin and more to do with shifting norms of whiteness in relation to hegemonic norms. The Irish are an example of a group that have been historically oppressed in the global ecumene, but now find themselves (mostly) accommodated in the folds of whiteness. They have been both victims of (neo-)colonialism and its perpetrators. There is a history of relationships between Ireland, Britain and its former colonies where, on the one hand, the Irish partook in brutal oppression as part of colonial structures: one of the more extreme examples being that of General Reginald Dyer and Lieutenant Governor Michael O'Dwyer who together were responsible for the massacre of hundreds in the Jallianwala Bagh incident in India in 1919. On the other hand, however, the freedom struggle of the Republic of Ireland against British colonialism, especially in the 1920s, allowed for alliances between Irish activists and political figures in India (Holmes and Holmes 1997; Kapur 1997). It is not incidental that some of the British women working in India against imperialism, such as Margaret Cousins and Annie Besant, were Irish (Visweswaran, cited in Grewal 1996: 9). The nationalist struggles against colonialism in both countries were often mutually supportive. The travels of Udham Singh from colonial India to London in the late 1930s, coming with ambitions to assassinate the former Lieutenant Governor of the Punjab, is renowned for his fraternization of Irish pubs, comrades and girlfriends. His was a revenge attack against O'Dwyer's role in the massacre at Jallianwallah Bagh.

Alongside the politics, came the representations: the easy replacement of the 'Paki' or the 'Hindoo' with the derogatory Irish signifier of 'Paddy' was all too prevalent in the racist colonial menagerie. This kind of attitude persisted, after India's independence, in the failing heart of the (post-)imperial capital, London, when notices were put up around several hotels in the 1950s and 1960s: 'No Blacks, No Irish, No Dogs' – quite ironic as we were always led to believe that the Englishman's best friend was his dog. It was no surprise that it was largely earlier migrants such as the Irish who had accommodation available for rent to people from the newly independent, former colonies.

In contemporary times, such histories are easily forgotten in the racial antagonisms of the moment. One notable example is that while signs of a relatively more benign relationship between Irish Protestants and Catholics emerge in Northern Ireland, the number of racist attacks against Ireland's minorities (both in Northern Ireland and the Republic of Ireland) are escalating.[14] This may well be due to the increased attention to racial matters, especially in light of the belated 1997 extension of the UK Race Relations Act of 1976 to Northern Ireland. The dual processes of overcoming Catholic–Protestant divides and finding other 'demons' to serve imperial interests are not entirely unrelated (*Fortnight*, May 1998). It is still the Orange and Green emblems that predominate in the fractured Christian and white image of Ireland. Parallels such as comparing racism against the Asians and the Irish in England, or proclaiming the Irish as the 'Blacks of Europe' are limited: 'Black' remains an opportunistic category for the Irish, one which they can easily slip out of as and when they want to, unlike Blacks and/or Asians who carry indelible markers on their skins. Furthermore, to present the Irish as autochthonous 'Blacks' is to promote a dubious politics of indigeneity, and to add further violence to state legislation and policy against people of colour. Noel Ignatiev (1995) charts out the ambivalent position of the Irish *vis-à-vis* British imperialism, and how in latter-day times there has not only been an Anglicization of Irish identity, but also a transfer of the privileges accorded on to Irish people. The Irish accent may well be conspicuous, but it can be watered down or modulated, at will, if the person sees fit. The language, after all, was the same, which in places like Southall, as noted earlier, was a further means of identification against Asians whose vernacular languages acted as a barrier. At any rate, with the appeal of postmodern difference, there appears to be a fetishization of the 'loveable Irish rogue'.

The case of the large Irish-American diaspora presents another distinct and, occasionally, similar set of circumstances. Most Irish have 'assimilated' into the American lifestyle while holding on to their ethnic flavour of Celtic roots in their self-fashioned hyphenated identities. The process of Irish accommodation was ascendant with the rise of the Civil Rights movement from the 1950s where black–white binaries overtook other ethno-racial differentiations. After these politically turbulent decades subsided, the Irish-American contingent that had not departed from radical politics still presented a special case when compared to other diasporas of secondary whiteness. Irish distinctiveness is sustained by two main features. The first is the symbolic currency of a transnational 'Anglo-Celtic' culture.[15] The second is American-Irish activism, fund-raising and lobbying for the autonomy of the North of Ireland.[16]

For the Irish diaspora in Europe there is also the wider discourse of the European Union to take onboard (Shore 2000). Les Back and Anoop Nayak (1993) focus on the racist logic of pan-European whiteness that underpins debates about 'Fortress Europe':

> It is quite clear that these institutionalized forms of immigration control are premised on a racialized idea of what a European looks like: the prevailing common sense is that Europeans are white, while non-Europeans are black. What is emerging is a shift from national forms of ethnocentric racism to a Eurocentric racism which is being established and institutionalized in all EC member states. (Back and Nayak 1993: 4)

The Irish have also become card-carrying members of this imagined yet highly territorial Europe. So here we have an example of a diaspora with contingent relations to hierarchies of race/ethnicity. While the Irish have been oppressed politically, culturally and racially, they are mobile in the sense that, due to factors of skin colour, language, the political discourse of European identity and also the broader church of Christianity, they are deemed as more able to 'assimilate' in England than, for instance, British-Asian Muslims.

Encouraged by the work on race by Ignatiev, Ware notes that 'some ethnic groups demonstrate a more complex and ambivalent relationship to both blackness and whiteness and have historically been eligible to move between the two' (Ware 2002b: 162). Clearly, a focus on the Irish diaspora reveals whiteness as a process, rather than a static field of power relations. Once seen as 'black' in the political sense of being colonially oppressed, the Irish diaspora has overwhelmingly been promoted to being considered as 'white'. The example is a vindication of Matthew Jacobson's (2000) observation that Jewish, Italian, Greek and other diasporas not from Anglo-Saxon Europe may be viewed as 'probationary whites' or what we have described above as examples of secondary whiteness.[17]

White or not quite?

Shifting formations of power and identity mean that promotion to whiteness is not necessarily a linear, static or straightforward process. The experience of the Jews in the twentieth century provides a striking example of this phenomenon, where, as Matthew Jacobson observes, the Second World War saw a significant turning point in their transformation towards whiteness

(2000: 241). In contrast, in the late nineteenth century, the Jews were the reviled group, seen as morally and physiognomically 'black' or at least 'swarthy' in ethnological literature (Gilman 2000: 231).[18] Morally, the 'blackness' of the Jew was a mark of racial inferiority and an indicator of a supposedly diseased nature. Physiognomically, skin colour and external markers were used as indices of difference. They were likened to Africans, seen to interbreed, and designated as part of the 'ugly' races of humankind (Gilman 2000: 232). This view jostled with the idea that it was generally not their 'blood' but their religion that marked the Jews as a people apart (Jacobson 2000: 241). Depending upon the geographical location of their residence, they began to be seen as 'adaptive' people (Jacobson 2000: 233). But even though they were seen to blend in, people still held the view that they were a separate and distinct racial category. As Sander Gilman notes: 'The nose becomes one of the central loci of difference in seeing the Jew' (2000: 235). The facial protuberance was seen as a visual talisman for shrewdness, turning around profits, and having an aptitude for insight into character. Similarly, Jacobson argues:

> ...visible Jewishness in American culture between the mid-nineteenth and mid-twentieth centuries represented a complex process of social value *become* perception: social and political meanings attached to Jewishness generate a kind of physiognomic surveillance that renders Jewishness itself discernible as a particular pattern of physical traits (skin color, nose shape, hair color and texture, and the like – what Blumenbach called 'the fundamental configuration of face'. (Jacobson 2000: 241, original emphasis)

As a residue of history and of the contemporary ideologies of extreme far right-wing organizations, these views still hold purchase. Jews continue to be persecuted by far right-wing parties in racial terms. Numerous examples are provided by a search of neo-Nazi groups on the internet. The site run by the British-based Combat 18 announced 'Death to ZOG, 88' (Zionist Occupation Government) after the murder attempt upon President Jacques Chirac in Paris on 14 July 2002.[19] Neo-Nazis repeatedly bark on about the 'Jewish-led conspiracy' that is believed to run the world and which threatens the future of the 'white race'. This is despite transparent attempts by far right-wing organizations to appear democratic from the 1990s.[20] The professedly democratic far-right party, with which [the neo-Nazi] Maxime Bruneries is linked, condemned his actions (Lichfield 2002).[21]

This view, however, rankles with efforts to transform Jews into whites. The main features of this transformation in post-war USA were due to: black–white racial binaries taking over other ethnic divisions; the geographical dispersal of Jews to 'whites only' suburbs aided by their entrepreneurial successes; and the establishment of the Israeli state which, along with US support, had the consequence of 'whitening' Jews. Effectively, 'America's client state in the Middle East became, of ideological necessity and by the imperatives of American nationalism, a *white* client state' (Jacobson 2000: 249, original emphasis). Along with the secularization of Jews in the USA, 'Jews gradually became Caucasians over the course of the twentieth century' (Jacobson 2000: 238). This Caucasian identity needs be qualified by what can generally be seen as the *cultural markers* of Jewish ethnicity, rather than the assumed biological traits of 'race'. This discursive transition from 'race' to ethnicity was fuelled by the Holocaust of the Second World War, when theories of racial biologization took on genocidal extremes and were therefore discredited.[22] Such contradictions have led critics to query:

> 'Are Jews white?' asks Sander Gilman. The question gets at the fundamental instability of Jewishness as racial difference, but so does its wording fundamentally misstate the contours of whiteness in American political culture. From 1790 onward Jews were indeed 'white' by the most significant measures of that appellation: they could enter the country and become naturalized citizens. Given the shades of meaning attaching to various racial classifications, given the nuances involved as whiteness slips off toward Semitic or Hebrew and back again toward Caucasian, the question is not *are* they white, nor even how white are they, but how have they been both white and Other? What have been the historical terms of their probationary whiteness? (Jacobson 2000: 241)

The dialectic between whiteness and Otherness is succinctly expressed in the formation of the Israeli nation-state (created as a compensation for the Holocaust of the Second World War), but it has effectively become a representative of white supremacy with strong backing from the US government and a sanctioned, systematic oppression of (displaced) Palestinians. This is a situation that has perplexed many. As Linda Grant (2002: 4) surmises: 'How could the Jews who experienced the Holocaust behave like this towards the Palestinians?'. Whereas Jewish diasporas are complex, multifarious, accompanied with differing attitudes towards Zionism, once embodied in the Israeli state as the 'homeland' par exemplar, these dynamics appear to be not so diverse.

Zionism relies on some notion of Jewish purity that, while being the alterity of Aryan, shares a set of common presuppositions with white supremacy. Here is an example of anti-hybridity which seeks to expunge the common Arab ancestry of many Jews, Christians and Muslims. The privileges associated with whiteness, rather than its invisibility, will always be a facet of Jewish experience while the state of Israel remains Zionist. Most troubling, of course, is the extent to which this maintenance of Jewish purity requires the expulsion of the Palestinian Other from the land. Here, we see that the 'problem' of Palestine is not one of reproducing the interactions and cultures that gave rise to the varieties of Judaism, Christianity and Islam, but rather a deadly quest for purity which resonates with that of white supremacy to the detriment of all. The multi-ethnic, multinational, multilingual nature of the Israeli population is therefore reduced to a privilege that asserts domination of Jews over Muslims and to an extent Christians. It is ironic that the term 'diaspora' is so closely associated with the Jewish experience, when Israel defends its boundaries as a nation-state with the most advanced, American-funded military weaponry.

But it is falling into the trap of Zionist discourse to talk in terms of a Jewish diaspora in the first place (with the mythical homeland of Jerusalem).

Several studies have looked to the finer negotiations of Jewish diasporas from all areas of the world in a variety of locations. Sarah Abrevaya Stein (1997), for instance, provides an instructive reminder on the diversity of features which characterized North African, Middle Eastern and Balkan Jewry histories. These narratives, however, have not been reflected in the literature, which relies upon constructing holistic objects – that is, of the Sephardi and Middle Eastern Jewries, who are assumed to be colonized by European Jewry. Stein's work is a caution against Zionist-influenced studies which do not take on board the specificities of different diasporic histories, host populations and their mutual entanglements. Other interesting cases, often overlooked in the general literature on Jewish diasporas, are provided by the likes of Joel Beinin (1992) with his article on 'the Rome Group' of Egyptian-Jewish communist exiles. This group had been prominent in the development of Egyptian Marxism before the creation of Israel, but were expelled or left voluntarily after 1948 when the nation-state was founded. It is also a worthwhile reminder that not all Jewish diasporas entailed move-ments into areas that could be designated as part of the West. Clearly, even within particular Jewish diasporas, there are differences in relation to an engagement with Zionism, to the Israeli state and to structures of whiteness such that the diaspora is not homogeneous and its hybridity is already conflicted and multiple.

Interactions

The Jewish case highlights the contradictions within a conceptualization of diaspora which can produce both inward-looking and often xenophobic formations, while at the same time producing a counter to absolutist notions of identity. In practice, however, there are a variety of interactions with the host society, as indeed with other diasporic populations, that mitigate against a culturally exclusivist lens.[23] As we have already mentioned in Chapter 1, Brah (1996) discusses the need to consider 'diaspora spaces' as locations for the interchange between migrants and those considered 'indige-nous' to the region. This would mean that ethnic particularisms are eroded in a diasporic space, where interactions of various kinds can be envisaged and realized. Here, we cannot assume that it is only the marginal or sub-ordinate groups that are transformed in processes of hybridity. As Anthias put it, culturally dominant groups need to be 'open to transforming and abandoning some of their own central cultural symbols and practices of hegemony' (Anthias 2001: 12; see also Chapter 4). It is from the latter perspective, often overlooked in discussions on hybridity, that this chapter proceeds.

The emergence of Anglo-Indian communities in colonial South Asia is a case in point. They are, of course, not a consolidated group, but nevertheless they fall into the rubric of hybridity – as 'race' mixture – which was discussed in Chapter 4.[24] Indeed, our analysis attempts to take seriously the call to examine specificity dialectically and with an eye to political mobilization and efficacy. Does Anglo-Indian identity have a mission here? Or does the hybrid confound both hybridity and diaspora as process?

A by-product of colonial British (and to some extent French and Portuguese) sexual exchange with native peoples, in post-colonial times, Anglo-Indians have been virtually institutionalized as another ethnic/racial community in the subcontinent.[25] The category of Anglo-Indian emerged as one of the descriptions for the offspring of liaisons between European men and native women: 'Eric Stracey, a 63 year-old Anglo-Indian said, "The Anglo-Indians owe their origin to the coincidence of Man's need for women!"' (cited in Younger 1987: 10). By 1776, Anglo-Indians outnumbered the British, in the Raj. They found themselves in an ambivalent position: on the one hand, they were mistrusted by Indians for their British heritage and orientations and, on the other, they were seen as a threat by the British, particularly as in the early days, as shareholders of the East India Company wanted their sons and not Anglo-Indians to be appointed to the high posts in India. Indeed, the ambiguous status of the Anglo-Indian reflected the Victorian obsession with 'race' mixture. This is well demonstrated by the fact that Rudyard Kipling's *Kim*, first published in 1901, is the story of Kimball O'Hara, the orphaned son of an Irish soldier and Indian woman. This Anglo-Indian spends his childhood as a vagabond in Lahore, no doubt providing a self-fulfilling prophecy about the inadequacy of hybrid populations. A latter-day equivalent would be Hari Kunzru's *The Impressionist* (2002), which itself takes the blended politics of identity as plot and theme.

It was with the Indianization of employment in the government services, much of which was consolidated by the time of the Montagu–Chelmsford Report in 1919, that Anglo-Indian community consciousness crystallized. It appeared that while Anglo-Indians wanted the privileges accorded to those native to India, they also saw themselves as British by virtue of their language, religion, lifestyle and education. However, the British were not so welcoming:

> Rather, [Anglo-Indians] were viewed as representing the dark side of the Raj, the product of sexual promiscuity. The advent of the Victorian age ushered in a preoccupation with racial purity and the ascendance and superiority of the racially pure over the mixed blood. The half-caste was believed to embody the worst of both races, his inferior blood set the Eurasians apart and he was popularly believed to be indolent, slovenly, heartless, vicious, self-seeking and unscrupulous. (Younger 1987: 16)

Due to their uncertain positions in a time of high nationalism and fading colonialism, many Anglo-Indians migrated to Britain and other Commonwealth countries. The first wave of migration of Anglo-Indians was in 1946–47. This was largely due to the fear and uncertainty that Anglo-Indians felt about their status in the newly Independent India. The second wave was after 1965 when Hindi became India's official language – a period that saw much unrest and language riot. In the contemporary era, there are only about 100–125 000 Anglo-Indians left in India, concentrated in the urban centres and mainly comprising those who are too old and/or too poor to migrate.

If we cast our eyes westwards, we see the emergence of yet another kind of 'Anglo-Indian' population, but this time a mis-named alliance between Europeans and Native Americans from the seventeenth century. Traders who lived among the Indians often had '"Indian wives", women who provided sexual companionship and domestic services for the duration of the traders' residence in the community' (Godbeer 1999: 91). The women enabled inroads for trade. As Gary Nash points out: 'They became the very symbol of mestizo America – *metissage* is the French term (comparable to the Spanish *mestizaje*) for the joining of English or French traders and their Indian wives, and their offspring were *metis*' (Nash 1999: 13).

Some of these relationships were more permanent. The adventurer, John Rolfe, married Pocahontas, daughter of Powhatan, in the first recorded interracial marriage of the seventeenth century.[26] Nevertheless, 'prejudice and violence blocked the way toward what might have become a mixed-race American republic' (Nash 1999: 11). Despite the racism, multiracial alliances continued unabated. In fact, Nash argues that:

> On the peninsula comprising Delaware, eastern Maryland and eastern Virginia, deep-rooted mixtures of red, white, and black peoples created triracial communities. Still today, from Alabama to New York, the Lumbees, Red Bones, Wesorts, Brass Ankles, and many other triracial societies maintain their distinctive identities. (Nash 1999: 15)

Such phenomena have been effectively erased from the history books, reflecting the mood of institutional anti-miscegeny of the day. This belies the fact that millions of white people in the USA have multiracial roots. It is a consequence of the sharing of diasporic spaces, where European travellers dealt with Native Americans on what has been described by Richard Godbeer as the 'middle ground'. This middle ground 'bore witness to the many possibilities of intercultural contact: it embodied not only the violence of colonial appropriation but also the mutual and successful accommodation of different peoples' (Godbeer 1999: 92). It was not only Native Americans who were transformed, but also European travellers in very physical and tangible ways despite their ideologically-loaded thesis of purity being next to godliness.

Whiteness is tainted in these encounters, as racial hierarchies are disrupted and reformed around the multiple terms given for peoples who more honestly reflect the actual genetic make-up of humanity. Groups designated as mulatto, hybrid, mestizo are paradigmatic of the diasporic condition, but such mixture is also the unacknowledged condition of the generic 'white' as well. In a state of heightened ambivalence, the 'mixed race' is falsely and doubly excluded as not really belonging to native society, and as not being fully accommodated in the folds of whiteness due to regimes of racial purity and exclusivity. In the North American case, not only were native, raced populations transformed under an (incipient) colonialism, but there was also the fundamental alteration of white populations. Yet the conservative contingent still live in denial of their histories in a bid to present themselves as superior and racially distinct from black or native populations. The assertion of supremacy, as we have repeatedly stated in this chapter, relies on ideological and political structures that render those powerful as white, and in this section the story remains the same. Whiteness remains stubbornly blind to colour, even that which is its own.

Not 'what about me?'

Throughout our journey in this chapter, we have cast our gaze on the ways in which whiteness is constructed in relation to diaspora and hybridity. We noted how diasporic studies tends to avoid whiteness, as a focus, in its preoccupation with minority racialized groups or ethnicized communities of secondary whiteness. There are a number of reasons for this absence. First, it is in part due to the naturalization and normative associations of whiteness with legitimate citizenship of the West. Second, as has been noted in numerous studies on whiteness, white people are rendered invisible in the maintenance of hegemonies that encompass the West. Third, there has been a kind of implicit arrogance in that the movement of white people is not taken to represent a 'problem' in terms of assimilation and integration as other travelling populations may be.

It is important to stress that by singling out whiteness in a book on diaspora and hybridity that we do not intend to reinscribe its hegemony by recentring it in analysis. This would invite a 'what about me?' school of response or, as Richard Dyer puts it, 'me-too-ism', 'a feeling that, amid all this attention being given to non-white subjects, white people are being left out' (1997: 10). This could be counterproductive to the lessons learnt from such a critical enquiry. To focus on journeys of whiteness is not to throw oneself into this bag of academia, to become just another added ingredient to the self-affirming credentials of whiteness. Rather, it is to shake the ground, so that common-sense assumptions and prejudices are undermined both inside and outside the academy. If we do not interrogate whiteness, we leave it to be imagined as neutral and natural:

> thus missing differences between racism (which oppresses and privileges) and race as a system of classification that is overdetermining the modern nation-state, supported by systems of knowledge, juridically coded, constituting and constituted by other social categories, and intersecting with the interests of global capital. (Socialist Review Collective 1995: 6)

Triangulating whiteness with diaspora and hybridity, at least presents an opportunity to expose some of the hidden assumptions in each of these areas of thought and analysis. However, as in other chapters in this book, we also need to ask to what extent exposing the power structures that maintain whiteness enable a response to the resurgence of far right-wing parties and activities throughout Europe and North America. The gains of the British National Party in Britain, the Freedom Party in Austria, Pim Fortuyn in the Netherlands and Le Pen in France, illustrate a growing tide of xenophobic, white supremacist political parties. In collaboration with the White militia in the USA, these formations provide the bedrock of an assertion of whiteness that in its more violent and virulent forms is unlikely to be tested by merely stating 'we are all hybrid' or that autochonous claims are false. What we have presented in this chapter certainly provides some of the ammunition with which engagement with these parties can take place, but as we have already repeated in previous chapters, the strategic and organizational logic to combat the rise of the far right still needs some working out.

Notes

1 Patrick Barkham, 'No Waltzing in Woomera', *The Guardian Weekend*, 25 May 2002: 24–31. See also Alison Dellit (2001) 'Philip Ruddock: Minister for Racism', *Green Left Weekly*, No. 433, www.greenleftweekly.org.au/back/2001/433/433p10.html and our discussion of Woomera in Chapter 5.

2 One exception is Karen O'Reilly's (2000) study on the British in the Costa del Sol in Spain, to which we return below.

3 Incidentally, the *Mayflower* ferrying the 'pilgrim fathers' was not the first ship to leave people on the soils of the Americas. The oppression of indigenous Native Americans is another inconvenience brushed under the carpet of the American mainstream narrative of belonging.

4 Back comments:

> Technological advances such as the Internet have provided a means for contemporary fascists within Europe and the white diasporas of the New World to garner a digitally enhanced translocal culture in cyberspace and a truly international market. The Internet provides much more than just another publishing tool for propaganda, for it has offered an immediate and direct form of access to people with networked personal computers and a means to participate interactively in racist movements without face-to-face contact. (Back 2002a: 94–95)

Here, technologies enable the imagination of a diasporic transnation where European history and heritage acts as a literal and/or mythical homeland. Three main points are made:

> (i) that the notion of whiteness promotes a racial lineage plotted through and sustained by cyberspace;
> (ii) that whiteness has a relational 'other'/'others', and that these images of alterity vary – Turks in Germany, Blacks and South Asians in Britain, for instance, with Jews acting like an invisible force everywhere; and
> (iii) that there is a sense of the minoritization of whiteness, where the 'white race' is seen as the new global minority. (Back 2002a: 130–132)

5 Southall has attracted migrants from all parts of the world. By the 1970s, it was predominantly Asian but many of these families have moved out to be replaced by recent arrivals from Somalia, Eastern Europe and Afghanistan.

6 The relation between notions of the English and the Irish is itself a complex arena, particularly for mixed families, second- or third-generation Irish. How these impinge upon race or cultural ethnicity is a further complication (see McGarry 1990).

7 In Ellison's novel, black invisibility also provides the potential for a kind of spectral power.

8 Critical incursions, however, have been made on the general theme of the invisibility of whiteness. Charles A. Gallagher argues that white students in a US urban university are

conscious of their race in a very tangible manner: '[They] experience their whiteness as a "real" social category that intrudes on most of their everyday activities. Race matters for these students because they have been weaned on a brand of racial politics and media exposure that has made whiteness visible as a racial category while simultaneously transforming whiteness into a social disadvantage' (Gallagher 1995: 166). This condition may well not be characteristic of the majority of white people residing in the West, but when situated among designated 'Others', white people become overly aware of their imbrication in the discourse of whiteness. This is at a time when affirmative or positive discriminatory policies favouring minority groups in the West have resulted in a spectral fear of 'whiteness-under-seize' – that is, the belief that white people's rights are being eroded in light of a perceived favouritism towards non-white minority groups.

9 Susan Koshy (1998) provides further perspectives by showing how discourse between South Asian-American and mainstream ideas sometimes uncomfortably converge. Koshy notes that while some South Asian-Americans and scholars have neglected the saliency of race, other South Asian-Americans and scholars have treated displays of South Asian colour-consciousness as equivalent to white racism. Ironically, she suggests that both groups end up choosing to construct racial identification – in the process, inadvertently reproducing the American ideology of self-making, even though the evidence suggests that South Asian-Americans have been ineluctably racialized. Their middle-class and 'model minority' status buffers a serious engagement with the politics of race and, in this case, differs from the majority of the cases of South Asians in Britain. These differences arise not just from the differences in composition of the respective diasporas, but also the differential needs and management strategies of host states.

10 On a variant note, Rosemary Marangoly George's (1997) study on middle-class Indian-Americans in Southern California points out that they could deploy ethnocultural categories based on essentialist and religious terms to avoid the overriding discourse of the mainstream for migrants defined by skin colour, chromatics or race.

11 There is another perspective to marking out whiteness as a racialized formation. Les Back points out how such discourse is governed by regimes of visuality. If we were to consider the realm of aurality, slightly different conclusions may be reached. In his study on white blues musicians in the southern states of the USA, Back notes how the arguments about cultural imperialism and exploitation of black musicians' music distorts the actuality of guys hanging out in studios jamming and belting out tunes. He proposes that 'the contribution made by these players to soul music cannot be reduced to their whiteness, but, paradoxically, in order to make sense of this story, it is necessary to know that these musicians are white' (Back 2002b: 232). Racialization is overly determined by visuality where aural cultures do not neatly fall into its limited repertoires. Defying ideas about 'redneck' hostility in the southern states of the USA, Back points out that among these musicians colour did not matter. What mattered was whether one could play an instrument in a compelling and inspirational manner. Where these dynamics got distorted, however, was at the point of record company involvement and the widespread marketing of the sound, where invariably in the conservative USA it was white musicians who were favoured over black.

12 Interestingly, the word 'refugee' came into the English language after the expulsion of the skilled religious minority of the Huguenots from France in 1685 (Fletcher 1992), a group whose only ticket to ethno-racial marginality in the contemporary era seems to reside in French-sounding surnames.

13 This was alongside a discourse about the 'splendours of the East', magnificence that was to trigger the 'envy of the eye'. Mary Pratt, in her book *Imperial Eyes* (1992), considers how even though Europeans may feel that they are innocently recording the outside world, their accounts are shot through with recurrent images which, in effect, end up producing 'the rest of the world for European readerships at particular points in Europe's expansionist trajectory?' (1992: 5). These accounts more often than not encode and legitimate the aspirations of economic expansion and empire.

14 Similarly, the arrival of Asians into the then English- and Irish-dominated area of Southall, West London, led to the further sharpening of racial difference (McGarry 1990). It is apparent that next to a predominately Asian or African-Caribbean population, the Irish are not positioned closer to white than they are black.

15 See Paul Arthur's (1991) exploration of transnational 'Anglo-Celtic' culture in his reviews of two books by D.H. Akenson on the Irish diaspora in South Africa and New Zealand.

16 Another article by Arthur (1992) analyses Irish-American attempts to influence US policy in Northern Ireland and notes the limits of intervention in international affairs when lobbyists lack unanimity and their target is a US ally, such as Britain, rather than the Arab states, the latter being the target of the Jewish American lobby (see Chapter 7).

17 However, a qualification is in order when considering the case of Greek diasporas in particular: even though seen as part of the poorer countries of South Europe, invocation of ancient Greek classical culture acts as a passport to the higher ranks of whiteness. Gregory Jusdanis, for instance, tries to reclaim this past by arguing that Greek Americans imagine themselves in relation to the cultural capital that ancient Greece represents in the West. Nevertheless, there continues the systematic exclusion of various phases of Greek history – as with the extermination of pagan Greek culture – and of modern Greece from the memory of a Europe that celebrates classical Athens in the fashioning of European identity. Evidently, the holy grail of whiteness is Western Europe, and claims to that status depend on the symbolic and geographical imagining of Europe. Europe is not just a geographical entity, which itself has very unclear boundaries despite the 'Fortress Europe' reality for non-Europeans, but it is also an imagined space, one that conjures up imagery of classical history, artistic and cultural heritage and notions of civilization. Scholars such as Louis A. Ruprecht Jr. (1994) go on to argue that it is not only Hellenic culture which defines the idea of Europe, but also Hebraic cultures. He argues that Europe as we know it today was initiated in cultural synthesis that originated in the Levant region, when the two cultures co-existed in war and peace for centuries.

18 Nancy Foner (1997) observes that, as she puts it, 'white ethnics', who were seen as part of racial groups, were reviled in the period of 'the last great wave' of migration in 1880–1923 to the USA. She also demonstrates that transnationalism is not just a contemporary phenomenon. There were high rates of return and repeat migration for Jews and especially Italians.

19 '88' refers to the eighth letter in the alphabet, an abbreviation for *Heil Hitler!*

20 See Back's chapter, 'Guess Who's Coming to Dinner? The Political Morality of Investigating Whiteness in the Gray Zone' (Ware and Back 2002: 33–59).

21 Maxime Bruneries was a member of the neo-Nazi organization, Groupe Union Defence, and ran for political office in 2001 under the National Republican Movement (MNR) party.

22 Rich Cohen also points out in his book, *Tough Jews: Fathers, Sons and Gangster Dreams* (1998), how the Jewish gangster past was buried by the end of the 1940s, particularly as they had their own legitimate collection of tough guys in the Israeli army.

23 Several scholars have noted the dialectic between essentialist and hybrid forms of identities and cultural productions in diasporic locations. Khachig Tölölyan (2000), for instance, considers the example of the Armenian diaspora since its formation in the eleventh century and an analysis of its passage, in the past two decades, from exilic nationalism to diasporic transnationalism.

24 See Phoenix and Owen (2000) for an analysis of the power dynamics that underline discussions of 'race-mixture'.

25 This was also the case for 'Coloureds' in South Africa and the Creoles in the Caribbean.

26 Interestingly, the monarch at the time, King James I, was not irked about interracial marriage, but fretted about whether a commoner such as Rolfe was entitled to wed the daughter of a king. Plainly, this is at a time when nineteenth-century scientific racism had not yet taken root in elite European thinking.

7

Transnational Terror

When we begin to consider the ideologies of corporate capital and the world market, it certainly appears that the postmodernist and postcolonialist theorists who advocate a politics of difference, fluidity and hybridity in order to challenge the binaries and essentialism of modern sovereignty have been outflanked by the strategies of power. Power has evacuated the bastion they are attacking and has circled around the rear to join them in the assault in the name of difference. ... There is no need to doubt the democratic, egalitarian and even at times anticapitalist desires that motivate large segments of these fields of work but it is important to investigate the utility of these theories in the context of the new paradigm of power. (Hardt and Negri 2000: 138)

The new paradigm of power has an old name in the contemporary era: colonialism. The occupation of Afghanistan and Iraq and the installation of a colonial governor in the former Yugoslavia points to an undermining of sovereignty that was prevalent in the era of formal colonialism. In the influential book, *Empire* (2000), Michael Hardt and Antonio Negri spend much time trying to explain the new strategies and circuits of power that they see constituting the late twentieth-century capitalist condition. However, events have rendered that part of their analysis redundant and defunct. While there is much to agree with as to the co-option and reworking of terms such as hybridity and diaspora, and associated cultural and political forms, ultimately we find that Hardt and Negri's theoretical approach lacks much use for those in combat with colonizing forces. In this concluding chapter we will demonstrate the re-assertion of the imperial nation-state in contrast to an amorphous empire, by considering two defining issues in the aftermath of the attacks on the World Trade Center and the Pentagon: homeland (in)security in the USA and the treatment of asylums-seekers and refugees in Europe. In these cases, we see a clamp down on transnational links though assertion of the rhetoric of purity and xenophobia, with no serious challenge on the part of diaspora and hybridity theorists to culturalist-militarist demonization at home and abroad. A key linking theme between these arenas is the mobility of human subjects and how this can be seen as dangerous and so in need of totalitarian controls.

The restitution of colonialism following the attacks on the twin symbols of US global hegemony might have been a prime opportunity for those engaged in diaspora theory, in particular, to offer mechanisms for progressive mobilization. In the midst of a crisis where the themes we have been discussing have often been prominent – global movement, transnational co-constitution of here and there, the increasingly productive exchange, for better or worse, of cultural difference – it is the rhetoric of the 'clash of civilizations' and of 'bringing liberation, freedom and democracy' to the Muslim world that has dominated attention. Even where a transnational dimension can be acknowledged, this has been in the shape of an enemy. It is 'transnational' terrorists who are the new demons. Those 'others' who stand 'with' the USA, those who sign on as the safe 'communities of diaspora', distancing themselves from 'Muslims' and others who might look like them, are displayed as examples that serve to illustrate the compact where everyone can be brought into the modern ecumene of democracy. In this way, they are also giving a warning to those quiescent diasporic groups that expression of dissent is in itself an act of treason (Chomsky 2003).

The US-initiated war on terror, as war on Islam, finds its theoretical home in the 'clash of civilizations' thesis promoted most recently by Samuel Huntington (1996, 1997). Of course, Huntington's actual interest was to divide the world in such a way so as to attack liberal US, domestic, cultural politics.[1] Migrant groups within Western societies (Huntington cannot call them settlers) are the crux of the problem, specifically their rejection of assimilation and adherence to customs of their 'home' societies. For Huntington, this inevitably leads to an irreconcilable dual loyalty, which means, by way of a paranoid logic, that orginary 'home' governments rather than the USA are supported by immigrant nationals. Actual evidence for such fixed support is limited and any support is often manipulated by the US State Department, but this does not seem to matter in circumstances where the rhetoric covers much wider geo-political investments: 'The enemy (immigrants, blacks, poor people) at home is in cahoots with the enemy abroad (Muslims, communists, drug cartels)', goes the simplistic refrain. As a consequence of these difficult times, we witness the triumph of civilizational thinking inaugurated and rationalized in the context of 11 September. David Palumbo-Liu comments:

> Crucially, in the present incarnation of civilizational thinking, the dichotomy between national identity and international civilizational thinking has collapsed, the two positions intermingling and recombining into a potent ideological position, now mobilized by the events of September 11th. To the enemy within (ethnic and diasporic populations) is now added a viable enemy without, something Huntington pined for in order to solidify the nation just a few years before. The enemy will be civilizational: It will be Islam. (Palumbo-Liu 2002: 122)

It is illustrative of the fragile base from which much post-colonial, diasporic and multicultural theorizing takes place that so many have had to 'deconstruct' Huntington or at least include his work in debate. It was not the words of hybridity and modernities that were taken up when President Bush described the American mission following September 11, but rather of the old imperial mission of civilizing the savage. In contrast, the counter-arsenal to civilizational thinking of buzzwords and conceptual niceties are not at the forefront of self-defence squads formed to protect mosques under attack or to defend migrant/diasporic taxi drivers from 'backlash', or to extract detainees from detention camps in Guantanemo Bay.

The plight of Arab-Americans is indicative. In an article entitled 'Cracking down on Diaspora', Sally Howell and Andrew Shryock (2003) detail the multiple ways in which the Arab population of Detroit have found themselves transformed from 'model minority' to the 'terrorists within'. The passage of the aptly named Patriot Act,[2] and the creation of an Office of Homeland Security in the predominantly Arab suburb of Dearborn – the first place in American to have such an establishment – all point to the containment of once transnational communities, in effect de-diasporization. The ability of the US state to revoke citizenship and to force the registration of Arab non-US citizens under the assumption of enmity are all part of an effort to revoke, remove and reshape transnational ties. Links in place that service US domestic and foreign policy will be tolerated but no others:

> As the U.S. solidifies its control over Iraq, the relationship between Arab Americans and Iraq will be subordinated to the demands of military occupation. Any movements of expertise, money, technology, or information that might support opposition to the American presence will be deemed illegal, then rigorously disciplined, both 'here' and 'there'. (Howell and Shryock 2003: 459–460)

In the Iraq context, the US has gone one step further in the use of the Iraqi diaspora; half of the appointed governing council of Iraq has either an American or European passport. Indeed, for some of those newly anointed for stewardship of that country, an Iraqi passport was something in their distant past.[3] Those economic and political aspects of diaspora which can foster progressive links are being vigorously circumscribed, not only in the USA but also in Europe.[4] In the meantime, theorists of hybridity and diaspora, such as Pnina Werbner, can remark how the US government is deemed to be willing to 'tolerate cultural pluralism, dual citizenship, and transnational activism as never before' (Werbner 2000: 6). Even though this comment was written before September 11, it displays a shocking naivety of the historical practices of the US state.

It concerns us that Howell, Shyrock and Werbner, despite contrasting perspectives, share an assumption that there was a time when the activities of other diasporas were not subject to surveillance, control and violence. The history of US colonialism and imperialism in Central and Latin America should be sufficient to recognize that only the name of the enemy has changed, rather than any major transformation in the workings of the state.[5] Indeed, William Blum has written extensively on this subject in *Killing Hope* (1995) and *Rogue State* (2000). What is quantitatively different is that the Patriot Act potentially exerts controls over white citizens that were formerly reserved for blacks and non-Americans. In the land that prides itself as being made up of immigrants, the passing of the Patriot Act has meant the aggressive sealing off of borders, the stiffening of immigration rules and the creation of laws which strip away any vestige of civil liberties for those targeted and named/maimed as terrorists. In moves that would make the old anti-communist Joseph McCarthy proud, the American state has enacted measures such as extra-judicial trial and detention that have created the detainee and the terrorist as another tier of legally designated and consequently stereotyped, bound and gagged, demotic sub-humanity. We now add these folk devils to the already long list of refugee, exile, asylum-seeker.

Legislative onslaught and consequential renaming such as this invokes a break with the hybrid identifications which accompany diaspora that were considered in Chapter 4. In the wake of the 'war on terror', Arab-Americans and South Asian-Americans were required to undo the hyphen and drape themselves in the US flag as a sign of their unadulterated patriotism. As we heard and saw on the nightly news after September 11, each and every US household was engaged in some display of the flag. In this context, imagining a post-national situation and a world of cosmopolitan hybrids freely circulating along the circuits of capitalism remains in the domain of idealism. When the F16s start bombing there is no canopy of hybridity and no bomb shelter of diaspora to protect those beneath the flight paths. In the aftermath of the fifth Afghanistan war (Prashad 2002b), categories of traditional and modern were deployed in equal measure, with the bombing of those who were seen as essentialist and fundamentalist shamelessly perpetuated by those who were also essentially fundamentalist, and both with God on their side. As Dube notes:

> In most denunciations of the Taliban's action, the simplicity of the story line marked one world from another, construing critical antinomies: we are progressive, they are backward; we are tolerant, they are intolerant; we are modern, they are medieval; we are we/us, they are they/them. (Dube 2002: 730)

Vijay Prashad cites the example of Benjamin Barber's book *Jihad versus McWorld* (1996), which attempts to create a strong contrast between jihadis (traditional) and globalizers (modern). In what could mischievously be called a hybrid turn, Prashad crumples the traditional/modern distinction and argues that it is right-wing and fundamentalist regimes, such as the Bharatiya Janata Party in India and the Partido Revolucionario Institutional in Mexico, that have embraced the entry of transnational capitalism and 'IMFundamentalism' so that it 'might be better to collapse the dialectic couple Jihad and McWorld into the category of McJihad' (Prashad 2002b: 81). He further explains:

> McJihad is along the grain of neoliberalism: weak regulation of certain sectors of the economy, coupled with a strong repressive apparatus and with cultural nationalism intended to draw upon popular legitimacy just as the regime sells its national interests to transnational corporations. (Prashad 2002b: 84)[6]

Prashad's examination touches on the relationship between the political economy and the antinomies of modernity that come to classify groups of people as modern and traditional. Moving out of the sphere of culture, he is able to present a materialist analysis that more often than not is lacking in contemporary culturalist commentary.

It is significant that the practices of activists in the USA post-September 11 have forced them to look beyond cultural exchanges, which to some extent were fairly minimal, towards new coalition-building. Drawing upon her experience of the formation of multiracial anti-war coalitions in California, Nadine Naber identifies how Japanese, Latin American and Black groups worked with South Asian and Arab groups to organize anti-war resistance. The difficulties these groups had with mainstream left and liberal groups focused upon their insistence on linking the anti-war struggle with the plight of the Palestinian people. As Naber poignantly and obviously states: 'US Imperialism is an extension of US domestic policies' (Naber 2002: 234). Any opposition to the war had to take into account the struggles against US imperialism at home and abroad. This could still be read as evoking a diasporic politics of mobilization, but to do so would limit the intent and motivation, reducing it from an explicit, necessary and united opposition to imperialism to some sort of culturalist code. The anti-war movement in Britain has also engaged in coalition-building between Muslim groups, peace campaigners and sections of the left, with mixed results. However, where they have attracted intellectual attention, writers such as sometime *Guardian* columnist and anti-globalization movement commentator, George Monbiot, and the former International Marxist Group activist Tariq Ali have focused upon the conflation of baddies (Bush and Taliban, Saddam and Rumsfield) in their writing, rather than on strategies for organizing. Gore Vidal has probably been the most entertaining of these critical voices, pointing out the business links between Bush senior and the bin Laden family, reminding everyone that the USA had armed and trained Saddam in the first place and, given Blair and Bush's rather idiosyncratic religious views, pointing out the scary notion that these two men with vast military power at their whim also both think that Jesus might want them for sunbeams.[7]

The cover of Tariq Ali's *Clash of Fundamentalisms* (2002), depicting George W. Bush with turban in Taliban guise, was perhaps a formal attempt to use hybridity to portray the equivalence of the US neo-conservatives and the Islamicist far right.[8] But actually, this type of juxtaposition does a disservice to a critical analysis by portraying the Taliban and George Bush as equivalents. The basis of an adequate critical response would be one that can equate the impact of US imperialism – all-pervasive and linked with capitalist exploitation – to that of the Taliban – terrible for the already impoverished people of Afghanistan but still localized. Vidal is clear and persuasive: 'In these several hundred wars against communism, terrorist, drugs or sometimes nothing much, between Pearl Harbor and Tuesday September 11th, 2001, we tended to strike the first blow. But then we're the good guys, right? Right' (Vidal 2002: 40). If we consider merely the quantitative impact of US imperialism and the Taliban simply in terms of the numbers of people killed, or whose lives have been made miserable, then there is no equivalence.[9] This could be too crude an analysis if the long civil war in Afghanistan is counted as an internal concern, but the evidence is there that the USA played the great game in Afghanistan from the beginning (Prashad 2002b).

Tariq Ali might argue that all his cover image is trying to do is depict the fact that both Bush and the Taliban are the enemy of those who would fight for liberation. Equally, of course, it was important to provide solidarity with the Iraqi people against the repressive regime and to organize against the American and British occupation of that country. These are in themselves correct, but tell us little about strategy and priority. This is where an older style of politics might ask us who and at what time is the greater enemy. Hybridity does not provide an answer here and therefore leads those who wish to do more than comment on a situation into a state of elegantly worded paralysis.

There is another perspective which might be depicted in an image from the television scenes of wartime coverage, a perspective commensurate with the view that there are greater and lesser enemies and these should be tackled in that sequence. This ordering would be summed up in the picture of the Iraqi peasant, at the height of the US invasion, holding up his AK47, with which he claims to have shot down an American fighter helicopter besides which he is standing.[10] This time the image was not created in the virtual world of digital manipulation, and was one that cannot easily be read as hybrid. Rather, the Western media purported to demonize the rabid fervour of the Saddam loyalist. But the image sent another message of the possibility of emancipation from one's enemies by an active and well-organized people. Of course, once again there is no equivalence between the fire power of the gun and the helicopter, but the coding articulated by the picture is also one that argues that resistance is possible and, perhaps more importantly, that the enemy can be defeated.

While the picture of Bush in Taliban guise may cause humour or sardonic laughter, it does not present a call to action. Opposing the war on Iraq and Saddam Hussein's regime does not enable a positive response. Implicit in these kinds of position is a *de facto* support for those regimes engaged in the occupation of Iraq. The defeat of imperialism and the dominant nations actually means those involved in the anti-war mobilizations, in the advanced capitalist nations, having to lose something themselves, not just their representatives or elites. Inadequate and inconsequential thoughts born of insecurity, the theoretical concepts of diaspora and hybridity, which should be delivering so much to those engaged in struggle, are left bereft. Does it help us much to think of those men who have some affiliation to Al Qaeda as a diasporic grouping? It would perhaps be better than the state preference of international terrorists or the Islamicist *umma*. But it would not help those held in jail on colonized Cuban land (Guantanamo Bay), as they are now people for whom no law – national or international – applies. Indeed, those captives at Camp X-Ray, at Bagram Airbase and in detention under the US Patriot Act have no status, just like another group of peoples who fall through the slip of hybridity and diaspora – asylum-seekers, refugees, sex workers and undocumented migrants.

Making–breaking borders

If Arabs, Muslims and brown folks in general are the new enemy within the nation for the US state, then Europeans have taken this formulation to a new level with the conflation of those seeking asylum and refuge with international terrorists. The death of a policeman in Manchester in January 2003, while carrying out a raid on the home of 'suspected' terrorists, led to a furore of media attacks on asylum-seekers and refugees. The fact that only a handful of those arrested had come to Britain through the asylum system had no bearing on the media coverage, which was intense and hostile. The vitriolic outpourings that this event generated are the most extreme end of a general attitude towards new immigrants (if we read those seeking asylum into this category) which illustrates a schizophrenic xenophobia. At the very same time that hybridity is celebrated in the ingestion of Chicken Tikka Masala (see Chapter 5), there is a nauseating response to those who are coming to Britain in extreme circumstances and plight. It is our contention that hybridity is unable to help us resolve cultural discrepancy in theory, and as a practical antidote to xenophobia it seems deeply ineffective.

A worrying convergence of the attitudes found in the media with those of groups such as the neo-fascist British National Party can be found when the BNP proudly proclaims on its website that the 'British press help[ed] spread the BNP message', following the incident in Manchester. The message of making Britain white, a pure nation unsullied by immigration, is explicitly declared by these far-right groups. This then becomes a reading of the message provided in newspapers such as the *Daily Mail* and *The Daily Telegraph*. Contradictions run deep in this context. Diasporic groups, once settled into the patterns of a benign multiculturalism, which does not test any limits of a stereotypical English nationalism, are increasingly presented as acceptable in the media. In contrast, there is a uniform representation of asylum-seekers and refugees that focuses on the negative, most cogently seen in the conjunction that unites terrorists with asylum-seekers and with Muslims.

If we were to take a wider internationalist perspective, then the link between asylum-seekers, terrorists and criminality in general actually does hold some weight. This is so if we consider that the activity of nation-states against citizens can itself be terrorist and that the criminal consequence of state (colonialist) terror is to produce refugees. The greatest number of asylum-seekers to Britain follows the imperialist wars instigated by the dominant nations. In 1998, it was Kosovans, Albanians, Yugoslavs and Bosnians who were the subject of vilification, while their countries were being liberated by the humanitarian bombing of NATO. This was followed by a trickle of Afghanis and Iraqis, their countries being subject to direct military interference and years of UN sanctions and military repression. In the course of this redefining process, we also need to address the fundamentals of what the asylum-seeker and refugee are ultimately escaping from. As Sivanandan remarks:

> Even genuine refugees and asylum-seekers are being sent back to the countries they have escaped from on the grounds that they are economic and not politi- cal refugees, which overlooks the fact that it is the authoritarian regimes main- tained by western governments, in Third World counties, on behalf of transnational companies, that throw up refugees on western shores. It is your economics that makes our politics that makes us refugees in your countries. (Sivanandan 1997)

No distinction is drawn between economic and political refugees because, indeed, all refugees are to some extent escaping the problems generated by multinational capital. On the one hand, asylum-seekers are forced into the role of a reserve army of labour, accepted into the low-wage, no regulation side of the European economy. On the other hand, they are vilified and excluded when demand for labour is low. This is immigration law regulat- ing for capitalist gain. The treatment of asylum-seekers masks the demand they fulfil for labour that can operate outside the minimum wage system, outside the formal arenas of citizenship and diaspora. In the same way that undocumented Mexican workers ensure that the Californian economy remains afloat, so asylum-seekers and other undocumented immigrants in Europe maintain those sectors which pay below what is already an unlive- able wage. Removing the right to work of asylum-seekers is ostensibly a measure designed to discourage economic migrants, but this actually serves the domestic economy by creating a class of labour outside the rules of the welfare state. This, at an even more basic level, is a re-creation of the classic proletarian who has no other recourse than to sell her/his labour power. But in this era there are few organizations to mobilize this group and the work they do is in those sectors which carry no political clout, such as catering and domestic work.

The argument that it is economic motivation that drives asylum-seekers is risible in the light of direct military intervention in those parts of the world from where refugees come. Sivanandan makes the point succinctly: 'The distinction between political refugees and economic migrants is a bogus one – susceptible to different interpretations by different interests at different times' (www.irr.org.uk/2000/august/ak000001.html). In an era where labour is required, then there is no need to distinguish between who is allowed in and who is not. In a situation where a minimum wage is in oper- ation, then illegal and undocumented workers are the best solution to provide labour for the worst jobs. The history of migration from Commonwealth countries to Britain has oscillated between being economically necessary and politically expedient. So the draconian legislation in the British 2002 Nationality and Immigration Act, which essentially renders asylum-seekers as non-people and refugees as marginal citizens, also contains within it the provision for the selective import of skilled and entrepreneurial migrants.

This is perhaps the most important point to make, that while states make the movements of certain people more difficult, they grant more intrusive access to a whole range of foreign economic interests in the shapes of business people, bankers, etc. (Sassen 1996).

We do not think that the concepts on offer in academic debate can combat laws that degrade and dehumanize asylum-seekers, or create terrorists out of all Muslims. The potentiality that migration and hybridity are granted by theorists such as Hardt and Negri seems a little hollow if the practicalities of strategy and mobilization are ignored. If it is possible to 'take control of the production of mobility and stasis, purities and mixtures' (Hardt and Negri 2000: 156) and that a multitude in 'perpetual motion' subject to 'hybridization' (2000: 60) is capable of 'smashing' all old and new boundaries and borders with a 'nomad singularity' and the 'omnilateral movement of its desire' (2000: 363), then migration becomes the forefront of the struggle against capitalism. However, the condition of possibility of the world market is the same 'circulation, mobility, diversity and mixture' which also 'overwhelms any binary division' and as 'uncontainable rhizome' cannot ever be 'completely subjugated to the laws of capitalist accumulation' (2000: 397). The very displacements, dispersal and exodus advocated by Hardt and Negri in *Empire*, which point to a model for resistance, are also the same stuff of which the enemy is made. With their figure of displacement, they suggest a general desertion from the global apparatus of power. We are all to be refugees (some more than others!). Hardt and Negri's conception of hybridization and a mobile multitude is an attempt to put a positive spin on what, when blocked by the passports, visas, border patrols, asylum and immigration laws and detention centres of the state, is a limitation on the integrated labour force that Marx anticipated would lead to the political awakening of the proletariat – 'workers of the world, unite' he wrote.

It is not that migration does not create active, militant and political workers' organization. Janitors in California and taxi drivers in New York City have shown militant activism in the 1990s which belies both the view that those in the service sector and those who are new immigrant workers are quiescent (see Prashad 2002a). But this kind of organizational ethos is lost in the analytical pot. For example, Saskia Sassen (1998) wishes to alert us to new transnational forms of political organization through NGOs, cross-border struggles around human rights, the environment, arms control, women's rights, labour rights and the rights of national minorities. Her point is that the 'secretaries' and the 'cleaners of the buildings where the professionals do their work' should be put back into the analysis:

> In the dominant account, the key concepts of globalisation, information economy, and telematics all suggest that place no longer matters and that the only type of worker that matters is the highly educated professional. This account favours the capability for global transmission over the concentrations of established infrastructure that make transmission possible; favours information outputs over the workers producing those outputs, from specialists to secretaries;

and favours the new transnational corporate culture over the multiplicity of cultural environments, including reterritorialized immigrant cultures within which many of the 'other' jobs of the global economy take place. (Sassen 1998: 7)

In Sassen's work, the agency of the working class, the organizational threat to capital which forces the compromise of the welfare state buy-off of the advanced industrial workers, and the 'fruits of frequently violent labour struggles' are reduced to consequences of a particular phase of economics that has now passed. The current conjuncture is then characterized as including a new flexibility, fluid labour markets, more part-time and temporary jobs, high unemployment, casualization and 'new types of social divisions' (Sassen 1998: 102). By way of sharp contrast, Prashad focuses not on the absence/irrelevance of organized labour in the USA, but on the ways it needs to change to support a wider range of struggles:

> If unions do not take up the issues of the people (racism, sexism, etc.) then they will be unable to fight beyond the narrow confines of the workplace and will not be able to fashion a program for widespread social change. ... [But] without the militancy of organized labor, the threat to the capitalist elite would make little impact, but without the concern for social change, the union movement would be unable to lead the entire society away from the barbarism of the present. (Prashad 2002a: xvii and xx)

The analysis of the new types of worker may be the same but the prescription provided by Sassen and Prashad could not be more different. Placing migration at the heart of a progressive project of redistribution favours those instances where militant worker unity, such as that seen in Britain among black workers, has generated cross-union support and enables international solidarity. If these examples of progressive moments render a positive evaluation of mobility, they still need to be tempered by recognition that reactionary forces also mobilize transnationally and that there is no inherent quality (as Hardt and Negri would argue) in migration that enables progressive outcomes.

Another possibility

> Anti-colonialism, like postcolonialism, was partly driven and predominantly articulated by these diasporic figures, the product of the movements across borders of intellectual-politicians who typically incorporated the experience of western as well as indigenous ideas into their thinking. (Young 2001: 178)

Robert Young goes on to give examples of such figures as Franz Fanon and Mahatma Gandhi, though he could have created a longer list of names in his excellent agenda-shifting volume, *Postcolonialism: An Historical Introduction* (2001). In the anti-colonial period, diasporic figures played a crucial role in mobilizing movements and articulating ideologies. Indeed, it could be said, perhaps if only to evoke the purchase of the terms, that a hybrid Marxism emerges from the activities of these diasporic figures. We see in the figure of the travelling comrade a link between the two main themes of this book that we may look to as crucial for our interest in social justice. We recall Prashad's narration of the meeting of Ho Chi Minh with Marcus Garvey in Harlem and think this is profound (Prashad 2001: 67). For us, a reading of these moments in history as diasporic and hybrid enhances the material changes that the anti-colonial movements wrought on the world.[11] But to maintain these links with social justice requires a similar association and critical interrogation of concepts as that which we have illustrated throughout this book. Our approach to hybridity and diaspora remains critical, however much we think the terms and issues are still the key terrain of politics today. Contemporary social movements such as the anti-capitalists, the 'Stop the War' campaigners and those defending asylum-seekers do not use this language for mobilization or defence. We understand why this is the case, but at the same time regret that linkages which could be made are not.

So what is the best on offer: diaspora and hybridity in a mulitcultural world of recognition of difference? An enlightened attitude of tolerance to be sure, but tolerance is not much if we start from a degree of inequality hitherto equivalent to the worst humanity has devised. Recognition and tolerance of difference implies a notion of the norm, of the centre. Even a decentred centre, one that is also a margin, the margin of the margins, retains the centre as the privileged site from which tolerance is deployed and difference is defined. Diaspora and hybridity recognize the disruption of that privilege, but do not offer the means to displace it, and the massive military-legalistic forces that ensure its continuity.

Notes

1 It is as if we were talking of the bin Laden of the seminar room – highly trained in the application of rhetorical tropes, ensconced in a secure bunker, armed with an unassailable belief in the righteousness of his own cause.

2 The Patriot Act is a series of legislation that re-enforce existing legislation within the USA in terms of increasing the rights of the government to engage in surveillance of citizens and to remove those deemed a threat to security.

3 In an even more absurd example the new Pakistani Prime Minister (elected July 2004) did not even have Pakistani citizenship (his American passport being sufficient credentials for this post).

4 The shutting down of the informal banking or *Halwa* system is an example of the way in which global financial institutions are able to apply governance on flows of money, something deemed not possible when it comes to much more damaging currency fluctuation. But here it is the interests of the West that are conflictual.

5 The wholesale deportation of thousands of communists from the USA in the 1920s merits only a minor mention in the immigration museum of Ellis Island, New York, where the deportees were processed. Today, does it seem not so very long ago that the evil empire was dressed in cassocks and astrokhans rather than in kurtah and kaftan?

6 Certainly, the presence of McDonalds at the exit to the *Kabbah*, the holiest of places for Muslims, in Mecca is a good example supporting Prashad's point of view. See Sayyid (2000b) for a couplet or two on this part of the Muslim pilgrimage, the Hajj.

7 Gore Vidal usefully excoriates these terminologies while worrying that the god-bothering evangelical Christianity of Bush and Blair means that the world is being run by two boys who

think 'Jesus wants them for sunbeams' (Vidal, interview with Amy Goodman on Pacifica Radio, 13 May 2003).

8 There is no doubt that at the ideological level, Bush's support for fundamental Christianity and the Taliban's *wahabbi*'ized Islam share some frightening similarities and both need opposing, but our argument is that they are not of the same consequence, beyond the level of the mundane.

9 Kovel (1997) documents the many millions killed in US wars against communism.

10 See news of 25 March 2003.

11 It may be worth expressing the inarticulation of diasporic or hybrid themes during the anti-colonial struggle, this being a twenty-first century re-reading of those times. The notion of 'The Internationale' and of 'the internationalist' were never sufficient to contain those ambitions. But our critique of the nation in earlier chapters also illustrates the need to go beyond a narrow focus on the national and, of course, to work out the aspirations of those denied statehood. All of these facets of diaspora still leave us with a difficulty in articulating basic demands, sometimes for *roti kapra aur makan* (food, clothing and housing), sometimes for justice and equality.

References and Bibliography

Adorno, Theodor (1991) *The Culture Industry, Selected Essays on Mass Culture*, London: Routledge.

Adorno, Theodor (1998) *Critical Models: Interventions and Catchwords*, New York: Columbia University Press.

Ages, Arnold (1973) *The Diaspora Dimension*, The Hague: Martinus Nijhoff.

Akers, Ronald L. (1977) *Deviant Behaviour: A Social Learning Approach*, 2nd edition, Belmont, CA: Wadsworth.

Akers, Ronald L., Krohn, Marvin D., Lanza-Kaduce, Lonn and Radosevich, Marcia (1979) 'Social Learning Theory and Deviant Behaviour: A Specific Test of a General Theory', *American Sociological Review*, Vol. 44, No. 4, pp. 636–655.

Alexander, Claire (1996) *The Art of Being Black: The Creation of Black British Youth Identities*, Oxford: Clarendon Press.

Alexander, Claire (2000) *The Asian Gang: Ethnicity, Identity, Masculinity*, Oxford: Berg.

Alexander, Claire (2002) 'Beyond Black: Re-thinking the Colour/Culture' *Ethnic and Racial Studies*, Vol. 25, No. 4, pp. 552–571.

Alexander, Priscilla (1997) 'Feminism, Sex Workers, and Human Rights', in Jill Nagle (ed.), *Whores and Other Feminists*, London: Routledge, pp. 83–97.

Ali, N. (2002) 'Kashmiri Nationalism Beyond the Nation-State', *South Asia Research*, Vol. 22, No. 2, pp. 145–160.

Ali, Tariq (2002) *Clash of Fundamentalisms: Crusades, Jihads and Modernity*, London: Verso.

Alleyne, Brian (2002) *Radicals Against Race*, Oxford: Berg.

Amin, Samir (1997) *Capitalism in the Age of Globalization: The Management of Contemporary Society*, London: Zed Books.

Andall, Jacqueline (1999) 'Cape Verdean Women on the Move: "Immigration Shopping" in Italy and Europe', *Modern Italy*, Vol. 4, No. 2, pp. 141–157.

Anderson, Benedict (1983) *Imagined Communities*, London: Verso.

Anderson, Benedict (1994) 'Exodus', *Critical Inquiry*, Vol. 20, No. 2, pp. 314–327.

Anthias, Floya (1992) *Ethnicity, Class, Gender and Migraiton: Greek Cypriots in Britain*, Aldershot: Averbury.

Anthias, Floya (1998) 'Evaluating "Diaspora": Beyond Ethnicity?', *Sociology*, Vol. 32, No. 3, pp. 557–580.

Anthias, Floya (2001) 'New Hybridities, Old Concepts', *Ethnic and Racial Studies*, Vol. 24, No. 4, pp. 619–641.

Anthias, Floya and Yuval-Davis, Nira (1989) *Woman–Nation–State*, London: Macmillan.

Anwar, Muhammad (1979) *The Myth of Return: Pakistanis in Britain*, London: Heinemann.

Anwar, Muhammad (1998) *Between Cultures: Continuity and Change in the Lives of Young Asians*, London: Routledge.

Anzaldúa, Gloria (1987) *Borderlands = Frontera: The New Mestiza*, San Francisco: Aunt Lute Books.

Appadurai, Arjun (1990) 'Disjuncture and Difference in the Global Cultural Economy', *Public Culture*, Vol. 2, No. 2, pp. 1–24.

Appadurai, Arjun (1996) *Modernity at Large: Cultural Dimensions of Globalization*, Minneapolis: University of Minnesota Press.

Arthur, Paul (1991) 'Our Greater Island Beyond the Seas', *Diaspora*, Vol. 1, No. 3.

Arthur, Paul (1992) 'Diasporan Intervention in International Affairs: Irish America as a Case Study', *Diaspora*, Vol. 1, No. 2, pp. 143–162.

Axel, Brian (2002) 'National Interruption: Diaspora Theory and Multiculturalism in the UK', *Cultural Dynamics*, Vol. 14, No. 3, pp. 235–256.

Back, Les (2002a) 'Wagner and Power Chords: Skinheadism, White Power Music, and the Internet', in Vron Ware and Les Back, *Out of Whiteness: Color, Politics, and Culture*, Chicago: Chicago University Press, pp. 94–132.

Back, Les (2002b) 'Out of Sight: Southern Music and the Coloring of Sound', in Vron Ware and Les Back, *Out of Whiteness: Color, Politics, and Culture*, Chicago: Chicago University Press, pp. 227–270.

Back, Les and Nayak, Anoop (1993) *Invisible Europeans: Black People in the New Europe*, London: Routledge.

Banerjea, Koushik (1999) 'Ni-Ten-Ichi-Ryu: Enter the World of the Smart Stepper', in Raminder Kaur and John Hutnyk (eds), *Travel Worlds: Journeys in Contemporary Cultural Politics*, London: Zed Books, pp. 14–29.

Banerjea, Koushik (2002) 'The Tyranny of the Binary: Race, Nation and the Logic of Failing Liberalisms', *Ethnic and Racial Studies*, Vol. 25, No. 4 (July), pp. 572–590.

Banerjea, Koushik and Barn, Jatinder (1996) 'Versioning Terror: Jallianwala Bagh and the Jungle', in Sanjay Sharma, John Hutnyk and Ashwani Sharma (eds), *Dis-Orienting Rhythms: The Politics of the New Asian Dance Music*, London: Zed Books, pp. 193–216.

Barber, Benjamin (1996) *Jihad vs. McWorld*, New York: Ballantine Books.

Bard, Julia (1992/93) 'Women against Fundamentalism and the Jewish Community', *Women against Fundamentalism Journal*, No. 4, pp. 3–5.

Barkan, Elazar and Shelton, Marie-Denise (eds) (1998) *Border, Exiles and Diasporas*, Stanford, CA: Stanford University Press.

Barth, Fredrik (1969) 'Introduction' in F. Barth (ed.), *Ethnic Groups and Boundaries*, Bergen: Universitetsforlaget.

Bataille, Georges (1988) *The Accursed Share: Volume 1: Consumption*, New York: Zone Books.

Bates, Elizabeth (1979) *Mental Disorder and Madness: Alternative Theories*, Brisbane: University of Queensland Press.

Baudrillard, Jean (1968/1996) *The System of Objects*, London: Verso.

Bauman, Zygmunt (2000) *Liquid Modernity*, Cambridge: Polity Press.

Baumann, Gerd (1996) *Contesting Culture: Discourses of Identity in Multi-Ethnic London*, Cambridge: Cambridge University Press.

Behdad, Ali (1997) 'Nationalism and Immigration in the United States', *Diaspora*, Vol. 6, No. 2, pp. 155–178.

Beinin, Joel (1992) 'Exile and Political Activism: The Egyptian–Jewish Communists in Paris, 1950–59', Vol. 2, No. 1, pp. 73–94.

Benjamin, Walter (1968) *Illuminations*, H.S. Zohn (trans.), New York: Shocken Books.

Berlant, Lauren and Warner, Michael (1994) 'Introduction', in David Theo Goldberg, *Multiculturalism: A Critical Reader*, Cambridge: Blackwell, pp. 107–113.

Bhabha, Homi (ed.) (1990) *Nation and Narration*, New York: Routledge and Kegan Paul.

Bhabha, Homi (1994) *The Location of Culture*, London: Routledge.

Bhabha, Homi (1996) 'Culture's In-Between', in Stuart Hall and Paul du Gay (eds), *Questions of Cultural Identity*, London: Sage, pp. 53–60.

Bhachu, Parminder (1985) *Twice Migrants: East African Sikh Settlers in Britain*, London: Tavistock.

Bhachu, Parminder (1995) 'New Cultural Forms and Transnational South Asian Women: Culture, Class and Consumption among British South Asian Women in the Diaspora', in Peter van der Veer (ed.), *Nation and Migration: The Politics of Space in the South Asian Diaspora*, Philadelphia: University of Pennsylvania Press, pp. 222–244.

Bhatt, Chetan (1997) *Liberation and Purity: Race, New Religious Movements and the Ethics of Postmodernity*, London: UCL Press.

Bhatt, Chetan and Mukta, Parita (2000) 'Introduction: Hindutva in the West: Mapping the Antinomies of Diaspora Nationalism', *Ethnic and Racial Studies*, Vol. 23, No. 3, pp. 407–441.

Bhattacharya, Gargi, Gabriel, John and Small, Stephen (2002) *Race and Power: Global Racism in the Twenty-first Century*, London: Routledge.

Blum, William (1995) *Killing Hope: U.S. Military and CIA Interventions since World War II*, London: Zed Books.

Blum, William (2000) *Rogue State: A Guide to the World's Only Superpower*, London: Zed Books.

Bowker, Geoffrey C. and Star, Susan Leigh (1999) *Sorting Things Out: Classification and Its Consequences*, Cambridge, MA: MIT Press.

Brah, Avtar (1996) *Cartographies of Diaspora: Contesting Identities*, London: Routledge.

Brah, Avtar and Coombs, Annie (2000) *Hybridity and its Discontents*, London: Routledge.

Brennan, Tony (2001) 'World Music Does Not Exist', *Discourse*, Vol. 23, No. 1, pp. 44–62.

Bromley, Roger (2000) *Narratives for a New Belonging: Diasporic Cultural Fictions*, Edinburgh: Edinburgh University Press.

Butler, Judith (1994) 'Introduction: Against Proper Objects', in More Gender Trouble: Feminism Meets Queer Theory, *Differences: A Journal of Feminist Cultural Studies*, Summer–Fall, pp. 1–26.

CARF (2000) 'Refugees from Globalism', *Campaign Against Racism and Fascism*, No. 57, pp. 3–4.

Castells, Manuel (1996) *The Rise of the Network Society*, Oxford: Blackwell.

Castles, Stephen (1991) 'Italians in Australia: Building a Multicultural Society on the Pacific Rim', *Diaspora*, Vol. 1, No. 1, pp. 45–66.

Castles, Stephen and Kozack, Godula (1973) *Immigrant Workers and Class Structure in Western Europe*, London: Oxford University Press.

CCCS (Centre for Contemporary Cultural Studies) (1982) *The Empire Strikes Back*, London: Hutchinson.

Chambers, Iain (1994) *Migrancy, Culture, Identity*, London: Routledge.

Chambers, Iain (1996) 'Signs of Silence, Lines of Listening', in Iain Chambers and Linda Curtis (eds), *The Post-colonial Question*, London: Routledge, pp. 47–62.

Chambers, Iain and Curtis, Linda (eds) (1996) *The Post-colonial Question*, London: Routledge.

Chatterjee, Partha (1995) *The Nation and Its Fragments: Colonial and Postcolonial Histories*, Princeton, NJ: Princeton University Press.

Chomsky, Naom (2003) *Hegemony or Survival*, London: Hamish Hamilton.

Chow, Rey (1993) *Writing Diaspora*, Bloomington: Indiana University Press.

Chow, Rey (1998) *Ethics After Idealism*, Bloomington: Indiana University Press.

Chua, Beng-Huat (1998) 'Culture, Multiracalism, and National Identity in Singapore', in Kuan-Hsing Chen (ed.), *Trajectories: Inter-Asia Cultural Studies*, London: Routledge, pp. 186–205.

Clarke, Colin, Ceri, Peach and Steven, Vertovec (1990) *South Asians Overseas: Migration and Ethnicity*, Cambridge: Cambridge University Press.

Clifford, James (1994) 'Diasporas', *Cultural Anthropology*, Vol. 9, No. 3, pp. 302–338.

Clifford, James (1997) *Routes: Travel and Translation in the Late Twentieth Century*, Cambridge, MA: Harvard University Press.

Clifford, James (2000) 'Taking Identity Politics Seriously: "The Contradictory Stony Ground …"', in Paul Gilroy, Lawrence Grossberg and Angela McRobbie (eds), *Without Guarantees: In Honour of Stuart Hall*, London: Verso, pp. 94–112.

Cohen, Phil (1999) 'Rethinking the diasporama', *Patterns of Prejudice*, Vol. 33, No. 1, pp. 3–22.

Cohen, Rich (1998) *Tough Jews: Fathers, Sons and Gangster Dreams*, London: Cape.

Cohen, Rina (1999) 'From Ethnonational Enclave to Diasporic Community: The Mainstreaming of Israeli Jewish Migrants in Toronto', *Diaspora*, Vol. 8, No. 2, pp. 121–136.

Cohen, Robin (1997) *Global Diasporas: An Introduction*, London: UCL Press.

Creed, Barbara (1993) *The Monstrous Feminine: Film, Feminism, Psychoanalysis*, London: Routledge.

Dellit, Alison (2001) 'Philip Ruddock: Minister for Racism', *Green Left Weekly*, No. 433, www.greenleftweekly.org.au/back/2001/433/433p10.htm.

Deleuze, Gilles and Guattari, Felix (1972/1984) *Anti-Oedipus: Capitalism and Schizophrenia*, London: Athlone Press.

Derrida, Jacques (1992) *Given Time: Counterfeit Money*, Chicago: University of Chicago Press.

Derrida, Jacques (1996/1998) *Monolingualism of the Other, or The Prosthesis of Origin*, Stanford, CA: Stanford University Press.

Derrida, Jacques (2001) *On Cosmopolitanism and Forgiveness*, London: Routledge.

Dinnage, Rosemary (1997) 'Out of the Ruins', *New York Review of Books*, Vol. 44, No. 13, (August 14), pp. 14–15.

Donald, James and Rattansi, Ali (eds) (1992) *'Race', Culture and Difference*, Newbury Park, CA: Sage.

Dube, Saurabh (1999) 'Travelling Light: Missionary Musings, Colonial Cultures and Anthropological Anxieties', in R. Kaur and J. Hutnyk (eds), *Travel Worlds: Journeys in Contemporary Cultural Politics*, London: Zed Books, pp. 29–50.

Dube, Saurabh (2002) 'Introduction: Colonialism, Modernity, Colonial Modernities', *Nepantla, Views from the South*, Vol. 3, No. 2, pp. 197–219.

Dutton, Michael (1998) *Streetlife China*, Cambridge: Cambridge University Press.

Dyer, Richard (1997) *White*, London: Routledge.

Ellison, Ralph (1947) *Invisible Man*, Harmondsworth: Penguin.

Eltringham, Nigel (2004) *Accounting for Horror: Post-Genocide Debates in Rwanda*, London: Pluto Press.

Esmail, Anees, Everington, Sam and Doyle, Helen (1998) 'Racial Discrimination in the Allocation of Distinction Awards?', *British Medical Journal*, No. 316, pp. 193–195.

Fletcher, John (1992) 'The Huguenot Diaspora', *Diaspora*, Vol. 2, No. 2, pp. 251–260.

Foner, Nancy (1997) 'What's New about Transnationalism? New York Immigrants Today and at the Turn of the Century', *Diaspora*, Vol. 6, No. 3, pp. 355–376.

Fortier, Anne-Marie (1998) 'The Politics of "Italians Abroad": National, Diaspora and New Geographies of Identity', *Diaspora*, Vol. 7, No. 2, pp. 355–375.

Fortier, Anne-Marie (2003) 'Making Home: Queer Migrations and Motions of Attachment', in S. Ahmed, C. Castañeda, A.-M. Fortier and M. Sheller (eds), *Uprootings/Regroundings: Questions of Home and Migration*. Oxford: Berg.

Foucault, Michel (1975/1982) *Discipline and Punish: The Birth of the Prison*, Harmondsworth: Penguin.

Frankenberg, Ruth (1993) *The Social Construction of Whiteness: White Women, Race Matters*, Cambridge: Cambridge University Press.

Furedi, Frank (1997) *Population and Development: A Critical Introduction*, Cambridge: Polity Press.

Fuss, Diana (1991) 'Inside/Out', in Diana Fuss (ed.), *Inside/Out: Lesbian Theories, Gay Theories*, London: Routledge, pp. 1–10.

Gabaccia, Donna R. and Ottanelli, Fraser (1997) 'Diaspora or International Proletariat? Italian Labor, Labor Migration, and the Making of Multiethnic States, 1815–1939', *Diaspora*, Vol. 6, No. 1, pp. 61–84.

Gallagher, Charles A. (1995) 'White Reconstruction in the University', *Socialist Review*, Vol. 24, Nos 1 and 2, Special Issue: *Arranging Identities: Construction of Race, Ethnicity and Nation*, pp. 165–187.

Garcia Canclini, Nestor (1995) *Hybrid Cultures: Strategies for Entering and Leaving Modernity*, Minneapolis: University of Minnesota Press.

Garcia Calclini, Nestor (2000) 'The State of War and the State of Hybridization', in Paul Gilroy, Lawrence Grossberg and Angela McRobbie (eds), *Without Guarantees: In Honour of Stuart Hall*, London: Verso, pp. 38–52.

Geertz, Clifford (1973) *The Interpretation of Cultures*, New York: Basic Books.

Geertz, Clifford (1988) *Works and Lives: The Anthropologist as Author*, Cambridge: Polity Press.

Gellner, Ernest (1983) *Nations and Nationalism*, London: Verso.

George, Rosemary Marangoly (1997) '"From Expatriate Aristocrat to Immigrant Nobody": South Asian Racial Strategies in the Southern Californian Context', *Diaspora*, Vol. 6, No. 1, pp. 31–60.

Gibson, Pamela Church (2001) '"You've been in my life so long I can't remember anything else": Into the Labyrinth with Ripley and the Alien', in Matthew Tinkcom, Mathew Villarejo and Amy Villarejo (eds), *Keyframes: Popular Cinema and Cultural Studies*, London: Routledge, pp. 35–51.

Gillespie, Marie (1995) *Television, Ethnicity and Cultural Change*, London: Routledge.

Gilman, Sander L. (2000) 'Are Jews White? Or, the History of the Nose Job', in Les Back and John Solomos (eds), *Theories of Race and Racism: A Reader*, London: Routledge, pp. 229–237.

Gilroy, Paul (1987) *There Ain't No Black in the United Jack*, London: Routledge.

Gilroy, Paul (1988) 'Cruciality and the Frog's Perspective: An Agenda of Difficulties for the Black Arts Movement in Britain', *Third Text*, No. 5, pp. 33–44.

Gilroy, Paul (1991) '"It Ain't Where You're From, It's Where You're At …": The Dialectics of Disasporic Identification', *Third Text: Third World Perspectives on Contemporary Art & Culture*, No. 13, pp. 3–16.

Gilroy, Paul (1993a) *The Black Atlantic: Modernity and Double Consciousness*, London: Routledge.

Gilroy, Paul (1993b) *Small Acts: Thoughts on the Politics of Black Cultures*, London: Serpent's Tail.

Gilroy, Paul (1994) 'Black Cultural Politics: An Interview with Paul Gilroy by Timmy Lott', *Found Object*, Vol. 4, pp. 46–81.

Gilroy, Paul (2000) *Between Camps*, Harmondsworth: Penguin.

Gluckman, Max (1955) *Custom and Conflict in Africa*, Oxford: Basil Blackwell.

Godbeer, Richard (1999) 'Eroticizing the Middle Ground: Anglo-Indian Sexual Relations along the Eighteenth-century Frontier', in Martha Hodes (ed.), *Sex, Love, Race: Crossing Boundaries in North American History*, New York: New York University, pp. 91–111.

Gold, Steven J. (1995) 'Gender and Social Capital among Israeli Immigrants in Los Angeles', *Diaspora*, Vol. 4, No. 3, pp. 267–301.

Gordon, P. and Klug, F. (1986) *New Right New Racism*. London: Searching Publications.

Goulbourne, Harry (1991) *Ethnicity and Nationalism in Post-Imperial Britain*, Cambridge: Cambridge University Press.

Gramsci, Antonio (1971) *Selections from the Prison Notebooks*, New York: International Publishers.

Grant, Linda (2002) 'Defenders of the Faith', *The Guardian Review*, 6 July.

Grewal, Inderpal (1994) 'Autobiographic Subjects and Diasporic Locations: *Meatless Days* and *Borderlands*', in Inderpal Grewal and Caren Kaplan (eds), *Scattered Hegemonies: Postmodernity and Transnational Feminist Practices*, Minneapolis: University of Minnesota Press, pp. 231–254.

Grewal, Inderpal (1996) *Home and Harem: Nation, Gender, Empire, and the Cultures of Travel*, Durham, NC: Duke University Press.

Guha, Ranajit (1983) *Elementary Aspects of Peasant Insurgency*, Delhi: Oxford University Press.

Gupta, Rahila (2004) *From Homebreakers to Jailbreakers*, London: Zed Books.

Gutierrez, Gonzales (1999) 'Fostering Identities: Mexico's Relations with its Diaspora', *Journal of American History*, Vol. 86, No. 2, pp. 545–557.

Hall, Stuart (1989) 'New Ethnicities' Black Film', British Cinema *ICA Documents* 7, London: Institute of Contemporary Arts.

Hall, Stuart (1990) 'Cultural Identity and Diaspora', in Jonathan Rutherford (ed.), *Identity: Community, Culture, Difference*, London: Lawrence and Wishart, pp. 222–238.

Hall, Stuart (1992a) 'The Question of Cultural Identity', in S. Hall, D. Held and A. McGrew (eds), *Modernity and its Futures*, London: Polity Press, pp. 273–326.

Hall, Stuart (1992b) 'What is this "Black" in Black Popular Culture', in Gina Dent (ed.), *Black Popular Culture*, California: Bay Press, pp. 21–33.

Hall, Stuart (1995) 'Black and White Television', in June Givanni (ed.), *Remote Control: Dilemmas of Black Intervention in British Film and TV*, London: British Film Institute, pp. 13–28.

Hall, Stuart (1996) 'When was the Postcolonial: Thinking about the Limit' in Iain Chambers and Linda Curtis (eds), *The Post-colonial Question*, London: Routledge, pp. 242–260.

Hall, Stuart and Tony Jefferson (eds) (1974) *Resistance through Rituals: Youth Subcultures in Post-War Britain*, Birmingham: Centre for Contemporary Cultural Studies.

Hamon, Evelynn (1994) 'Black (W)holes and the Geometry of Black Female Sexuality', in More Gender Trouble: Feminism Meets Queer Theory, *Differences: A Journal of Feminist Cultural Studies*, Summer–Fall, pp. 126–145.

Haraway, Donna (1997) *Modest_witness@Second_Millennium.FemaleMan©_Meets_OncoMouse™*, New York: Routledge.

Hardt, Michael and Negri, Antonio (2000) *Empire*, Cambridge, MA and London: Harvard University Press.

Harindranath, Ramaswami (2003) 'Reviving Cultural Imperialism', in Linda Parks and Shanti Kumar (eds), *Planet TV*, New York: New York University Press, pp. 155–168.

Hebdige, Dick (1979) *Subculture: The Meaning of Style*, London: Methuen.

Hebdige, Dick (1987) *Cut 'n' Mix: Culture, Identity and Caribbean Music*, London: Comedia.

Held, David, McGrew, Anthony, Goldblatt, David and Perraton, Johnathon (1999) *Global Transformations: Politics, Economics and Culture*, Cambridge: Polity Press.

Holmes, Michael and Holmes, Denis (eds) (1997) *Ireland and India: Connections, Comparisons, Contrasts*, Dublin: Folins.

Hoagland, Sarak (1988) *Lesbian Ethics*, Palo Alto, CA: Institute of Lesbian Studies.

Home Office (2003) *Nationality, Immigration and Asylum Act*, London: HMSO.

hooks, bell (1990) *Yearning: Race, Gender, and Cultural Politics*, Boston, MA: South End Press.

hooks, bell (1997) 'Representing Whiteness in the Black Imagination', in *Displacing Whiteness: Essays in Social and Cultural Criticism*, Durham, NC: Duke University Press, pp. 165–179.

Howell, Sally and Shryock, Andrew (2003) 'Cracking Down on Diaspora: Arab Detroit and America's "War on Terror"', *Anthropological Quarterly*, Vol. 76, No. 3, pp. 443–462.

Huntington, Samuel P. (1996) *The Clash of Civilizations and the Remaking of World Order*, New York: Simon and Schuster.

Huntington, Samuel P. (1997) 'The Erosion of American Interests', *Foreign Affairs*, Vol. 76, No. 5, pp. 28–49.

Hutnyk, John (1996) *The Rumour of Calcutta: Tourism, Charity and the Poverty of Representation*, London: Zed Books.

Hutnyk, John (2000) *Critique of Exotica: Music, Politics and the Culture Industry*, London: Pluto Press.

Hutnyk, John (2004) *Bad Marxism Capitalism and Cultural Studies*, London: Pluto Press.

Hutnyk, John and Kalra, Virinder (1998) 'Diasporic Music and Politics', *Postcolonial Studies*, Special issue, Vol. 1, No. 3.

Hutnyk, John and Sharma, Sanjay (2000) 'Music and Politics', *Theory, Culture and Society*, Special issue, Vol. 17.

Ignatiev, Noel (1995) *How the Irish Became White*, London: Routledge.

Jacobson, Matthew F. (2000) 'Looking Jewish, Seeing Jews', in Les Back and John Solomos (eds), *Theories of Race and Racism: A Reader*, London: Routledge, pp. 238–252.

Jayawardena, Kumari (1986) *Feminism and Nationalism in the Third World*, London: Zed Books.

Jayawardena, Kumari (1995) *The White Woman's Other Burden*, London: Routledge.

Kalra, Virinder S. (2000) *From Textile Mills to Taxi Ranks: Experiences of Migration, Labour and Social Change*, Aldershot: Ashgate.

Kalra, Virinder S. (2000a) 'Vilayeti Rhythms: Beyond Bhangra's Emblematic Status to a Translation of Lyrical Texts', *Theory, Culture and Society*, Vol. 17, No. 3, pp. 83–105.

Kalra, Virinder (2006) 'Locating the Sikh Pagh', *Journal of Sikh Studies*, Vol. 1, No. 1, forthcoming.

Kalra, Virinder and Hutnyk, John (1998) 'Brimful of Agitation, Authenticity and Appropriation: Madonna's "Asian Kool"', *Postcolonial Studies*, Vol. 1, No. 3, pp. 339–355.

Kapur, Devesh (2001) 'Diasporas and Technology Transfer', *Journal of Human Development*, Vol. 2, No. 2, pp. 265–286.

Kapur, Narender (1997) *The Irish Raj: Illustrated Stories about Irish in India and Indians in Ireland*, Antrim: Greystone Press.

Katz, Nathan (ed.) (1999) *Studies of Indian Jewish Identity*, New Delhi: Manohar.

Kaur, Raminder (1999) 'Parking the Snout in Goa', in Raminder Kaur and John Hutnyk (eds), *Travel Worlds: Journeys in Contemporary Cultural Politics*, London: Zed Books, pp. 155–172.

Kaur, Raminder (2003) 'Westenders: Whiteness, Women and Sexuality in Southall, UK', in Jacqueline Andall (ed.), *Gender and Ethnicity in Contemporary Europe*, Oxford: Berg, pp. 199–217.

Kaur, Raminder and Banerjea, Partha (2000) 'Jazzgeist: Racial Signs of Twisted Times', *Theory, Culture and Society*, Vol. 17, No. 3, pp. 159–180.

Kaur, Raminder and Hutnyk, John (eds) (1999) *Travel Worlds: Journeys in Contemporary Cultural Politics*, London: Zed Books.

Kaur, Raminder and Kalra, Virinder (1996) 'New Paths for South Asian Music and Creativity', in Sanjay Sharma, John Hutnyk and Ashwani Sharma (eds), *Dis-Orienting Rhythms: The Politics of the New Asian Dance Music*, London: Zed books, pp. 217–231.

King, Russell, Williams, Alan and Warnes, Tony (2000) *Sunset Lives: British Retirement Migration to the Mediterranean*, New York: New York University Press.

Klein, Christina (2004) '*Crouching Tiger, Hidden Dragon*: A Diasporic Reading', *Cinema Journal*, Vol. 43, No. 4, pp. 18–42.

Klein, Naomi (2000) *No Logo*, London: Flamingo.

Koshy, Susan (1994) 'The Geography of Female Subjectivity: Ethnicity, Gender, and Diaspora', *Diaspora*, Vol. 3, No. 1, pp. 69–84.

Koshy, Susan (1998) 'Category Crisis: South Asian Americans and Questions of Race and Ethnicity', *Diaspora*, Vol. 7, No. 3, pp. 285–320.

Kovel, Joel (1994) *Red Hunting in a Promised Land*, New York: Basic Books.

Kumar, Amitava (2000) *Passport Photos*, Berkeley: University of California Press.

Kumar, Amitava (2002) *Bombay London New York*, New York: Routledge.

Kunzru, Hari (2002) *The Impressionist*, Harmondsworth: Penguin.

Leonard, Karen (1992) *Making Ethnic Choices: California's Punjabi Mexican Americans*, Philadelphia: Temple University Press.

Lévi-Strauss, Claude (1955) *Tristes Tropiques*, New York: Jonathan Cape.

Lichfield, John (2002) 'Combat 18 website praises Chirac's attacker', *The Independent*, 17 July, p. 9.

Lovink, Geert (2002) *Dark Fiber: Tracking Critical Internet Culture*, Cambridge, MA: MIT Press.

Lowe, Lisa (1996) *Immigrant Acts: On Asian American Cultural Politics*, Durham, NC: Duke University Press.

Lugones, Maria (1991) 'On the Logic of Pluralist Feminism', in C. Card (ed.), *Feminist Ethics*, Lawrence, KS: University of Kansas.

MacCormack, Carol and Strathern, Marilyn (eds) (1981) *Nature, Culture and Gender*, Cambridge: Cambridge University Press.

MacCullum, Mungo (2002) 'Girt by Sea', *Quarterly Essay* 5, Melbourne: Black.

Mandel, Maud S. (1995) 'One Nation Indivisible: Contemporary Western European Immigration Policies and the Politics of Multiculturalism', *Diaspora*, Vol. 4, No. 1, pp. 89–103.

Mankekar, Purnima (1994) 'Reflections on Diasporic Identities: A Prolegomenon to an Analysis of Political Bifocality', *Diaspora*, Vol. 3, No. 3, pp. 349–371.

Mao Zedong (1975/1928) 'Report From Hunan', in *Selected Works*, Vol. 1, Peking: Foreign Languages Press.

Marquese, Mike (1996) *Anyone but England: Cricket and the National Malaise*, New York: W. W. Norton & Company.

Marshall, Barbara L. (1994) *Engendering Modernity: Feminism, Social Theory and Social Change*, London: Polity Press.

Marx, Karl and Engels, Fredrik (1848/1987) *Collected Works*, Vol. 3, London: Lawrence and Wishart.

McClintock, Anne (1996) *Imperial Leather: Race, Gender, and Sexuality in the Colonial Context*, London: Routledge.

McDowell, Jane (ed.) (2003) *Diaspora City*, London: Arcadia.

McGarry, T. (1990) 'A Study of the "Irish" in Southall', Department of Human Sciences BA Dissertation, Brunel University.

Melvern, Linda (2004) *Conspiracy To Murder: The Rwandan Genocide*, London: Verso.

Mercer, Kobena (1994) *Welcome to the Jungle: New Positions in Black Cultural Studies*, London: Routledge.

Modood, Tariq (1992) *Not Easy Being British: Colour, Culture and Citizenship*, London: Runnymede Trust and Trentham Books.

Moody, Roger (1990) *Plunder*, London: Partizans.

Morley, David (2000) *Home Territories: Media, Mobility and Identity*, London: Routledge.

Murray, Alison (1998) 'Debt-bondage and Trafficking: Don't Believe the Hype', in K. Kempadoo (ed.), *Global Sex Workers: Rights, Resistance and Redefinition*, New York and London: Routledge, pp. 51–64.

Naber, Nadine C. (2002) 'So Our History Doesn't Become your Future: The Local and Global Politics of Coalition Building Post-September 11th', *Journal of Asian American Studies*, Vol. 5, No. 3, pp. 217–242.

Nader, Laura (ed.) (1996) *Naked Science: Anthropological Inquiry into Boundaries, Power, and Knowledge*, New York: Routledge.

Naficy, Hamid (2001) *An Accented Cinema: Exilic and Diasporic Filmmaking*, Princeton, NJ: Princeton University Press.

Nagle, John (2003) 'The Transmission and Reception of Irish Traditional Culture in a London-Irish Arts Centre', unpublished PhD thesis, Queen's University Belfast.

Nash, Gary B. (1999) 'The Hidden History of Mestizo America', in Martha Hodes (ed.), *Sex, Love, Race: Crossing Boundaries in North American History*, New York: New York University Press, pp. 10–32.

Neu, Dean and Therrien, Richard (2003) *Accounting for Genocide: Canada's Bureaucratic Assault an Aboriginal People*, Black Point, NS: Fernwood Publishing.

Newmeyer, Frederick J. (1986) *The Politics of Linguistics*, Chicago: University of Chicago Press.

Noriega, Chon A. (2001) '"Waas sappening?": Narrative Structure and Iconography in "Born in East L.A."', in Matthew Tinkcom and Amy Vallerejo (eds), *Keyframes: Popular Cinema and Cultural Studies*, London: Routledge.

Nugent, Stephen (1994) *Amazonian Coboclo Society: An Essay on Invisibility and Peasant Economy*, Oxford: Berg.

O'Hanlom, Rosalind and Washbrook, David (2000) 'After Orientalism: Culture, Criticism and Politics in the Third World', in Vinayak Chaturvedi (ed.), *Mapping Subaltern Studies and the Postcolonial*, London: Verso, pp. 191–219.

O'Reilly, Karen (2000) *The British on the Costa del Sol: Transnational Identities and Local Communities*, London: Routledge.

Ong, Aiwa (1999) *Flexible Citizenship: The Cutural Logics of Transnationality*, Durham, NC: Duke University Press.

Ostergaard-Nielson, Eva (2000) 'Trans-State Loyalites and Politics of Turks and Kurds in Western Europe', *SAIS Review*, Vol. 20, No. 1, pp. 23–38.

Palme Dutt, Rajani (1949) *Britain's Crisis of Empire*, London: Lawrence and Wishart.

Palumbo-Liu, David (2002) 'Multiculturalism Now: Civilization, National Identity and Difference Before and After September 11th', *boundary 2*, Vol. 2, No. 29, pp. 109–127.

Panagakos, Anastasia N. (1998) 'Citizens of the Trans-Nation: Political Mobilization, Multiculturalism, and Nationalism in the Greek Diaspora', *Diaspora*, Vol. 7, No. 1, pp. 53–74.

Papastergiadis, Nikos (1998) *Dialogues in the Diaspora: Essays and Conversations on Cultural Identity*, London: Rivers Oram.

Papastergiadis, Nikos (2000) *The Turbulence of Migration: Globalization, Deterritorialization and Hybridity*, Cambridge: Polity Press.

Parker, David (2000) 'The Chinese Takeaway and the Diasporic Habitus: Space, Time and Power Geometries', in Barnor Hesse (ed.), *Un/Settled Multiculturalisms: Diasporas, Entanglements, Transruptions*, London: Zed Books, pp. 55–68.

Parmar, Pratibha (1982) 'Gender, Race and Class: Asian Women in Resistance', in Centre for Contemporary Cultural Studies, *Empire Strikes Back*, London: Hutchinson.

Pascoe, R. (2000) 'Third Culture Kids Are Left a Complex Legacy', www.internetforschools. co.uk/global/expatliving/adfamily7.html.

Penley, Constance (1997) *Nasa/Trek*, New York: Verso.

Phoenix, Ann and Owen, Charlie (2000) 'From Miscegenation to Hybridity: Mixed Relationships and Mixed Parentage in Profle', in Avtar Brah and Annie Coombs (eds), *Hybridity and Its Discontents*, London: Routledge, pp. 72–95.

Phillips, Mike and Phillips, Trevor (1999) *Windrush: The Irresistible Rise of Multi-Racial Britain*, London: Harper Collins.

Prakash, Gyan (2000) 'Can the Subaltern Ride? A Reply to O'Hanlon and Washbrook', in Vinayak Chaturvedi (ed.), *Mapping Subaltern Studies and the Postcolonial*, London: Verso, pp. 120–238.

Prashad, Vijay (1995) 'Roots: A Manifesto for Overseas South Asians', *Sanskriti*, Vol. 6, No. 1. Available at: www.foil.org/resources/sanskriti/dec95/vijay.html.

Prashad, Vijay (2000) *The Karma of Brown Folk*, Minneapolis and London: University of Minnesota Press.

Prashad, Vijay (2001) *Everybody was Kung Fu Fighting: Afro-Asian Connections and the Myth of Cultural Purity*, New York: Beacon Press.

Prashad, Vijay (2002a) *The American Scheme: Three Essays*, New Delhi: New Left Books.

Prashad, Vijay (2002b) *War Against the Planet: The Fifth Afghan War, Imperialisms and Other Assorted Fundamentalisms*, New Delhi: Left Word.

Prashad, Vijay and Mathew, Biju (1999–2000) 'Satyagraha in America: The Political Culture of South Asians in the U.S.', *Amer-Asia Journal*, Vol. 25, No. 3, pp. ix–xv.

Pratt, Mary (1992) *Imperial Eyes: Travel Writing and Transculturation*, London: Routledge.

Puar, Jasbir (1995) 'Resituating Discourses of "Whiteness" and "Asianness" in Northern England: Second Generation Sikh Women and Constructions of Identity', *Socialist Review*, Special Section: Arranging Identities – Constructions of Race, Ethnicity, and Nation, Vol. 24, Nos 1 and 2, pp. 21–53.

Puar, Jasbir (2002) 'A Transnational Feminist Critique of Queer Tourism', *Antipode*, Vol. 34, No. 5, pp. 935–946.

Puar, Jasbir and Rai, Amit (2002) 'Monster, Terrorist, Fag: The War on Terrorism and the Production of Docile Patriots', *Social Text*, Vol. 20, No. 3, pp. 117–148.

Purewal, Navtej (2003) 'Re-producing South Asian Wom(b)en: Female Feticide and the Spectacle of Culture', in N. Puwar and P. Raghuram (eds), *South Asian Women in the Diaspora*, Oxford: Berg, pp. 137–157.

Radhakrishnan, Rajagopalan (1996) *Diasporic Mediations: Between Home and Location*, Minneapolis and London: University of Minnesota Press.

Ramdin, Ron (2000) *Arising from Bondage: A History of the Indo-Caribbean People*, New York: New York University Press.

Rasanah Kharberie (2000) *News from NAZ London*, November, Issue 11, London: NAZ Project.

Rayaprol, Aparna (1997) *Negotiating Identities: Women in the Indian Diaspora*, Delhi: Oxford University Press.

Rothenberg, Celia (1999) 'Proximity and Distance: Palestinian Women's Social Lives', *Diaspora*, Vol. 8, No. 1, pp. 23–50.

Roy, Arundhati (1997) *The God of Small Things*, New York: Random House.

Roy, Arundhati (1999) *The Cost of Living*, London: Flamingo.

Roy, Arundhati (2001) 'The Progressive Interview, with David Barsamian', *The Progressive*, April, pp. 33–39.

Ruge, Uta (1992) 'Female Genital Mutilation and the Position of African Refugee Women in Britain', *Women Against Fundamentalism Journal*, Vol. 3, pp. 7–8.

Ruprecht, Jr., Louis A. (1994) 'On Being Jewish or Greek in the Modern Moment', *Diaspora*, Vol. 3, No. 2, pp. 82–102.

Rushdie, Salman (1992) *Imaginary Homelands: Essays and Criticism 1981–1991*, London: Granta, in association with Penguin.

Rutherford, Jonathan (1997) *Forever England: Reflections on Race, Masculinity and Empire*, London: Lawrence and Wishart.

Ruthven, Malise (1991) *A Satanic Affair: Salman Rushdie and the Wrath of Islam*, London: Chatto & Windus.

Ryan, Chris and Hall, C. Michael (2001) *Sex Tourism: Marginal People and Liminalities*, London: Routledge.

Safran, William (1991) 'Diasporas in Modern Societies: Myths of Homeland and Return', *Diaspora*, Vol. 1, No. 1, pp. 83–99.

San Juan, Jr., E. (2001) 'Interrogating Transmigrancy, Remapping Diaspora: The Globalization of Laboring Filipinos/as', *Discourse*, Vol. 23, No. 3, pp. 52–74.

San Juan, Jr., E. (2002) *Racism and Cultural Studies: Critiques of Multiculturalist Ideology and the Politics of Difference*, Durham, NC: Duke University Press.

Sassen, Saskia (1996) *Losing Control? Sovereignty in an Age of Globalisation*, New York: Columbia University Press.

Sassen, Saskia (1998) *Globalization and its Discontents: Selected Essays 1984–1998*, New York: New Press.

Sayyid, Salman (1997) *A Fundamental Fear: Eurocentrism and the Emergence of Islamism*, London: Zed Books.

Sayyid, Salman (2000a) 'Bad Faith: Anti-Essentialism, Universalism and Islamism', in Avtar Brah and Annie Coombs (eds), *Hybridity and Its Discontents*, London: Routledge, pp. 257–271.

Sayyid, Salman (2000b) 'Beyond Westphalia: Nations and Diasporas – the Case of the Muslim *Umma*', in Barnor Hesse (ed.), *Un/Settled Multiculturalisms: Diasporas, Entanglements, Transruptions*, London: Zed Books, pp. 33–51.

Schumaker, Lynne (2001) *Africanizing Anthropology: Fieldwork, Networks, and the Making of Cultural Knowledge in Central Africa*, Durham, NC: Duke University Press.

Seabrook, Jeremy (2001) *Travels in the Skin Trade: Tourism and the Sex Industry*, London: Pluto Press.

Segal, Ronald (1996) *The Black Diaspora*, New York: Noonday Press.

Seth, Vikram (1994) *A Suitable Boy*, London: Perennial.

Shain, Yossi (1994) 'Marketing the Democratic Creed Abroad: US Diasporic Politics in the Era of Multiculturalism', *Diaspora*, Vol. 3, No. 1, pp. 85–111.

Shain, Yossi (1999) *Marketing the American Creed Abroad: Diasporas in the US and their Homelands*, Cambridge: Cambridge University Press.

Shain, Yossi (2002) 'The Role of Diasporias in Conflict Perpetuation or Resolution', *SAIS Review*, Vol. 22, No. 2, pp. 115–144.

Sharma, Ashwani (1996) 'Sounds Oriental: The (Im)Possibility of Theorizing Asian Musical Cultures', in Sanjay Sharma, John Hutnyk and Ashwani Sharma (eds), *Dis-Orienting Rhythms: The Politics of the New Asian Dance Music*, London: Zed Books, pp. 15–31.

Sharma, Sanjay (1996) 'Noisy Asians or Asian Noise?', in Sanjay Sharma, John Hutnyk and Ashwani Sharma (eds), *Dis-Orienting Rhythms: The Politics of the New Asian Dance Music*, London: Zed Books, pp. 32–57.

Sharma, Sanjay (2005) 'Asian Sounds', in Nasreen Ali, Virinder Kalra and Salman Sayyid (eds), *Postcolonial People: South Asians in Britain*, London: Hurst.

Sharma, Sanjay and Housee, Shirin (1999) '"Too Black Too Strong"? Anti-racism and the Making of South Asian Political Identities in Britain', in Tim Jordon and Adam Lent (eds), *Storming the Millennium: The Politics of Change*, London: Lawrence and Wishart.

Sharma, Sanjay, Hutnyk, John and Sharma, Ashwani (eds) (1996) *Dis-Orienting Rhythms: The Politics of the New Asian Dance Music*, London: Zed Books.

Shohat, Ella and Stam, Robert (1994) *Unthinking Eurocentrism: Multiculturalism and the Media*, London and New York: Routledge.

Shore, Cris (2000) *Building Europe: The Cultural Politics of European Integration*, London: Routledge.

Sivanandan, Ambalever (1981) 'From Resistance to Rebellion: Asian and Afro-Caribbean Struggles in Britain', *Race and Class*, Vol. 23, pp. 111–151.

Sivanandan, Ambalever (1982) *A Different Hunger: Struggles for Racial Justice*, London: Pluto Press.

Sivanandan, Ambalever (1987) 'Closing the Door, the Clampdown on Refugees', on *Homebeats* (CD-ROM), London: Institute of Race Relations.

Sivanandan, Ambalever (1997) 'On Fortress Europe', Speech. Available at: www.irr.org.uk/sound/people/siva.ram

Socialist Review Collective (1995) 'Arranging Identities: Framing the Issue/s', *Socialist Review*, Special Section: Arranging Identities – Constructions of Race, Ethnicity, and Nation, Vol. 24, Nos 1 and 2, pp. 1–19.

Southall Black Sisters (1990) *Against the Grain: A Celebration of Survival and Struggle*, London: SBS.

Spivak, Gayatri Chakravorty (1987) *In Other Worlds: Essays in Cultural Politics*, New York: Methuen.

Spivak, Gayatri Chakravorty (1993) *Outside in the Teaching Machine*, New York: Routledge.

Spivak, Gayatri Chakravorty (1996) *The Spivak Reader*, London: Routledge.

Spivak, Gayatri Chakravorty (1999) *Critique of Postcolonial Reason: Towards a History of the Vanishing Present*, Cambridge, MA: Harvard University Press.

Spivak, Gayatri Chakravorty (2000a) 'The New Subaltern: A Silent Interview', in Vinayak Chaturvedi (ed.), *Mapping Subaltern Studies and the Postcolonial*, London: Verso, pp. 324–340.

Spivak, Gayatri Chakravorty (2000b) 'Thinking Cultural Questions in "Pure" Literary Terms', in Paul Gilroy, Lawrence Grossberg and Angela McRobbie (eds), *Without Guarantees: In Honour of Stuart Hall*, London: Verso, pp. 335–357.

Srinivas, M.N. (1962) *Caste in Modern India and Other Essays*, Bombay: Media Promoters and Publishers.

Stein, Sarah Abrevaya (1997) 'Sephardi and Middle Eastern Jewries: History and Culture in the Modern Era', *Diaspora*, Vol. 6, No. 1, pp. 96–111.

Stoler, Ann Laurer (1991) 'Carnal Knowledge and Imperial Power: Gender, Race and Morality in Colonial Asia', in Micaela di Leonardo (ed.), *Gender at the Crossroads of Knowledge: Feminist Anthropology in the Postmodern Era*, Berkeley: University of California Press, pp. 51–101.

Stoler, Ann Laura (1995) *Race and the Education of Desire: Foucault's History of Sexuality and the Colonial Order of Things*, Durham, NC: Duke University Press.

Stoler, Ann Laura (2000) 'Sexual Affronts and Racal Frontiers: European Identities and the Cultural Politics of Excluson in Colonial Southeast Asia', in Avtar Brah and Annie Coombs (eds), *Hybridity and its Discontents*, London: Routledge, pp. 19–55.

Sykes, Roberta (1989) *Black Majority*, Hawthorn, Vic.: Hudson.

Szasz, Thomas (1970) *The Manufacture of Madness*, London: Harper and Row.

Tatla, Darshan Singh (1998) *The Sikh Diaspora: The Search for Statehood*, London: UCL Press.

Taussig, Michael (1980) *The Devil and Commodity Fetishism*, Chapel Hill, NC: University of North Carolina Press.

Tessman, Lisa (1995) 'Beyond Communitarian Unity in the Politics of Identity', *Socialist Review*, Special Section: Arranging Identities – Constructions of Race, Ethnicity, and Nation, Vol. 24, Nos 1 and 2, pp. 55–83.

Thiara, Ravi K. (2003) 'South Asian Women and Collective Action in Britain', in Jacqueline Andall (ed.), *Gender and Ethnicity in Contemporary Europe*, Oxford: Berg, pp. 132–161.

Thomas, Nicholas (1988) 'Hybrid Histories: Gordon Bennett's Critique of Purity', *Communal/Plura*, Vol. 6, No. 1, pp. 23–45.

Thomas, Nicholas (2000) 'Technologies of Conversion: Cloth and Christianity in Polyesia', in Avtar Brah and Annie Coombs (eds), *Hybridity and Its Discontents*, London: Routledge, pp. 198–215.

Tölölyan, Khachig (1996) 'Rethinking Diaspora(s): Stateless Power in the Transnational Moment', *Diaspora*, Vol. 5, No. 1, pp. 3–36.

Tölölyan, Khachig (2000) 'Elites and Institutions in the Armenian Transnation', *Diaspora*, Vol. 9, No. 1.

Trinh, T. Minh-ha and Morelli, Anamaria (1996) 'The Undone Interval', in Iain Chambers and Linda Curtis (eds), *The Post-colonial Question*, London: Routledge, pp. 3–16.

Vertovec, Steven (1999) 'Three Meanings of "Diaspora", Exemplified by South Asian Religions', *Diaspora*, Vol. 6, No. 3, pp. 277–300.

Vidal, Gore (2002) *Perpetual War for Perpetual Peace*. New York: Thunders Mouth Press/ Nation.

Visvanathan, Shiv (1997) *A Carnival for Science: Essays on Science, Technology and Development*, Delhi: Oxford University Press.

Visweswaran, Kamala (1997) 'Diaspora by Design: Flexible Citizenship and South Asians in US Racial Formations', *Diaspora*, Vol. 6, No. 1, pp. 5–30.

Wahlbeck, Osten (2002) 'The Concept of Diaspora as an Analytical Tool in the Study of Refugee Communities', *Journal of Ethnic and Migration Studies*, Vol. 28, No. 2, pp. 221–238.

Ware, Vron (2002a) 'Otherworldly Knowledge: Towards a Language of Perspicuous Contrast', in Vron Ware and Les Back (eds), *Out of Whiteness: Color, Politics, and Culture*, Chicago: Chicago University Press, pp. 15–32.

Ware, Vron (2002b) 'Room with a View' in Vron Ware and Les Back (eds), *Out of Whiteness: Color, Politics, and Culture*, Chicago: Chicago University Press, pp. 271–289.

Ware, Vron and Back, Les (eds) (2002) *Out of Whiteness: Color, Politics, and Culture*. Chicago: Chicago University Press.

Watson, James (1977) *Between Two Cultures: Migrants and Minorities in Britain*, Oxford: Basil Blackwell.

Wayne, Michael (2002) 'The Critical Practice and Dialectics of Third Cinema', in Rasheed Araeen, Sean Cubitt and Ziauddin Sardar (eds), *The Third Test Reason on Art, Culture and Theory*, London: Continuum.

Weidenbaum, Murray and Hughes, Samuel (1996) *The Bamboo Network*, New York: The Free Press.

Werbner, Pnina (2000) 'Introduction: The Materiality of Diaspora – Between Aesthetic and "Real" Politics', *Diaspora*, Vol. 9, No. 1, pp. 5–20.

Westwood, Sallie (1995) 'Gendering Diaspora: Space, Politics and South Asian Masculinities in Britain', in Peter van der Veer (ed.), *Nation and Migration: The Politics of Space in the South Asian Diaspora*, Philadelphia: University of Pennsylvania Press, pp. 197–221.

Willis, Paul (1977) *Learning to Labour*, Farnborough: Saxon House.

Wolfe, Patrick (1999) *Settler Colonialism and the Transformation of Anthropology: The Politics and Poetics of an Ethnographic Event*, London: Cassell.

Worsley, Peter (1964) *The Third World*, London: Weidenfeld & Nicholson.

Young, Lola (2000) 'Hybridity's Discontents: Reading Science and "Race"', in Avtar Brah and Annie Coombs (eds), *Hybridity and Its Discontents*, London: Routledge, pp. 154–170.

Young, Robert (1995) *Colonial Desire: Hybridity in Theory, Culture and Race*, London: Routledge.

Young, Robert (2001) *Postcolonialism: An Historical Introduction*, London: Blackwell.

Younger, C. (1987) *Anglo-Indians: Neglected Children of the Raj*, Delhi: B.R. Publishing.

Zack, Naomi (1993) *Race and Mixed Race*, Philadelphia: Temple University Press.

Filmography

Aliens, dir. James Cameron (1986)
Alien 3, dir. David Fincher (1992)
Alien Resurrection, dir. Jean-Pierre Jeunet (1997)
Babymother, dir. Julian Henriques (2000)
Bend It Like Beckham, dir. Gurinder Chadha (2002)
Bhaji on the Beach, dir. Gurinder Chadha (1994)
Bladerunner, dir. Ridley Scott (1982)
Born in East L.A., dir. Richard Marin (1987)
Crouching Tiger, Hidden Dragon, dir. Ang Lee (2000)
Decoder, dir. Muscha/Maeck (1984)
Drugstore Cowboy, dir. Gus Van Sant (1989)
Encoding/Decoding, dir. Megan Legault (2000)
Gattica, dir. Andrew Niccol (1997)
Handsworth Songs, dir. John Akomfrah (1986)
I'm British, But, dir. Gurinder Chadha (1990)

Lousy Little Sixpence, dir. Alec Morgan and Gerry Bostock (1982)
Mission to Mars, dir. Brian de Palma (2000)
My Beautiful Laundrette, dir. Stephen Frears (1985)
Rabbit-Proof Fence, dir. Phillip Noyce (2002)
Red Planet, dir. Anthony Hoffman (2000)
Sammy and Rosie Get Laid, dir. Stephen Frears (1987)
The Fifth Element, dir. Luc Besson (1997)
The Passion of Remembrance, dir. Sankofa Film Workshop (1986)
The Thin Red Line, dir. Terrance Mallick (1998)

Index

absolutism
  ethnic 16
  racial 91–2
academic debate 135
acculturation 74
activists 92
Adorno, Theodor 40, 100
Afghanistan 131–2
African Women's Welfare Group
  (AWWG) 58–9, 60
African-Caribbeans 53–4
Ahmed, Hadiyah 59, 60
Al Qaeda 132
Alexander, Claire 54
Ali, Tariq 131–2
Alien movie series 80–1
aliens 99
alliances
  hybridity 92
  Irish and Indian 115
America
  Anglo-Indians 122
  Hindus 46
  imperialism 129–32
  mestizo 122
  nationalism 15
American-Irish activism 117
American-Jewish diaspora 20
Amritsar, Golden Temple 21
Anderson, Benedict 20, 31
Anglo-Celtic culture 117
Anglo-Indians 120–2
Anglo-Saxon
  hybridity 89
  ideals 106
Anthias, Floya
  Cypriots 21
  ethnic absolutism 16
  gender 51, 57
  host society interactions 120
  hybridity 95
  political problems
  whiteness 110–11
anthropological syncretism 73–4, 97

anti-colonial period 136–7
anti-colonial struggles 26
Anzaldúa, Gloria 5
apartheid era 10
Appadurai, Arjun 22, 31, 36
Arab-Americans 129
Asian dance music 39, 40
Asian Dub Foundation 83, 86n
Asian women
  objectification 55–6
  South 39
  stereotypes 67
Asian Youth Movements 97
asylum seekers 133–4
Australia
  aboriginal policy 74–5
  liberation of detainees 96–7
authenticity, racial 82
AWWG *see* African Women's
  Welfare Group
Axel, Brian 32

Back, Les 117
Banerjea, Koushik 54–5, 93, 113
Bangladesh 19
Barth, Fredrik 16
Baudrillard, Jean 80
Behdad, Ali 109
Beinin, Joel 120
belonging 29–34
Berlant, Lauren 92
'between cultures' 56, 112
Bhabha, Homi 37, 43–4,
  71, 89, 102–3
biology of hybridity 72
Black/Asian British 41
'Black Atlantic' 36
Black category 90
Black politics 88
black/white divide 15
Blacks of Europe 116
Blum, William 129
BNP *see* British National Party
Bollywood 41

Booker Prize 46
border exchanges 95–7
boundaries
    diasporic group 51
    ethnicity 16
Brah, Avtah 11, 12, 33, 96
brain-drain 23, 24
brain-gain 24
Brennan, Tony 39
Bretton–Woods organizations 34, 49n
Britain
    Asian Youth Movements 97
    citizenship 36, 49n
    Greek Cypriots 57
    imperialism 23
    minority ethnic groups 16
British Asian films 40
British Empire 23, 114
British Greek Cypriot diaspora 57
British National Party (BNP) 133
British Nationality and Immigration
    Act 2002 134
British Raj 121–2
British Sikhs 21–2
Burroughs, William 78
Bush, George W. 131

capitalism
    globalization 42
    hybridised 82
    transnational 35
categorization of ethnic groups 16
Chadha, Gurinder 40, 41
Chambers, Iain 71
Che-Leila 97, 104n
Chinese
    America 106
    entrepreneurial class 23
    film 42
Chow, Rey 100–1
Chua, Beng-Huat 93
circumcision, female 58–9, 60
citizenship
    Britain 36
    dual 18–19
civil rights movement, USA 26
clash of civilizations 128
class hierarchy 89–90
class status 112
Clifford, James 12, 30, 32, 43, 71
co-option 42
coalition-building 131
Cohen, Phil 8
Cohen, Robin 11–12

colonialism 26, 101, 127
commodification 37–40, 42, 45
communities
    authority 57
    fundamentalism 61
    virtual 32
conflicts, long-distance 22
contact zones 73–7
Coombs, Annie 96
corporate multiculture 102
creolization 75
cultural activists 92
cultural exchange 73, 93
cultural hybridity model 88
cultural identity 70
cultural orthodoxy 58
cultural production 37–44, 71, 83
cultural symbolism 51
culture 35–7
    British 31
    clash 75
    exchange 73, 93
    industry 36, 93, 102
    politics 15, 38
    products 37–43, 44, 71, 83
    studies 47
    wars 46–8
'cut "n" mix' 37, 38
cyborgs 77–8
Cyprus 21

Derrida, Jacques 76, 92
detainees 96–7, 130
deterritorialization 32–3
dialectics 102
diaspora
    cohesive tool 67
    conciousness 30
    frameworks 11–14
    imperial 111
    legal status 18–19
    in the making 65
    memory 26
    organizations 18
    process 29
    revolutionary 22–3
    space 36, 38, 43, 45, 120, 122
    studies 47
    white 105–7
differences 55–6, 100
displaced people 11
diversity 89–90
domestic labour 65–7
dual citizenship 18–19

dual loyalty 128
Dube, Saurabh 130
Dyer, Richard 106, 123
dynamism, transcultural 82

economic justice 93
economic migrants 134
economics 23–5
elite, transnationals 101
Ellison, Ralph 108–9
entrepreneurial networks 8, 23
equality 90
Eritrea 19
essentialism 16, 17, 90, 103n
ethnic absolutism 16
ethnic associations 16, 18
ethnic pluralisation 81
ethnic purity 73
ethno-cide 74
ethnocentrism 74
Eurocentrism 54
European Union 117
Europeans
    abroad 113–14
    American 122
exchange, cultural 73, 93
exile, forced 10
expatriates 111–13
exploitation zones 101
extra-judicial trials 130

family values 63
fatwa 60–1
female circumcision 58–9, 60
feminists 51
Filipina 47, 50n
films 40–3, 94
food, hybrid 93
forced exile 10
Fortress Europe 117
fundamentalism 61, 130

Garcia Calclini, Nestor
    85, 97–8, 100
Garvey, Marcus 10
gay studies 63–4
Geertz, Clifford 75–6
gene mapping 80
genital mutilation 58–9, 60
Gibson, Pamela Church 80–1
Gilman, Sander 118
Gilroy, Paul
    creativity 82
    cultural moves 36

Gilroy, Paul *cont.*
    hybridity 71, 72–3
    music 38
    nation-state 87
    new racism 31
    racial absolutism 91–2
    'roots and routes' 29
    slavery 10
    urbanization 97
global capitalism 24
global identity 84
global technology 43
globalization 27, 42–3, 135–6
going native 94–5
Grant, Linda 119
Greek Americans 126n
Greek Cypriots 57, 110
Green Revolution 74
Grewal, Inderpal 62

Hall, Michael 65
Hall, Stuart 30, 37, 40,
    42, 73, 81–2
Hamon, Evelynn 63
Haraway, Donna 77–8
Hardt, Michael 77, 127, 135
Harindranath, Ramaswami 101
Harvey, Alfred ('King Dick') 54
Hebdige, Dick 37
hegemonic formations
    90, 92, 95, 107
hierarchies
    class 89–90
    racialized 10, 15, 25–6, 39, 105
    white 107
Hindu 46
Hoagland, Sarah 62
Holocaust 119
home culture 88–91
homeland 12, 19, 23–4
    newly created 19
homosexuality 61–4
host culture 88
Howell, Sally 129
Human Rights Watch 65, 66
humanism 37
Huntington, Samuel 128
Hussein, Saddam 131–2
Hutnyk, John 114
hybridity
    anchor 87
    identification 14–15
    identity 87
    use of term 70–85

hybridization 81–2
  process 85
  tranquillizing 100
hyphenated identities 33, 89

ICTs *see* Information communication
    technologies
identities 30, 33
  collective 17
  diasporas 22
  dynamic 64
  gender 54–5
  hybridity 70–2, 87
  politics 39
illegal workers 134
immigration 14–16, 109
imperial diasporas 111
imperial nation-state 127
imperialism 35, 48
  American 129–32
  British 23
India
  diaspora 12, 28–9
  dual citizenship 19
  Europeans 113–14
  Kashmir 21-22, 27n
industry, culture 36, 93, 102
information communication
    technologies (ICTs) 19
interface, colonial-cultural 71
internationalism 97
internet
  hybridity 78
  virtual communities 19
  white diaspora, 107, 124n
interpreter, anthropologist 75–6
investment in homeland 23–4
invisibility 105, 108-109, 124n
Iraq 132
Irish
  American diaspora 116–17
  London 108
  whiteness 115–17
Israel 20, 118

Jacobson, Matthew 117–18
Jews, whiteness 117–20
justice
  economic 93
  social 137

Kalra, Virinder 76, 89
Kapur, Devesh 23, 24
Kashmiris 21-2

Kaur, Raminder 89
Klein, Christina 42
Kumar, Amitava 84
Kurds, Euro-America 21
Kureshi, Hanif 41

labour
  domestic 65–7
  migration 12, 25
  organised 136
  power 52
  service sector 24–5
languages 43
  hybrid 71
  new 75, 76
legacy of colonialism 101
lesbians 62–4
liberal multiculturalism 47–8
literature 43–6
London
  English and Irish 108
  multicultural 99–100
long-distance nationalism 20
Lovink, Geert 85
Lowe, Lisa 53
loyalty 20, 31–2
  community 60
  dual 128
Lugones, Maria 62

machine-human hybrid 77–8
maid trade 52
Mankekar, Purnima 57
Marin, Richard ('Cheech') 94
Marxism 136
masculinity 52–5
mass consumption 40
media 133
memory, diasporic 26
Mercer, Kobena 71, 87–8
mestizo, America 122
Mexico 53, 57
middle-classes 100, 102, 110
Middle East 118–19
migration 11, 18
militant worker organizations 135–6
minority ethnic groups
  Britain 16
  internal problems 58–60
miscegenation 79–80
mixed-race 73, 79-80, 86n
model minority 110
modernism, religious 61
Morley, David 95–6

multicultural capital 99–100
multicultural clichés 41
multiculturalism
    corporate 102
    liberal 47–8
Murray, Alison 52, 66
music 38–40
    hybridity 82–3
    property rights 88
Muslims 128
    umma 9, 132
    underclass 54–5
myths
    Eurocentric 54
    purity 72

Naber, Nadine 131
Naficy, Hamid 41
Nash, Gary 122
nation-state 21–2, 28, 87–8
National Health Service, Britain 28
nationalism
    American 15
    long-distance 20
    unity 32
Nationality and Immigration Act
    2002, Britain 134
Native Americans, Europeans 122
Nayak, Anoop 117
NAZ project, London 63, 68
Negri, Antonio 77, 127, 135
neo-colonialism 107
neo-fascism 107
neo-liberalism 24, 25, 130
neo-Nazis 118
networks
    entrepreneurial 8
    small-scale 24
new racism 31
New World Order 21, 34

O'Reilly, Karen 114
organised labour 136
orthodoxy, cultural 58
Ostergaard-Nielson, Eva 21
Owen, Charlie 79

Pacific Island artefacts 90
Pakistan
    dual citizenship 19
    Kashmir 22
Palestine 119
Palme Dutt, Rajani 26
Palumbo-Liu, David 128
Pan-African Congress 22

Papastergiadis, Nikos 70, 84
patois language 75
patriarchal structures 52, 59
Patriot Act 129–30, 132
patriotism 31, 34
Phillips, Mike 53–4
Phillips, Trevor 53–4
Phoenix, Ann 79
pidgin language 75
planetary humanism 37
pluralism 91
pluralization, cultural 81
popular culture 93–4
post-colonialism 43, 87, 88
postmodernism 87, 88, 90, 93
Powell, Enoch 31
power, racialized 25–6
Prashad, Vijay 15, 130–1, 136
prejudices, stereotypical 58
privileges, whiteness 105, 107
property rights 88
prostitution 65–6
Puar, Jasbir K. 64
Punjabis 53, 57
purity
    Aryan 89
    culture 72–3

queer theory 63–4

races 92
    human 72
    mixture 73, 79–80, 86n
    purity 79–80
    terminology 79
racial absolutism 91–2
racial authenticity 82
racial violence 54–5
racialized difference 92
racialized hierarchies 10, 15,
    25–6, 39, 105, 107
racialized males 54
racism, new 31
Radhakrishnan, Rajagopalan 45
Raj, British 121–2
Ralph, Regan 65–6
rap 39
Rayaprol, Aparna 57
reciprocity 92
refugees 133
    Australia 96–7
    status 11
religious modernism 61
remittances 23–4
repatriation, Australia 96–7

resistance, women's issues 58–61
retirement migration 115
revolutionary diasporas 22–3
right-wing parties 123–4
Rock Against Racism 82–3
roots and routes 29
Roy, Arundhati 46, 84
Rushdie, Salman 45–6, 60–1
Rwanda 11, 27n
Ryan, Chris 65

San Juan, E. 47, 67, 96
Sassen, Saskia 97, 135–6
Sayyid, Salman 9, 34, 90
science, hybridity 72
science fiction
    hybridity 77–8, 80–1
    urbanization 99
Segal, Ronald 10
self-identity 30
September 11 2001 15-16, 54-5, 48n
service sector 24–5
settler colonialists 99, 113
sex trade 64–8
sexuality 61–4
Shain, Yossi 21
Sharma, Ashwani 92
Sharma, Sanjay 82
Shohat, Ella 83
Shyrock, Andrew 129
Sikhs 21–2
Sivanandan, Ambalever 26, 134
slave trade 10
slavery, agricultural 98
social justice 45, 137
social status 110–11
Somalis, British 60
South Africa 10
South Asian-Americans 125n
South Asians
    Punjabi men 53
    USA 110
    women 39
South Indian women 57
Southall, west London 108, 124n
Southall Black Sisters 58, 61
space
    diasporic 36, 43, 45, 120, 122
    political 61
    third 44
Spain, British 114–15
Spivak, Gayatri Chakravorty
    24, 26, 52, 95–6, 101–2
Stam, Robert 83
Star Trek, racial politics 77, 85n

stasis, hybridity 91, 92
Stein, Sarah Abrevaya 120
stereotypes 55–6, 67
Stoler, Ann Laura 79
subjectivity, heterogeneous 62
supremacy, white 105–9
symbolism, cultural 51
syncretism 70, 71, 73–4, 97
syntax 76

Taliban 131–2
Taussig, Michael 74
technology, global 43
technology-humanity interface 78
terminology of hybridity 72–3, 85
terror 127–36
'terrorists within' 129
Tessman, Linda 62
Third Culture Kid (TCK) 111–13
third space 71
Thomas, Nicholas 90
tolerance 137
tourism 113–14
trade, sex 64–8
trafficking women 64–8
trans-ethnic alliances 29–30, 33–4
transculturalism 82, 91
translation 43–4
    cultural 76
transmigration 96
transmitters, culture 56–8
transnational 12, 15, 27, 34–5, 107
    alliances 29–30
    capitalism 35
    elite 101, 104n
    non-territorial 36
    terror 127–36
transplantation 112
travel 113–14
triadic relationship 17–18
trials, extra-judicial 130
Trinh, T. Minh-ha 103
Turkey 21

Umma, Muslim 132
underclass, Muslim 54–5
union movement 136
unity
    across differences 83
    nationalism 32
urbanization 97–100
USA
    immigration policy 109
    multiracial roots 122
    nation of immigrants 28

USA *cont.*
  South Asians 110
  South Indian women 57

veil, stereotypes 55
verbal struggle 103
Vertovec, Steven 13–14
vessels of culture 52, 56–8
victims
  cultural stereotypes 55–6
  trafficking 66–7
Vidal, Gore 1, 131
violence, racial 54–5
virtual communities 19, 32
Visweswaran, Kamala 110

war on terror 128
Ware, Vron 109, 117
Warner, Michael 92
wars, culture 46–8
white diasporas 105–7

white supremacy 15, 105–9, 119, 124
whiteness, secondary 106, 117, 123
women 58–61
  carriers of culture 52, 56–8
  South Asian 39
  trafficking 64–8
Women Against Fundamentalism
    58, 61, 68
Woomera detention camp, Australia 96–7
worker organizations 135–6
World Trade Center, attacks 15–16
World Trade Organization 42

xenophobic nationalism 29

Young, Lola 90
Young, Robert 136
Yugoslavia 10

Zionism 119–20